D1053072

PRAYER WORKS

A LIFETIME SPIRITUAL JOURNEY

RICK HAMLIN

Guideposts

New York

Published by Guideposts a Church Corporation
39 Old Ridgebury Road, Suite 27
Danbury, CT 06810
Guideposts.org

This Guideposts edition is published by special arrangement with Hachette
Book Group, and Rick Hamlin.

Cover by W Design Group LLC.
Typeset by Aptara, Inc.

Printed in the United States of America
10 9 8 7 6 5 4 3 2 1

INTRODUCTION

The question had me stumped. A friend of a friend, a minister, had agreed to meet with me in his book-lined study. He had a reputation for being a scholar, a sort of gentleman's gentleman, so I expected a heady, intellectual conversation about faith. Nothing too personal. Instead, he asked me a question: "Do you know God?"

I fumbled for an answer. He stopped me and said these life-changing words: "You can't know God unless you spend time with him."

Spend time with God? How do you do that? "You pray," he said.

That conversation, which took place decades ago, set me on a lifetime spiritual journey that I explore in this book. *Prayer Works* comprises two memoirs originally published twenty years apart. Brought together into one volume, the parts form a whole that shows my evolution from a man learning to pray to a man learning to accept the prayers of others during a health crisis so debilitating that I found myself unable to communicate directly with God. When the habits of prayer I'd developed over the years failed me, the prayers of others sustained me.

Before that fateful conversation with the minister, however, I thought I knew something about prayer. I'd grown up going to church. Had memorized a few Bible verses in Sunday school, had been taught a bedtime prayer that my brother and I raced through to see who could finish it first. We never picked up our forks at the dinner table without listening to one of Dad's long rambling graces—dubbed the Six O'Clock News.

But did I spend time every day listening to God, looking for Him in my life, saying what was on my deepest heart? Well...no. How on earth do you listen to God?

That long-ago conversation got me started. I developed a prayer practice. Practice feels like the right word for it. Practice is not perfect. Practice is simply doing the thing day after day and trusting that if I'm present in this space, God is present too.

The best time to pray turned out to be during my subway train commute to work. This might sound insane or at least counterintuitive. Pray on a noisy train hurtling underground in the middle of a loud, clamoring city? Where is the much-lauded, sought-after silence in that?

But for me it worked. The rumble of the train, the jostle as the car bounced over the tracks, became my call to worship. The noise was soothing. I would start by reading a bit from a small pocket version of the Bible that I kept in my briefcase, a psalm or two. Then I would close my eyes. Check out to check in.

I was grateful for all that pastor taught me, but I felt he'd left out something important about praying. Finding time was good, but also finding a place was essential. The same place day after day. The external stimuli became internal stimuli.

For some people it's the birds singing outside their bedroom window. For me it was the click of the train on the tracks. It was like going to my desk and logging on to the computer. Time to work. That prayer place provided the same sort of signal—time to listen to the Spirit. Log on.

I happened to do it on the A train. Even wrote a book about it called *Finding God on the A Train—A Journey Into Prayer*, which makes up Part One of this book.

I've been asked: What do you do about interruptions? How do you handle distractions? What do you do to keep your mind from wandering?

Let it wander, I say. Just notice where it goes. If you start thinking about how much money you have in the bank and that difficult conversation you're going to have at work or that upsetting story you read in the newspaper that morning, put those worries in your prayer. Hear them, pray them. Then let them go. It's like catching a fish on a line and then releasing it. Catch and release. Let it off the hook. If you try not to think of the distraction, it'll only get bigger. Put it in God's hands. It might have come to your mind for that very reason.

On the A Train I've prayed for strength and guidance and understanding. I've prayed my way through family challenges and more than one health crisis. One of my hopes, one of my deepest desires, was that this regular inner workout—like going to the gym or jogging up the hills in the park, something I still do—would help me through those stark, spare times when God felt far away. If I was used to listening for Him on a crowded, noisy subway train, then I'd be ready to call on Him when I was in any sort of difficult situation.

That indeed felt true. For the longest time.

Until. Until the medical mishap I write about in the second part of this book, something that happened only three years ago. On a lovely September day at a time in my life when everything seemed to be going swimmingly, I landed in the hospital, hooked up to an oxygen tank, scrambling for every breath, my fever raging. The finest medical professionals couldn't figure out what was wrong with me. I was in despair. Worse than that, I couldn't pray. I couldn't find the necessary inner peace to do battle with my body and soul. So much for my so-called practice.

I was used to praying for others. It's something we do regularly here at Guideposts. Every Monday morning a group of us editors gathers around a conference room table and reads some of the requests people send in. I get emails, phone calls, and text messages, and pray for complete strangers. I do it for the people who are in need, who are suffering. I also do it for myself. Anytime you are asked to listen to someone else's struggles is an opportunity to grow in compassion. You can feel your soul being stretched. You can understand why the world asks for God's mercy.

But I didn't often ask for prayers for myself. Because I was too proud or too private or maybe because my needs paled in comparison with those of others.

Until that September day. My wife, Carol, sat by my hospital bed in the I.C.U. step-down unit and sent out emails about my dire condition. The word went out. People read it on Facebook. Friends and strangers alike shared my needs with their faith communities. People prayed for me.

Not for nothing is the second part in this book called *Pray for Me*. Most of my life, I'd heard that phrase only one way.

You have a need? You have a concern? You or some loved one is in trouble? I'll pray for you. I'll lift up that need and ask for God's help. As Jesus taught, wherever two or more are gathered, there Jesus is among us.

In the hospital, I discovered the second meaning in that age-old request "pray for me." It also is an opportunity to pray for someone who is struggling to find the right words or is in such despair that they don't know how to storm the heavens and can't feel God's presence. "Pray for me," we say because we can barely pray for ourselves. We need the help of others.

Because of all those prayers and because of a fine medical team and because of the wisdom of doctors and because of the tireless care of caregivers and because of the love of my wife, I came through. I recovered. I am back to running a few miles in the park (*slowly*) and singing in our church choir and praying on the subway and praying at home on our sofa in the morning (if our cat, Fred, will let me). I still stumble over memories of the trauma, but I am well and grateful, very grateful.

There is a lot more I could say about prayer, but most of it is in these pages that follow. May my words help you and sustain you in your prayer life.

This book is an expression of love for all those friends and strangers and Guideposts readers who did pray. It's what we all do—practicing day by day, growing in compassion and care, learning to love as we call on God's love because to love is to pray. Every day.

PART ONE

For Sweetie

CHAPTER ONE

This is my place. This is my time. This is my discipline. The subway rattles, shakes, and rolls. The tabloid headlines scream out in bold black letters, diverting my attention. Who was killed? Who was maimed? Who won the ballgame? The kids sitting next to me and standing above me are talking about school. One poor lone soul in baggy pants with the crotch at his knees is doing his homework, scratching the answers to algebraic equations in a workbook while trying to contribute to the conversation around him about girlfriends and teachers and music. Others have music plugged in their ears. Very loud. It sounds like rap, but all I get from where I sit is rhythm and bass.

At least the kids are easier to ignore than the old people. Old people standing on a crowded subway while I sit are the worst distraction of all. Old people who get on at 168th Street or 145th Street after I've settled into one of the few seats. Old people who can barely reach the metal straps that hang above my head. I hear their sighs. I feel their packages at my toes. Looking down, I can see their tired feet, the women in hose that bunch at the ankles. I avoid looking up, wary of meeting the gaze that will say, "Give me your seat, please." I avoid noticing how old they are by focusing on the small book in my lap or closing my eyes and thinking about God.

This is my place. This is my time. And if I really believed in the integrity of this devotional time, I would get up and offer my place to someone who probably deserves it more than I do. But that would mean stopping my prayer time for a moment, leaving off the meditation that I desperately crave. But I already have stopped. There's no choice. I look up and lock eyes. I offer my seat. The woman shakes her head no. I insist. She shakes it again. She says something to me in Spanish and indicates by her gestures that she doesn't mind standing. I look at what she's reading. I can make out a few words about God and prayer. I smile. This is her place too. We're not alone. *Where two or three are gathered in my name, I'm there with them.*

I close my eyes again and concentrate. Without even gazing around, I know there are others here too. I've come to know them by sight over the years. There's the woman with the red chapped hands who takes a rosary out of her frayed overcoat pocket and fingers the beads with one hand while holding on to a pole with the other (unless she, the fortunate one, has found a place to sit). There's the young Orthodox Jewish man with a thin brown beard barely covering his pink cheeks and chin. His prayer book is a mystery to me, the pages going back to front, the words right to left. There are Bible readers with black, well-thumbed books, passages circled and underlined in multicolored ink. I avoid their eyes because when they see what I'm reading they invite me to their neighborhood Bible study groups, and although I admire their commitment, this morning I don't want to hear their textual analysis. I don't even want to hear their witness, however moving their tales might be. This is not my time for community—except for the silent community that we create as we pray separately together on our journey south to make money for mortgages, rent, groceries, spouses and children, pizza and a movie on Saturday night.

4

Despite my best antisocial efforts, someone I know sits down next to me and I have to talk. My neighbor and I happen to find ourselves on the same train, in the same car, on the same bench, and although I can tell that he'd rather read the newspaper folded open in his hands and I'd rather look at the book in my lap, we make conversation. Of course, we could avoid talking about anything important by sticking to the weather, and then he could wander back to the front page and (if I proved brave enough to expose my fumbling efforts at faith) I might stray back to this little green-bound pocket edition of the New Testament and Psalms.

Instead, we connect. We discuss a mutual friend who's seriously ill. We talk about frustrations we have as parents of boys who are close in age. "How's your son doing in soccer this year?" "Is he planning to do baseball in the spring?" "What do you do when he doesn't do his homework?" We share our love of community and discuss the odd, awkward way our apartment building makes us a community.

At 59th Street, where we both get off the A express train— he goes upstairs to take another train and I wait for the local— we bid each other good-bye. How much time did we spend together? Twenty minutes at the most. But the time wasn't wasted. We're good friends. We exchanged news and advice. We talked. And as much as I'd dreaded the interruption of the business I'd set out to accomplish, I was grateful for it in the end.

"The Holy Spirit is the Lord of our time," a minister once said to me when we were discussing time management and how frustrating it was that you could never get done exactly what you planned to get done. "We give ourselves goals, deadlines, schedules, timetables," he explained, "but in the end, the Holy Spirit is the Lord of our time." I understood what he meant. The interruptions—the problem phone call, the crisis at home, the sick colleague whose job we must fill—are holy obligations as serious as the devotional time we've set aside to be with God. *Therefore, if you bring your gift to the altar and there remember that your brother or sister has something against you, leave your gift at the altar and go. First make things right with your brother or sister and then come back and offer your gift.*

So morning after morning I come to this place in a world of distractions, and I pray. I don't clock myself, but I use the subway stops as markers, guiding me in my ritual. I read from the 181st Street station to the 125th Street station, usually from the Bible, occasionally from what my wife calls a "God book"—a work by some metaphysical sage, recent or not so recent. Then at 125th Street I close my eyes. It's the express train, no more stops from there to 59th Street. At least five minutes (but as I say, I've never clocked it) of uninterrupted time. This is my time for God.

It's so little. I'm almost ashamed to admit to it on paper. There are other times too, I hasten to add. There are spot prayers uttered at work between taking a telephone call, making a trip to the water cooler, and wrestling with movable icons on the computer. There are letters that are really prayers as they capture a wish or a dream or a hope for someone else. There are formal prayers said at church on my knees, or grace at dinner with the children, thanking God for the minutiae of a day. There are those prayers I say in bed at night when I can't get to sleep because of worries about friends or work or family. And then there are songs that are prayers lingering in my head like the incense that clings to my jacket after a High Church festival Sunday with the thurifer swinging the billowing censer while smoke-sensitive choir members cover their mouths with handkerchiefs.

But this early-morning time of prayer feels like the most important. Without it my day would fall apart and I would forget whose I am and what I want to do and what I believe. It's the time without which I would exist only for myself, without which I would be consumed by petty demands on my time and petty distractions of my ego. I would be pulled into a thousand pieces by the various roles of life I play—friend, singer, son, do-gooder, student, worshiper, committee member, faithful correspondent, telephone talker, writer, editor, husband, father.

It's my time. It's my place.

CHAPTER TWO

I t all started about a dozen years ago, but I can think of a better place to start. Something my mother made me do when I was very young.

I was the third of four children. We were evenly spaced out, two years apart: girl, boy, boy, girl. We were raised in Southern California in the fifties and sixties. Whenever I see one of those family movies or classic TV sitcoms of the period, I'm briefly reminded of the world I grew up in. The people look and sound like sanitized versions of the neighbors I knew, the kids playing sandlot baseball on the cul-de-sac, the mothers hanging up laundry and gossiping over the back fence, morning newspapers arriving on the front porch and prize petunias blooming in back. The block on *Hazel* or *Leave It to Beaver* or *Ozzie and Harriet* could have been my block with its neat sidewalks, clipped hedges, cheerful green lawns, and open carports, illuminated by the bright, overexposed, yellowy sunlight of the L.A. Basin on a smoggy day.

I lived on a street that had been named by my grandfather when he lived in the neo-Spanish tiled house that dominated the block. That's where my mother was born. Then, a generation later, my grandfather built our one-story modern house behind a row of stucco tract homes. Next door was a vacant lot filled every winter with towering mustard weed that we used for making forts (making it easy to picture in Sunday school the startling scale of what comes from faith as small as a mustard seed). In the gully below our house ran a dry riverbed that had been covered over with cement so that it would take the runoff from hoses, sprinklers, and winter rains to the sea.

Dad worked as a salesman in my youngest days. He took long road trips up the Central Valley selling farm machinery and then flew back to the Midwest to visit the manufacturers he represented. Mom was often left on her own to rear her four children, and all told she did a good job. Especially when you consider that she herself had been reared by nannies, housekeepers, and a nervous neo-Victorian mother who was capable of warmth but no great spontaneity. My mother's mother lived for her regular games of golf and bridge at the country club. She was hopeless in the nursery or the kitchen. She actually had a nervous breakdown after my mother was born and took off to Europe for months to recover, leaving the children behind. So in many ways Mom started from scratch with us. And what she couldn't intuit she gathered from the popular advice dispensed in paperbacks and magazines.

In one of those publications, about the time I was born, Mom read an article suggesting that children needed time to be by themselves. Not just naptime or bedtime, but time during the day when a child could be behind a closed door (left slightly ajar, should the child call for help), sitting on a bed, gazing at the pages of a book or running a miniature car around a track on the chenille bedspread. With four energetic children, Mom appreciated the wisdom of advice that would allow her a few moments away from us. Once we were settled, she retreated to her bedroom for solitude. During hot September days when the Santa Ana winds blew from the desert, I remember her even resting in the bathroom. Given the lack of air-conditioning in our house, the white tile floor of that room was the coolest place around.

Many of my recollections from early childhood are images from this mandated rest time. I can remember looking out across the brick patio in the back to my brother's ramshackle treehouse. I can hear the sound of trucks driving on the main street that lay beyond the yellowing field of mustard. Sometimes I can hear the distant whistle of a train on the tracks that skirted our town's historic adobe mission. In midafternoon I can feel the heat of the sun melting my crayons as it shone through the large picture windows that looked out over the gully down to the concrete riverbed. But one of my key recollections isn't even from home.

We were at my grandparents' beach house. It sat high on a hill surrounded by ice plant and pink and white geraniums that gave off a bitter smell when we stepped on them. From the front we walked down a wooden path that snaked down the cliff to the surging Pacific. Waves pounded on the rock-strewn beach, carving out caves in the cliffs and bringing kelp to the sand. I didn't like to be on the beach, even when an adult held my hand. I found the water itself frightening and the noise of the waves terrifying. But from up on the cliff, looking down, I loved staring at the water.

That afternoon of my vivid memory I was in an upstairs bedroom for my twenty minutes alone. I crept up to the large plate-glass window, tinted green to keep out the glare, and I looked down to the lawn, the wooden chaise lounge draped with wet beach towels, the plastic bucket and shovel awaiting my return. Down the slope and beyond the sand and rock, the kelp beds sloshed up and down in the ocean like my mother's nylon stockings being washed in the kitchen sink. The waves rolled slowly, and the wind blew whitecaps across the tops. The sea stretched endlessly, going as far as the eye could see, finally disappearing in the haze of a gray fogbank. What had frightened me close-up now took on the luster of magic, the sunlight sparkling on the water like glitter spilled from a bottle or sequins on a majorette's gown in the Rose Parade.

As the wind blew and the waves rolled, I squinted, breaking the reflected light into a rainbow's prism. How long I stood there and gazed I don't know. Time stopped. I was left alone. *If children are lost in thought, leave them be.* That was my mother's blessing. It was a wonderful gift. She taught me how to love being by myself. She showed me what wonderful discoveries I could make on my own.

First there was the initial boredom. Then a moment of panic: "What if I don't have anything to do?" (I still get stuck at this step. I rush out of the house with a satchel overloaded with books and magazines for fear of an unfilled hour. Time lost. "Lost, yesterday, somewhere between sunrise and sunset, two golden hours, each set with sixty diamond minutes. No reward is offered, for they are gone forever," said Horace Mann. Victorian nonsense I still seem to live by.) Then, if I allowed myself to relax, I would rest silently and make friends of solitude. I would look with the inner eye and listen to the inner voice. My imagination opened up. Stories came to mind. A crack in the plaster ceiling took on shape. The rhythm of a rope flapping against the flagpole sounded the first notes of a symphony. It was my time, my time alone.

So prayer, when it was reintroduced to me, found fertile ground. I was used to listening to my soul. I'd discovered how solitude brought comfort that could be lost in the haranguing crowd. And at an early age I was given a solid sense of self that I kept with me so that I could disappear from the world (while still being in the world) and discover an inner world.

What a lost Eden! What an easy thing to allow to slip through your fingers! For it has come and gone and then come back to me. But I must never forget. Solitude has been my source of strength throughout the years, even in its most basic form, even without addressing a Supreme Being. I need to take time alone.

CHAPTER THREE

T ake time every day" was the advice of the man who set me on this spiritual journey a dozen years ago. I met him in his home office in his New York apartment, a room with dark-green walls, Oriental rugs, a cordovan sofa, wing chairs, and framed prints of the Holy Land done by nineteenth-century landscape painters. We met first thing in the morning, before work and after his church's morning prayer service. His wife usually left him some toast and marmalade on a silver tray and he ate as we talked—or rather *he* talked. He always offered me a piece of the toast with marmalade, which I ate hungrily.

He made me nervous because his eyes often wandered during our morning sessions: to his phone, which illuminated if anyone was on another line, to the view of treetops outside his window, to the well-worn books on the shelves that revealed his erudition, to the closed paneled doors. Behind those doors his family could be heard getting ready for the day. Did he listen to me? Or was he listening to his son complaining about having to wear a jacket on such a warm day and the baby-sitter receiving her marching orders and his wife fielding a call from a parishioner? And then just when I thought he hadn't heard a word I said, he turned his blue eyes on me and asked a perceptive question that showed he had followed every phrase.

He was a minister, and that was why I had been sent to him. A friend of a friend, he professed to be interested in my spiritual plight. I was not of his parish, I was not of his denomination, but at the recommendation of our mutual friend, I found myself in his office, studying the frayed threads of the Oriental rugs while his wandering gaze sometimes lingered on me.

"Do you know God?" he asked at our first session, not wasting any time.

"Do I what?"

"Do you know God?" he repeated. "You've got to be able to answer that question first."

It was the worst possible question, and it took me completely off guard. I didn't expect it of him. Partly because he was of that nice blue-blooded ministerial stock, Yale U. and Div. School, which seems more concerned with preserving the church's architectural heritage—shoring up buttresses and keeping dry rot out of the beams—than knowing God. He had the right society minister's looks: tall, tanned, rugged, and handsome, making a clerical collar the ultimate fashionable accessory, like a pectoral cross on a runway model. I had expected some fancy theological talk about a Higher Power and maybe a copy of Reinhold Niebuhr shoved across the table to me. To speak so frankly about faith, even for a minister, seemed in the worst of taste.

"I grew up going to church," I said; or something like that. I'd gone to Sunday school, I'd sung in choirs, I'd been baptized,...and at the appropriate age, I'd joined the church. Because I came at the tail end of the Right On generation, the end of the baby boomers, I had participated in church-sponsored peace rallies and marches to end world hunger. I had stayed up late in church basement coffee houses and had passed around petitions in favor of getting the United States out of Vietnam. I'd grown up in a congregation that was hip enough to have a bearded youth minister who rode a motorcycle and strummed a guitar, singing folk songs about the martyrdom of Abraham, Martin, and John. I'd sat through sensitive rap sessions in that same church basement, as we lounged on batik-print pillows around scented candles, talking about how friendship was like a bridge over troubled water. And I'd been in youth services of contemporary worship where we passed out daisies and danced before the altar.

But did I know God?

As his eyes wandered, I told him that I was still a church-goer, was even paid for it because I had a decent tenor voice (and in New York City if you had a good enough voice and could read music, you could get a Sunday job as a paid chorister). I didn't have to admit I was in church to find out more about God. It was a job. It was money. It was a small check every month.

He grabbed a piece of toast off the sterling-silver platter. He probably had a dozen things on his mind. A meeting with the ladies from the Altar Guild, a sermon to write, a hospital to visit? And I searched my mind for something to say.

The only analogy I could come up with was that if I knew God, it was the way you knew the parents of your best friend from high school. You'd been in their house hundreds of times (although not in their bedroom), and whenever you saw them, they asked you polite questions about what college you hoped to attend and what you wanted to study and what you wanted to be when you grew up, but no matter how often they insisted upon it, you couldn't bring yourself to call them by their first names.

"No, I don't really know God," I said after a time.

"You don't know God?" he repeated.

"I suppose I don't."

"Do you want to know him?"

"Yes. That's why I'm here."

"Good. Well, here's what you must do." He turned to me, his attention focused. Now I felt it coming, the salesman's canned spiel, the well-rehearsed pitch. He would give me some stapled pamphlet with stick-figure drawings and time-worn phrases. He would tell me the steps I needed to follow—one, two, three, four, five—and at the end he'd put one clammy hand on my head and ask me to open my heart.

Instead, he dusted the toast crumbs off his fingers and licked a swirl of marmalade from his thumb. "You must pray every day," he said. "Five minutes or an hour—it doesn't really matter how long. What's important is that you do it every day, even when you don't think you have anything to say. *God* will have something to say. Get yourself to a private place and pray."

"Should I read the Bible?"

"That would probably help."

"Should I get down on my knees?"

"If you'd like."

"Should I find a group of other people to pray with?"

"That can be a good idea."

I was asking questions simply to prolong the discussion, but he stood up to indicate that our session was over. He expected to see me again. He would be my spiritual director—that was the term he used. He would be glad to guide me in my exploration. Now the ball was in my court.

He prayed over me, brisk, godly words, and then gave me a bear hug, a warm gesture that took me by surprise. He stood back and smiled. I was free to go. No charge. It wasn't like a visit with a therapist. We would meet again. He turned to a page in his pocket calendar. Two weeks from now? Fine. Same time? Great.

The next morning, before the winter sunrise, I went into the office of our one-bedroom Upper Westside brownstone apartment and opened the Bible to a few psalms. I had set the alarm so I'd be sure to have enough time before the day began. But I woke up on my own at 6:30 on the dot, as alert as though I were about to leave for a jet trip across the country. I had that sense of anticipation you have before making a long journey. The bags packed, the plants watered, the refrigerator empty.

I raise my eyes toward the mountains. Where will my help come from?

I didn't kneel. It would have made me too self-conscious. I closed my eyes and kept my hands on the Bible.

My help comes from the Lord, the maker of heaven and earth.

I heard the radiator rattle and someone flush a toilet in the apartment one floor beneath us, the water surging through the pipes. I heard my wife pull the covers tighter around her on the futon on the floor in the next room. I heard the refrigerator switch on, the lights dimming slightly from the loss of power. I could hear my own breathing. What was there to say?

Inspired by the Bible, I reached for some exalted phrases. I could think of a few sick people to pray for. A friend's mother had cancer; another friend's grandfather was having open-heart surgery. And I knew plenty of people with money woes; I could pray for them. I could pray for my wife, Carol, and the book she was writing. And peace, I could pray for peace. But what did I really want with God? What did I want to say?

In the silence, in the old house's creaking and groaning as it woke up, something came to me. First a nothingness, as though I were a blank slate waiting to be filled. Then an uneasy feeling inside, like the gurgling I heard in the water pipes behind the walls. Finally a question as shaming as the anxiety that comes before entering a room full of strangers at a party: Would God have anything to say to me?

CHAPTER FOUR

Those first mornings in our apartment's office, as I thumbed through the psalms in my small pocket Bible and looked for God, I found gnawing evidence of my own inadequacy. The silence told me how little I liked myself, and as I kept telling God I wanted to serve him somehow, I felt very small. Would my life ever count for something? What did God want of me? Surely he must exist, for he was the only one who could help me. I felt so low that getting on my hands and knees and crawling under the desk would have suited me fine. Was this what it was to know God? I wasn't sure I liked it. And all those psalms. What was so exalting about their phrases? *I am a worm and no man.... Why do the heathen rage? Break thou the arm of the wicked and the evil man.* Nothing nice and sweet. Nothing pious and churchy.

I would have given up early in this pilgrimage but for my deep need and two things I had learned about myself.

First there was something I had discovered in my writing. During the first year of my marriage I was working at being a writer. That was my principal occupation. Every day, after prayer, after doing the breakfast dishes, I wrote.

Like all struggling writers, I had turned to the works of other, greater writers for inspiration and advice. At the time I had written an (unpublished) murder mystery. As a native Californian and Angeleno romantic, I read a lot of Raymond Chandler. I couldn't imagine writing as well as he did. I made my way through his novels and then, still searching for some

27

clue to how he worked, read a volume of his letters, a book I found on the shelf of my mother-in-law's home. Somewhere in a letter to a would-be writer he had this wise thing to say about writing fiction (I paraphrase):

If you want to be a writer, you must set some time aside every day to write. You don't have to write. But during that time you can't do anything else.

No reading magazines, no filing your fingernails, no looking up favorite chapters from books, even if you think that task will bring inspiration. No cleaning the bathroom sink or scrubbing the floor. No telephone calling—especially not that. Just sit there and…well, write. *You don't have to write. But you can't do anything else.*

Just try it sometime. You find yourself going bonkers doing nothing. You can't wait to get to the typewriter. Even with the most modest literary ambitions, you want to push your pen across the page or move the cursor along the computer screen. No matter how inadequate you find your imagination, you're forced to depend on it. You write. You listen to your inner voice. You write anything. Maybe for a long time you sit and study your cuticles and count the hairs on the back of your hand, but eventually you write. You *have* to.

"That's what it must be like to pray," I realized as I began my prayer journey. *This time is sacred. I might not have anything to say to God, but I'm not allowed to speak to anybody else. No phone, no books, only the Bible. Pray. I don't have to pray. But I can't do anything else.* There's an old paradox that goes, "Faith is a gift, but you *can* ask for it." During my prayer time I set myself to asking.

The other thing that helped me persist in my pilgrimage was an analogy made by my spiritual director relating to my marital life.

That winter, in the first year of our marriage, my wife rented a TV to watch the Winter Olympics. Every evening, instead of talking at dinner, we'd stare at skiing, skating, tobogganing, ski jumping. We'd watch the men's figure skating, the women's figure skating, the ice dancing. For four hours every night we watched TV. It was exciting, but after a few days I felt as though I were living with a stranger. We were both glued to the TV. During the commercials my wife and I conveyed some essential information, but we didn't talk long enough to communicate. We discussed the phone bill, the rent, and who was going to pick up macaroni and cheese at the corner grocery store or what to order from take-out Chinese for dinner, but we didn't connect. I didn't know what she was worried about, what she was dreaming about, what she cared about, and what made her angry. I had lost touch.

"We've got to talk," I finally said during one commercial.

"What do we have to say?" she wondered.

"We'll figure it out when we sit down to talk."

So we established the "half-hour rule," one we still abide by. According to that rule, we have to sit in each other's presence half an hour a day. No TV, no newspaper, no books. Maybe we don't think we have anything important to say. Perhaps the day doesn't seem very interesting. Perhaps our minds are empty of any witticisms. Tough. We sit and talk. And if we're there long enough, we discover that we have plenty to say. We hear each other. I find out about my wife's work and the article in the newspaper that irritated her and what her mother said on the phone that morning. She discovers that I have an irrational fear of the polar ice cap melting and an interest in the dollar's rise and fall on the international currency markets.

"Just as in marriage," my spiritual director told me, "you can take care of necessary business with quick petitions to God, but you're never going to get close and stay close unless you spend time together. You can't know God or even know what you want to say to him unless you commit yourself to praying. Not just here and there, or in passing. Set aside time every day to do it."

And if I did it every day, I just might find out who God was and who he was to me.

CHAPTER FIVE

L ook back to your childhood. Look for times when you felt close to God. Look for what your past says about you spiritually," my guide had said to me. I didn't have to look far. There was something in my oldest memory, at least the oldest one that I can date.

I wasn't three years old yet. My mother was very pregnant with my little sister, who was born a few weeks before my third birthday. When the baby kicked inside the womb, I was encouraged to hold my ear up to my mother's tummy. It was like listening for the sound of the sea inside a conch shell or being told to look through the telescope for a view of a distant island when all you can see is your eyelash squashed against the lens. Although I could never really hear my sister kicking (or hear the sound of the sea in the shell), I could feel the warmth of my mother, and that was enough.

That day was a Sunday and my mother was wearing a pink seersucker maternity dress. I wore scratchy wool shorts and a white cotton shirt with stiff short sleeves that stuck straight out like a paper doll's. We stood together on a small riser in the church nursery, looking out the window at the older children playing in the sandbox and swinging on the swings. It must have been one of my first times at the church, because I was afraid to be left alone with the stout lady in the starchy dress that crinkled like tissue paper and the children who played on the swings. But Mom stayed with me, my hand in her warm hand. I felt comforted. I felt safe.

Did I know God? "We get our first glimpse of what God's love is like from our parents," I was told. We learn intuitively about God's nurturing from their nurturing. We come to understand how our wants are served and our needs satisfied. Our parents on earth as our Father in heaven. This concept worries me, because I wonder if those who had rotten parents will ever know a loving God (a God beyond the stern lawmaker and author of all natural disasters). But the concept also explains why this image of Mom and me has lingered with such clarity. It's not just chance that this is my oldest memory or that the setting is a church. There in the nursery I was comforted. I was safe.

In time that church we were visiting became our church, and its architecture became the scene for my earliest inquiries about God. The building wasn't your usual ecclesiastical Gothic but a variation on California Tudor, the half-timbered walls of a well-scrubbed Stratford-upon-Avon surrounded by day lilies, poppies, night-blooming jasmine, and roses that blossomed eleven months a year (one month to regenerate—a very limited dark night of the soul).

On Sunday mornings we were delivered to Sunday school rooms that wrapped around a sunny courtyard. Sometimes we were allowed into the sanctuary, sanctum sanctorum, where the arched beams in the ceiling disappeared into darkness like the ribbed beams of my father's boat sinking down into the keel. From the central beam in the apse a microphone hung from a black wire that seemed to come out of nowhere, dropping from the sky. And despite my father's best explanations, I believed it took our prayers up to heaven.

The minister was a kindly white-haired man who shared my first name, and when I was baptized I felt his wide hand encompass my small head, the drops of water messing up the cowlick that Mom had rigorously shellacked with spit and comb only minutes before. He looked holy to me, a central casting version of the divine. In Sunday school, we'd been told that no one knows what God looks like, but I knew the teachers were wrong. I knew exactly what God looked like. I had seen his picture on the cover of the record album of the Broadway show *My Fair Lady*. It was a Hirschfeld drawing of Eliza Doolittle as a marionette manipulated by Henry Higgins, whose strings were pulled by a bearded George Bernard Shaw from the heavens. God as playwright, God as puppeteer, God pulling all the strings. It was more convincing than the saccharine illustrations of Jesus I was shown.

I proved to be a champion Sunday schooler. I loved the songs: "Jesus Loves Me," "He's Got the Whole World in His Hands," "Joshua Fought the Battle of Jericho." I loved the art projects: making Judean homes out of sugar cubes, stick shepherds out of pipe cleaners, mangers out of Popsicle sticks. I loved the stories we dramatized, putting on old bathrobes and binding scraps of sheets on our heads with old stockings, marching around a stack of chairs until the walls of Jericho really came a-tumbling down. I was attracted to some of the teachings, especially Jesus' message of turning the other cheek. Here was a philosophy that transformed my older brother's nightly thrashings of me into a glorious martyrdom. My brother might have thought he was destroying me, wrestling me to the floor. But I was the true victor. After all, I had turned the other cheek.

In Sunday school we learned about prayer. We were taught how to close our eyes and bow our heads, telling the Lord what we wanted. "Don't worry about what you have to say," we were instructed. "It's just like talking to God."

I quickly decided, however, that it wasn't just plain talking. It wasn't like chatting with your stuffed animals or some imaginary friend. You used big words like *thou* and *thee* and *shouldst* and *wouldst*. You couldn't say just anything. If there was something you wanted from God or a favor you needed done, it was more like talking to an adult, one who wielded all the power. You had to phrase your request carefully, gauging your remarks with the utmost caution. You had to be careful. I knew about talking to adults. I had listened to them a lot. Parents, even when they think they're being harmless, can say hurtful things.

From an early age I was an eavesdropper. I discovered that if I lay on the living room floor with a few toys or a picture book, I could listen to Mom and her bridge-club ladies talk. I could collect valuable nuggets of gossip. Or at the beach, if I lingered by the grownups' towels, pretending to be absorbed in a sandcastle, I could gather information not available to my contemporaries. Sometimes my mother observed me and interrupted her friends, saying, "Little pitchers have big ears." But most of the time I went unnoticed. I had enormous powers of concentration. I was usually absentminded and had to be reminded countless times to do the things I was supposed to do, so how could my mother tell I was eavesdropping? How would a parent know I had overheard a remark when I rarely paid attention to what I was supposed to hear?

What I learned is that adults talked like parents when they spoke to kids, but they talked differently among themselves.

They discussed with disarming frankness their offspring's shortcomings and received with gratitude the praise of their children's strengths. It was the praise I longed to hear—real praise, not just the flattery meant for my ears but a direct, unpatronizing, adult-to-adult compliment. (That it would be flattery for my parents never occurred to me.) "Such an unusual child." "He's very talented." "He paints very well for a boy his age." "Does he always sit there like that without saying a word, reading for hours?" "He has a lovely voice when he sings."

The sting came when I discovered adults laughing at me. I remember sitting on the bleachers at a college football game. Feigning fascination with the band's half-time show, I overheard my mother's dear friend repeat a remark I had made earlier: "He said to me, 'Do you know that we four kids are born exactly two years apart?' Can you imagine that?" Then both women laughed, my mother just as hard as her friend. I felt betrayed. That my mother would think it funny too! Of course, I didn't understand that I had made a precocious comment about my parents' family planning to a friend who had twice as many children. I knew only that I was hurt.

The sting could also be administered by adults who weren't family or friends. I remember an incident that happened in second grade. At the time I loved to go to the dime store, where I'd spend hours walking up and down the aisles, studying every plastic ray gun, clipper ship, and antique car before I'd spend my five cents on a piece of candy or a stick of bubble gum. The aimless daydreaming was half the pleasure. I could imagine owning all the toys, or debating over which would be the perfect thing to buy if I had a dollar or two.

Then one day, as I was gazing at a new model of an aircraft carrier, I overheard the woman who ran the store laughing at me with another customer. "He'll be here all afternoon and look at everything in the store before he buys something," she said. I felt cheated. Spied on. Found out. Deprived of my private delight. Quickly I bought my gum and walked out of that store, never to return again. I would deny myself pleasure rather than be laughed at. Pride goeth before a fall? My pride would rob me of delight.

The flip side of this was a painfully acute willingness to please and a hunger for a record of my success. The subtle, unintended effect of my early Sunday school experience was to learn that God liked us best when we took center stage and showed off. He expected us to be good in class, quick at raising our hands, prompt with the answers about God's love. We were adept at reciting any memorized Bible verses and confident in the solo we sang before a packed congregation at Sunday school graduation (where we were awarded certificates for perfect attendance). It was hard not to believe that God was interested only in goody two-shoes.

And yet what a place to shine! I loved my moments in the godly limelight. In particular I recall a church Christmas party at some member's house. All the other kids had retreated to another room for a round of Freeze Tag or Murder in the Dark. The sugar cookies with red and green icing had been eaten up and the pink punch in the crystal bowl was long gone, but I lingered with the adults at the piano as they sang all four verses of "We Three Kings" and grown-up carols like "Bring a Torch, Jeanette Isabella." I waited patiently for my opportunity.

"Rick, would you like to sing a solo?" the pianist finally obliged, answering my prayer. "Why not 'Silent Night'?"

Why not? I took my position in a corner of the carpet and sang in my clear boy soprano, the precise diction a result of imitating the English children in Mary Poppins. I was a little nervous, but not much. A hush came over the room. Everyone was listening to me. I hit the high notes without any problem. When I was finished, the applause came, the only clapping at the party, then the usual compliments: "What a nice voice! You sing so well. You should be on TV." I listened to the praise that came my way (and more important, the words that went to Mom and Dad); then I joined my own age group.

Later, in the car as we drove home, I asked my parents (disingenuously), "Did anyone like my singing?"

"Yes," they said, repeating what I had already heard. "They said you have a nice voice and you have perfect pitch." The words of praise were even sweeter the second time around. I could savor them in my mouth, as if licking divinity fudge off the sides of my teeth.

"Rick has a beautiful voice." Rick is rewarded. Rick is loved.

CHAPTER SIX

M aybe I picked up some odd notions about what it means to talk to God," I told my spiritual director.

"We often do," he said noncommittally.

"I came from a praying family."

"Tell me about it."

Every night at dinner, as we gathered around our Danish modern teak table in the family room, my father served up a smorgasbord of prayer. "Let us reflect on the day," he said, and we bowed our heads. Beginning with the news he had heard on the car radio coming home from work and continuing with the latest family crises, he threw out morsels of concern for God and us to mull over.

"Hear our thoughts, Lord," he'd say, and we heard his thoughts. "Please be with Uncle Charlie as he recovers from his operation. We're thankful for the doctors who performed the surgery.

"Remember the people in the Midwest who are suffering from terrible tornadoes.

"We're thankful for the coming elections—that we live in a country where we have the freedom to elect our leaders. We ask for your wisdom to guide and help us as we go to the polls on Tuesday. May those who win honor you in their service." (This was honest sentiment from a man who once told me it was a pleasure to pay taxes.)

"We were sorry to hear about the passing of Winston Churchill, but we trust that he's with you, and we're grateful for all the good things he did in his life."

And closer to home, he prayed for my sister to do well on a test the next day. Or he prayed for my brother to be able to finish his math homework before bedtime. Or he asked God not to make me too nervous on the night of my piano recital.

"It's the six o'clock news," one family friend said after hearing Dad's grace. "He keeps you up to date by mentioning everything he can think of."

He prayed us through the various space flights, the moon landing, the assassinations of Martin and Robert and John, the forest fires in the California foothills, the Vietnam War, and student protests. He prayed us through the deaths of beloved relatives and the births of distant cousins. He prayed us through Marilyn's overdose, the Nixon inauguration, the Watts riots, Watergate. He was encyclopedic in his approach. He included everything that came to his mind. It was his moment, his chance to address his Lord (and his captive dinner-table audience). With four talkative children, he wasn't likely to get another chance.

Sometimes he tantalized us with short references to the day's events, such as "We remember Cousin George," or "Thank you for the healing of Aunt Eleanor," or "Help the Haskin family." When we lifted our heads we had to ask, "What happened to Cousin George?" or "What was wrong with Aunt Eleanor?" or "Who are the Haskins?" Then for a few more moments the table was Dad's. He took the floor. He got to speak before mayhem resumed.

He had a fine theatrical instinct in his prayers. He used interruptions well. I was reminded of him once when I was at the opera and saw a diva respond with a shrug to a set that collapsed at the wrong moment. She gave it its due, the audience got rid of its embarrassed laughter, and then she went on with her aria. Instead of ignoring disruptions—which only would have drawn our attention to them—Dad incorporated them into his prayers. For instance, when my little sister and I started giggling, he asked God to bless our high spirits and good humor. When the German shepherd next door started to bark at some distant siren, he thanked God for the dog. And when our mutt responded, barking and leaping at the sliding-glass doors, Dad asked God to help us keep the pooch happy. When the telephone began to ring, as it always did for my older sister during her high school years, he thanked the good Lord for her popularity and requested a little more peace and quiet around the house. And when the timer went off in the kitchen, announcing that the rolls were ready to come out of the oven, he brought grace to a quick conclusion: "Bless us to thy service and this food to our use. And God bless the hands that hath prepared it." Then Mom would rush to the kitchen and rescue the rolls with her much-blessed hands.

What to do with interruptions in prayer? Include them, for goodness' sake. Maybe the interruptions are God's way of reminding us to add something or someone to our prayer list, the Holy Spirit once more clamoring for lordship over our time.

Dad's graces were a wonderful ritual, but when I think about them, they were holy in that nice way of church prayers. They were filled with graceful "thanks" and prayerful "pleases" and all-inclusive blessings. He would make the charming asides of a practiced preacher to elicit a laugh and be assured that we, his secondary audience, were still with him. But what about a praying person's aching request for love

or popularity or attention? What about the kind of prayers I
made in bed late at night, such as the wish not to have to sit
alone at lunchtime at school, or the hope that if the teacher
called on me in class I wouldn't get my words jumbled up, or
the heartfelt request that would God please not let the class
slugger hit the ball to me in left field? How did I know God
heard those prayers too? Did Dad ever make them himself?

The odd thing about these corporate prayers is that they
were a contrast to the violence of emotion I was discovering in
the psalms. In third grade I memorized the hundredth and the
twenty-third psalms. Before the congregation I recited "Make a
joyful noise to the Lord" and the pastoral "The Lord is my shepherd" with my classmates, earning myself a copy of the Bible, a
black embossed Revised Standard Version with colored maps of
the Holy Land in back. But no one asked me to learn such passages from the psalms as "Break thou the arm of the wicked
and evildoer," or "Break their teeth, O God, in their mouth,"
or "Let them be blotted out of the book of the living." Hadn't
I wished that sort of harm on Lyle Donovan, who stepped on
my sandcastles in nursery school, or on Brad Bruington, who
pelted me with rotten persimmons one day when I was on my
way home from school? Why didn't we memorize *those* passages?
What would that have done for our spiritual education?

I knew intuitively about the dark, lurking terrors of life.
Twice I'd had deep premonitions that seemed to be fulfilled—
like the horrors promised by the biblical prophets. Once I
woke up before the dawn, knowing that something bad was
going to happen to my family. That morning my brother,
Howard, broke his arm when he fell off his bicycle. Then one
Good Friday when I was filled with a similar fear, I was almost

relieved to learn that distant Alaska had been struck by the worst earthquake in years. As I stared out at the ocean, waiting for a tsunami to come, I almost wondered if my premonition had brought on the disaster. Were there no prayers big enough for such cosmic fears?

There's something else I find disturbing about my own prayers at this age. They were often phrased in a negative way. *God, don't make me have to catch that ball. God, don't make me have to eat this terrible casserole. God, don't let the house burn down while the baby-sitter is still here. God, don't let me be the last one chosen on the team.* Feckless, spineless, I lacked the courage of my convictions. It was as though I was afraid God would say no if I asked him for something really big and nearly impossible. I don't think I ever once had the gumption to pray, "God, make me a fabulous baseball player during P.E. today so that when the ball comes to me in left field I'll be able to throw it into home plate, making the runner out and turning me into the hero of the school."

I think I feared that if I asked for something big, my faith would be tested. I might stop believing in God—this little image of a weak, unterrible god. Safer to keep the petitions to a minimum. Safer to be less than anything I dreamed of. Safer not to have to risk being refused and rejected. Wasn't that my biggest fear? To ask God for something and then not get it?

As a child I knew only one confirmed atheist, my Aunt Gioia. My mother's older sister, she was a loud, opinionated, strong-willed woman with a machine-gun laugh and a chain smoker's mentholated breath. A single parent of four girls, she lived down the street from us, and our families assembled for every relative's birthday and every major holiday. At the dinner table she held forth, holding her beautifully manicured hands aloft like some Renaissance saint, the smoke from her cigarette rising as incense. But she didn't believe in God. And when we bowed our heads to listen to Dad's blessings, she kept her eyes open, staring blankly at the avocado Jell-O salad or the camellias around the birthday cake. (I noticed. I peeked.)

Why didn't she believe? The family story was told:

When Aunt Gioia was eight and her mother was expecting a child, she prayed and prayed for a little brother. She knew God would answer her prayers, for God answered all the prayers of fervent believers. Then came the big day and her mother went off to the hospital, but when her father came home, he announced that she'd been given a little sister instead—my mother. My aunt burst into tears. She wouldn't accept a sister. She went into her bedroom and slammed the door. When her mother came home from the hospital, Gioia locked all the doors and windows and wouldn't let the baby inside. Finally coaxed into reason, she unlocked the front door and held the newborn. In time she became a devoted sister to my mother, but she never forgave God and she never believed in him again.

Maybe that's what I feared. If I asked for something big, I'd end up like Aunt Gioia. Forever disappointed. I'd be like her at dinnertime: staring blankly at the avocado Jell-O salad during Dad's grace, or watching the smoke rise from her cigarette to a heaven she refused to recognize.

CHAPTER SEVEN

Y ou must have had some good influence, someone who set you on the right course."

"Like who?"

"A friend, a relative, a teacher.... What about Sunday school?"

There was one teacher among the horde of Sunday school teachers who brought me closer to God.

She taught a special Sunday school class that was held on Tuesday afternoons. I made a deal with my parents: if I went to the class on Tuesdays, I wouldn't have to go to Sunday school on Sundays. I could sit in church with Mom and Dad, or sing in the choir, or go see a (religious) movie with the older kids during worship. By then I was in fifth grade, and the teachers who taught regular Sunday school for my grade weren't to my liking. One was an ex-Marine with a buzz haircut and halitosis. His drill was the memorization of Bible verses and the unimaginative enforcement of a weekly Sunday school curriculum—notebooks, flannelgraph boards, puzzles, games, and dreary, moralistic stories. His partner was a dour woman who wore her hair in a French roll and had a streak of blue eyeshadow on her eyes. She didn't smile much, probably for fear of getting wrinkles. I didn't hesitate about what choice to make: I would attend Sunday school on Tuesdays with Mrs. Clarke.

It was a little embarrassing at first because of the unbalanced ratio of boys to girls—two or three to almost a dozen.

After all, what self-respecting preadolescent male would want to learn about the Bible on a sunny afternoon when he could be catching pop flies at the sandlot? I didn't mind so much as long as there was at least one other boy. But if I was the only boy who showed up on a Tuesday afternoon, it was sheer torture.

(That's always been a problem with the expression of faith in our society. Men are afraid that it's women's stuff. That's one reason why men's prayer breakfasts and men's Bible studies and football ministries and baseball chapels exist. To take off the womanly taint stuck to prayer and faith. To make God look a little more macho. To make men feel maybe that it's all right to talk about Christ. It's also the sad reason that the newly ordained ranks of female clergy often face such an uphill battle. Men feel awkward enough talking about God, but it's a little easier if the preacher looks like their high school football coach.)

In fifth and sixth grades I stuck it out. I was one of three boys in the class (if we all showed up), and Dura Clarke was my teacher.

Mrs. Clarke was a Texan with jet-black hair, long bony fingers, paper-white skin, and dark eyes that were so deeply set you could barely see her eyelids. At times when the strain of keeping us under control became too great, she took off her glasses, put them down on her dog-eared Bible, and rubbed her deep sockets until I thought she would erase her eyes. "I think the Enemy is in our midst," she would say as we fidgeted at the table, someone lobbing a spit wad across the room. She was so sincere, she caught our attention. "I want us all to bow our heads and ask God to restore us to our purpose."

Our main purpose was a glorious one. After juice and snacks, after hymn singing and Bible study, after making stained-glass windows out of colored tissue paper, we worked on making a movie. With her Super 8 camera Mrs. Clarke was filming the Bible, from the Creation to the Resurrection, soup to nuts. I came to this project fairly early. My first role was Abraham the patriarch, white cotton beard and blue robe over my corduroys and sneakers, footage of the Texas hill country spliced in later to represent the land of milk and honey. After practicing in the upstairs Sunday school room, we put on our costumes and went to the local park, where the key scenes were filmed. (I prayed no sandlot-playing classmate would see me in my biblical duds.)

The girls carried water vases on their heads and huddled around the pup tent that was Sarah's and my home. Sarah laughed her infectious giggle—the only humorous moment I could find in the Bible—when the angels without wings told her she would have a child. She was supposed to be even older than Dura Clarke, and at the time I thought that was ancient.

My great moment came with the sacrifice of Isaac. We actors walked to a fallen sycamore tree, the trunk white and gnarled. Isaac carried a bundle of kindling, and I had a kitchen knife hidden in my belt (we giggled when Mrs. Clarke called the belt a girdle). Mrs. Clarke shot a close-up of the knife, and then we walked to the tree trunk. Like any would-be Cecil B. DeMille, she gave her directions from behind the camera, for this was the era of silent home movies.

"Tie him to the trunk, Abraham. Good, good. Raise your knife and raise your face. You're bewildered, but you know that you must follow God's will, so you obey. Good. Now you hear

God's voice. He's telling you to stop. He won't make you take your son. You've passed the test. Look to the bushes. There you see a lamb—we'll splice it in later. You'll sacrifice the lamb instead. You're happy, overjoyed. You're a good servant of God."

I loved the acting. I relished playing Abraham's old age with arthritic fingers, stooped shoulders, and deeply furrowed brow. Like an old movie star in a silent film, I gave an exaggerated, histrionic expression of despair for Mrs. Clarke's rolling camera. My hand shook as I clutched the knife, and my eyes fluttered shut as I imagined the horror of it all. But when I heard the voice of God, a beatific, bewildered expression came over my face.

Later I played the aging Isaac, and then Jacob. Mrs. Clarke recognized my dramatic bent and encouraged it. Others carried water jugs on their heads or shepherds' crooks in their hands. I held a knife and spoke to God. More important, God spoke to me. That's what captivated me about these mini-dramas. God spoke. In the Bible, people heard God's voice and obeyed it. God spoke to them in their tents, in fields where they were "keeping watch over their flock by night," on the rooftops of those Judean houses I had built out of sugar cubes. As I pondered this notion, I wondered if God would speak to me. Would he address me between dinner and my allotted half-hour of TV? Would he swoop down on our palm-lined block, where I flew a kite and rode my bike? Would he make an appearance in the school auditorium after we said the pledge of allegiance before an assembly? It was Dura Clarke's great gift as a teacher and the work of acting that made me feel that maybe I wasn't so far from Abraham, Isaac, and Jacob. God spoke to them. Why wouldn't he speak to me?

That became my fervent prayer. It wasn't an ultimatum. I never went so far as to say, "If you don't speak to me, I won't believe in you." But I did make my firm demand. I had become fixated on it. What did God's voice sound like? If you heard it, was it like hearing the principal's voice over the loudspeaker at school? Was it like the voice of the ghost in the TV show *The Ghost and Mrs. Muir* or the mother in *My Mother the Car?* Was it something that only you heard, making everyone else think you were out of your mind? Did God say actual words, or was the message just a feeling that came over you? (And if that was all, did it really count?) I even asked Mrs. Clarke one day after class, when the others had gone outside, "How do you know if God speaks to you?"

"My dear child," she said, looking at me with those dark, deep-set eyes that disappeared into her head and connected directly to her soul. She knew I was in earnest. She wouldn't laugh.

"You'll know," she said. "You'll know."

Then one early evening on a clear, rain-washed winter day, I was bicycling home from my piano lesson. The smog that usually shrouded the San Gabriel Mountains had lifted or blown out to the desert. I was coming to a hill behind my school with an incline good for coasting around the corner and all the way to the next street. You could lift your feet off the pedals and sail on the wind. It was getting dark, and the mountains were crushed grape at the bottom and gold at the top. The royal palms bent with the breeze as I lifted my feet off the pedals. And in that moment God spoke to me.

He was in the mountains, in the sunlight, in the dead palm branches clapping against the trunk. He was behind the schoolyard's chain-link fence and above the lone Frisbee thrown into the air across the newly sodded field, the sweet smell of grass tickling my nose. He was in the street lamps that just that moment clicked on—or did I only notice them just then? He was in the Clementi sonatina that had just left my fingers and the smiley face and three stars it had earned from my piano teacher. He was in the meatloaf dinner that would be waiting at home and the Wednesday night elation of having got through more than half the week without any mishaps. He was in the approaching twilight and the fading pink. He was in the wind, the night, the day; he was in me. I knew God spoke to me, words no more profound and no less than the great "I am" echoing through the words of the prophets and the psalms. As I careened down the hill, borne by gravity and some strange emotion I had never known before, I cried because I knew God was.

CHAPTER EIGHT

It would be wrong of me to suggest that was the only transcendent moment in a childhood that had its share.

There were the times we watched *Peter Pan* on TV, the taped version of the Broadway play with Mary Martin in it. It was broadcast every spring in my childhood. I remember going over to my grandparents' house to watch it on a color TV with all my cousins, lying on a bearskin rug with my head on the dead bear's stuffed head as I watched Mary Martin fly, held aloft by an invisible wire like the one attached to the microphone in church. I remember when Tinkerbell drank the poison. The glass went empty and her light flickered, gradually going dim. Just then Peter flew in, discovering his dying comrade. The poison was meant for him, yet "Tink" (sacrificial soul) drank it to save him. At that magical moment Peter—Mary Martin in tights—turned to the camera and begged everyone in the TV audience to clap. "If you believe in fairies, clap," he (she) said. "If you want Tinkerbell to live, you have to show that you believe. Clap, clap, everyone clap!"

Back then I clapped. Everyone clapped. Even my brother, who when told that elbows on the dinner table squished the fairies usually pounded on the table hard with his elbows. But when he heard about Tink's demise, he clapped. And I clapped harder. I believed, and I wanted to show that I believed.

I was drawn to things that required faith. Willingly I suspended my disbelief. It was easy to appeal to my imagination. Some things appealed so readily to my fears that I dreaded them. They called up monsters in the twilight and made me shudder. The flying monkeys in *The Wizard of Oz*, the rumbling chords of "A Night on Bald Mountain," the kettledrums in "Peter and the Wolf." Monster movies were out of the question.

I was the ultimate sucker for TV appeals. I had to watch hours of Jerry Lewis's Labor Day weekend telethon for muscular dystrophy. When my brother insisted on changing the channel, I burst into tears. "But Howard," I tried to explain to him, "as long as we keep the TV on, the little boy in the wheelchair will live. But once we turn it off, it's all over. The TV *has* to stay on for him to live." Like Tinkerbell's flickering light going dim. Clap, clap. I believed. Clap, clap.

And then there were the great space-age milestones of our era, some bringing fear, some lending thrills. I learned early to dread the sound of the sonic booms that rattled our plate-glass windows and made me fear that the Russians really were coming this time. But how could anyone forget the magic of being carried outside in his pajamas on a summer evening and having his father point to the heavens at a moving star that was our first satellite flying overhead? I remember my father's excitement and the nighttime sky better than any speck of light.

When I was six, my mother took me to my first professional play, a bus-and-truck production of *The Sound of Music* at the old Biltmore Theater downtown, not far from the red neon sign near Pershing Square that declared, "Jesus Saves." It was the last show to play in the old theater before the place was torn down and turned into a parking lot. We sat in the top row of the upper balcony beneath a few frescoed *putti*. "The bloody-nose section," an older man sitting next to us observed. (It was years before I realized he was making a joke about the high altitude of our seats.)

The curtain rose. The Alps looked like cardboard, even from our distant vantage point. The Trapp family house was obviously made of fabric; a wall rippled when an actor slammed a fake door. One backdrop came down from the fly-space and almost bounced off the stage floor. My eye wasn't fooled. But I was transported by the music. The combination of orchestra in the pit and real people singing on stage moved me. I found it intoxicating that people could make music out of what they had to say and what they felt as the plot progressed from song to song. I was hooked on musical theater.

From then on, the years of my childhood could be marked by whatever musical I saw: a *Showboat* revival, Meredith Willson's *Here's Love*, *Brigadoon* in the round, a high school production of *Carousel* that left me sobbing, *Mame*, *Man of LaMancha*, *You're a Good Man, Charlie Brown*. I asked for tickets for my birthday; I bought all the records and spent hours in the music store, fingering the sheet music. A biography of Richard Rodgers was my favorite book at the library. The imprimatur "Original Broadway Cast" became for me what *nihil obstat* is to an orthodox Catholic reader. I turned on the record player, and if no one was looking I danced to the music on our family-room rug.

Soon every other word of conversation was a cue for a song in my head—not only the hummable refrains but the obscure introductions and multiple verses. I discovered the power of a song to transform my moods, always for the better. The heartbreaking songs—the likes of "From This Day On,"

"You'll Never Walk Alone," and "Somewhere"—had cathartic powers. I could be smarting from the familial injustices that came of having an older brother twice my strength, and still I could talk myself into well-being by rattling off the patter of a song like "Wouldn't It Be Loverly?" from *My Fair Lady*. The meaning of the words was unimportant. The rhythm and tune satisfied.

"He who sings prays twice," said a sign in Gothic script posted in our choir room at church. For a long time I stared at that during rehearsals and wondered what it meant. Then I understood it a little bit. When you sing a song, it stays with you; it sticks in your craw and repeats forever in your mind until you get a new song to get rid of it. It's like praying without ceasing. Throughout the day you do a thousand other things—you brush your teeth, solve a math problem, do your homework, run a cross-country race—but all the while you've been singing of the sublime beauty of "Dulcinea." Even when I wasn't sure I believed, I found phrases of hymns and religious songs repeating in my mind.

"O, clap your hands all ye people, sing unto God with the voice of triumph." It becomes impossible to separate a biblical text from a tune once you've learned to sing it. I read "If with all your heart ye truly seek me, ye shall ever surely find me" and hear Mendelssohn, or read "This is the record of John" and think Gibbons. "O Clap your hands with a voice of triumph" is Vaughan Williams. How can anyone hear the phrase "And he shall reign forever and ever" without humming Handel? You sing the words before they make any sense, like a child warbling "Round yon virgin, mother and child." The sense of it comes much later. You believe, clap, clap. You clap. You believe.

The most popular moment of each Sunday school session came at the very end of class when a green light went off next to the clock at the front. That was the signal that the adults were finished worshiping. We were free. We could grab our mimeographed sheets of Bible verses and our clay crèches and our tissue-paper stained-glass windows and race down the stairs to meet our parents. But what I loved even more, the signal I looked for, was the sound that came a few seconds before the light went on.

The ushers pushed open the side doors of church on the last verse of the final hymn (modulated up a half-step), and the lovely, thrilling roar of hundreds of people singing like all the Whos in Dr. Seuss's Whoville shook the casement windows and the branches of the magnolia trees. Clap, clap, they believed.

Because I knew how to sing, I knew how to praise God. I knew it inside of myself. I knew that bubble-up-inside-you feeling. I knew how in only a few bars you could go from minor to major, from sorrow to joy, from adagio to vivace. I knew how people sang from the stage, as though their lives depended on what they could put into music.

> Praise God with the blast of the ram's horn!
>   Praise God with lute and lyre!
> Praise God with drum and dance!
>   Praise God with strings and pipe!
> Praise God with loud cymbals!
>   Praise God with clashing cymbals!
> Let every living thing praise the Lord!

CHAPTER NINE

B ut you still don't know how to ask," my spiritual director
said. He had become impatient with me and my ram-
blings about my past, as though my faith had been frozen at
some preadolescent level without any of childhood's natural
trust. This was a hurdle I dreaded facing.

"Ask?" I wondered.

"Ask for what you want. You don't trust that God will give
it to you."

He quoted Scripture at me: *Therefore I say unto you, What
things soever ye desire, when ye pray, believe that ye receive them and
ye shall have them.*

*Verily, verily, I say unto you, Whatsoever ye shall ask the Father
in my name, he will give it you.*

"That doesn't seem fair," I said, sounding very much like a
child objecting to the arbitrary nature of parental rule. "The
onus is on the person praying. As though if you don't believe
hard enough in what you're asking, you won't get it. That
doesn't seem fair."

"How will you know if you don't ask?"

Ask? I shuddered at the memory of people on religious television shows asking God for houses, for cars, for vacations in
Hawaii; of people begging for first prize in the Publishers
Clearing House Sweepstakes. It's as though God were the ultimate home-shopping companion. Order anything you like
and then give him a few numbers from your moral stockpile of
goodness and devotion. Offer up your niceness as collateral.

Charge it on your good-values credit card. I remembered the
weird experience of going to a scientific, nonchurch church in
Hollywood. A friend had asked me to go with her. She had said
she found the place helpful.

I was led into a large, windowless room, like the meeting hall of a secret society. The walls were painted a surgical
green, the floor covered with beige wall-to-wall carpeting.
Organ music came from speakers hidden above the ceiling's
acoustical tiles. We sat in folding chairs while the "minister"
(who called himself a "doctor") led us in a "treatment." We
closed our eyes and visualized what we wanted.

"You want a cabin in the mountains?" the preacher/doc-
tor said. "See it; picture it; make it come true. Believe it." He
looked for a situation appealing to the Hollywood congregation. "You want to be a star on a television series? Imagine it.
Imagine the audition, the things you say, the people you meet.
Picture yourself on the set with the actors you want to work
with. Or you want to fly first class? See the experience in your
mind's eye. See that wide, soft first-class seat. See the steward-
ess serving you complimentary champagne. Hear the beautiful classical music playing on the headphones. If you believe in
it and ask for it, you can have it."

I squirmed uncomfortably. The treatment struck me as
sacrilege. Who was going to give us all these good things
we were asking for? Was just picturing them what it took
to have them? Would a well-directed, fertile imagination
suddenly bring us the starring role or the first-class seat? It
was nonsense. The nonfrocked minister in the beige linen
suit seemed a charlatan and his treatments a sham. But now
my own spiritual director, a tweed-suited, clerical-collared

divinity school graduate, seemed to be suggesting that I do the same thing.

"It's so materialistic to ask God for things," I complained.

"Well, aren't some of your needs materialistic?"

"Yes, but..." I looked for more objections.

"Don't you think God cares about what you eat, where you live, how you work?"

"Yes, but why should he bother listening to me? Doesn't he have much better things to do with his time?"

"You know that old gospel hymn, don't you? 'His Eye Is on the Sparrow.'" He hummed a bit. "That says it all. 'He watches over me.'"

"Well, if he watches over me so carefully, he knows what I want already. I shouldn't have to tell him. I shouldn't have to ask him. He should have it all figured out."

"Maybe," my spiritual director said, while eyeing the light that illuminated on his phone, "just maybe he wants to hear it from you. Maybe he wants to hear you say it yourself. Maybe he knows you need to say it. When you need a raise at work, you ask your boss for it. Like your boss, God needs to know you care."

I wasn't so sure. When I left the parsonage and made my way through the dusty park to the subway, I thought again of the Bible record. *The Father will give you whatever you ask in my name.* I hated asking anyone for anything, let alone my Father in heaven. As a kid, I hated to ask my own mother and father for things. Not that they weren't generous; not that there were strings attached. It's just that I could always think of good reasons why I shouldn't be given a new book or couldn't go to the movies or wouldn't be able to take acting classes in summer school. The more I wanted something, the worse it was. I didn't want them to know how badly I wanted something. I wanted to please. My imagination worked overtime so I wouldn't have to ask for things.

I can recall something that happened when we visited New York City for the first time. It was 1965, the year of the World's Fair, when so many kids I knew made the pilgrimage to New York. We didn't go to Flushing Meadows to see the fair because, as my father (California chauvinist to the core) explained, "We have Disneyland back home." Instead, we traipsed the city streets for twenty-four hours. I loved it—loved the dust, the noise, the bustle, the popcorny stench, the sweltering July heat. It even rained that night, a summertime novelty for a Southern Californian. We climbed the Statue of Liberty, took the elevator to the top of the Empire State Building, walked through Times Square, where through the windows of a darkened bar I spied go-go girls dancing. We threw coins in the fountain at Rockefeller Center, held our ears in a hurtling subway, ate breakfast in the basement of the Seagram's Building, inspected the Impressionist paintings at the Metropolitan Museum of Art, and hurled paper airplanes out of the window of our skyscraper hotel, watching them float out of sight.

But as we were walking the streets on the morning we left, I got a bad case of the hiccups. We passed a streetside vendor with a large cart and an umbrella. I hiccuped vigorously, and he held up a small carton of orange juice. Did I want some?

Standing on a corner of Fifth Avenue with my family, I was suddenly struck with indecision. What *did* I want? Would orange juice help?

"You can have some," my dad said. I looked at the short, white-haired vendor holding out the juice. It would mean a sale for him, money in his pocket. He looked sympathetic. Except that drinking orange juice didn't usually work to get rid of hiccups. Suddenly it embarrassed me that we were stopped on a New York sidewalk because of me, and I wanted to get moving.

"What do you want?" teachers asked when you raised your hand in class.

"What do you want?" parents asked if you interrupted their telephone conversation. "What do you want?" they wondered when you woke them up in the middle of the night because you had had a bad dream or felt sick or scared.

What did I want? I didn't know, and at that moment on that street corner I was frozen with indecision. Stymied by an excess of self-consciousness, caught in confusion, I wondered whom I should try to please: my mom and dad (what did they want?), the man selling juice, or me?

The memory of the moment startled me. At the time, my indecision won. It was easier to say no. I shook my head no at the vendor and shrugged off Mom and Dad's concern, hiccuping repeatedly as we crossed the street and continued down the sidewalk to one last New York landmark, a blast of air-conditioned cold attacking us whenever we passed an open door.

Indecision won then as it often did later in my life when I struggled over career choices, life choices, spiritual choices. Sometimes I was like a person who buries a "to do" list deep in papers on a desk, hoping that the onerous tasks would somehow be done when the missing note was unearthed months later. I would rather that someone else do the asking for me, or that the decision be made by proxy. Maybe it was because

I spent so much time wondering what the answer would be—second-guessing the response—that I talked myself out of decisiveness. I was the last person I knew to ever ask a boss for a raise or a promotion. Did I do that with God? Did I spend so much time trying to figure out what he was like and what he wanted that I gave up being honest about what I wanted?

Just maybe he wants to hear from you. Tell him. Be direct. Believe that he wants what you want. *Just ask.*

"But I've done that before," I told my spiritual director. There was a time when I boldly asked, believing that God would give me just what I wanted.

O God, I'm still stuck at this level. I hate to ask for things. What if you refuse me? What if you say no? My faith wavers constantly. "This must be what the Lord wants," I think. But can I ask for it? No. I'm afraid. Even now. Afraid of being rejected.

CHAPTER TEN

With the onset of puberty I flirted dangerously with not believing in God at all. Maybe it was hormonal. Maybe it was intellectual. Whatever the reason, religion for me was an on-again, off-again thing during adolescence. At one moment I was the star of our church youth group, leading the congregation in contemporary worship services, hoping to shock the oldsters with a rendition of "One Tin Soldier" that was meant to be a rabble-rousing call to peace, passing out daisies as we sang. At another moment—in fact, at almost the same moment—I was sharing lustful asides with my best friend in the choir stalls about the girl in the front row who wore a backless Hawaiian print dress.

At a time when I wanted desperately to believe, I went with great enthusiasm to a youth Bible study at a church that was more evangelical than ours. One evening I sat on a leather sofa next to a gas-fueled fake-log fire in the fellowship hall of that church and listened to the leader outline what it meant to believe in Jesus. I hoped to give my heart to Jesus too, but I felt something phony and manipulative in the guitar music and songs, and when one of my cohorts found some charismatic spirit that flung her to the tiled floor in holy ecstasy, I wanted to laugh, not sigh. (Secretly I wished she were wearing a backless dress.)

When I was back at my usual church, our youth group went to see the movie *Woodstock* and then held a weekly Bible study on the book of Galatians. "Christ has set us free for freedom . . .," Paul wrote, and our minister emphasized that this book of the Bible was about freedom, but all I could think of were those hippies in the Woodstock movie who (high on music and hallucinogens) had taken off their clothes in the rain and were dancing naked in the mud. Free? Is that what real freedom was?

In the church basement our youth minister led a sex education class, and for several weeks I sat with a group of fifteen- and sixteen-year-olds as we gingerly discussed our feelings for the opposite sex. At one point the psychologist leading the session made some passing reference to masturbation.

"What's that?" one fifteen-year-old asked. The room fell into a stunned silence. I don't know what embarrassed me more—the clinical explanation the psychologist gave or the mind-boggling possibility that one of my contemporaries didn't know what masturbation was.

Lust is a confusing thing. Sex seems a sure way to heaven. It's so close. The forgetfulness, being lost to yourself in someone else's arms. The drive for passion…what a lovely servant, what a dangerous god. Not until I was married could I ever come close to acknowledging the power it had over me. Not until then could I see Eros as one of God's gifts.

After that I wandered away from church. By the time I was a junior and senior in high school I had decided it wasn't cool to believe in God, and when I started college I figured it would be much more convenient to call myself an atheist.

As an atheist I wouldn't have to answer any awkward questions about who I was or what I believed. I could indulge in some modest hedonism without any qualms. I wouldn't have to go to chapel on Sundays, wouldn't have to defend

any unpopular positions, wouldn't have to think about Saint
Paul when I wanted to think about sex. I could be cool, hip,
existential (whatever that meant). I was traveling all the way
cross country for an Ivy League education, and I figured my
Christianity was excess baggage—like my California flip-flops
and hang-ten T-shirts. It could go.

I arrived eagerly on the campus, finding walls covered
with ivy (as advertised), long-haired classmates full of radical
notions about impeaching the president, the dormitory lounge
filled with late-night *I Love Lucy* fans ready to challenge orthodox notions about faith as quickly as they changed the TV
channel. But what else should I discover? That my roommate,
the valedictorian at his Pittsburgh high school, a straight-A
student, and a brilliant physics major, was literally a card-
carrying Christian. He kept three-by-five cards with him at
night when he read the Bible. On them he wrote down passages he found inspiring and passages that would help him
when he was arguing theology with any of the doubters in
the dining hall. His Christian friends from campus often met
in our room for group Bible study, and the quotes were mar-
shaled out after the strumming of guitars and the singing of
folk songs that I'd thought I'd left behind in California.

It was God's little joke, no doubt. You can't run away from
the Almighty. He's the hound of heaven. *Where could I go to get
away from your spirit? Where could I go to escape your presence?*
God knew I was faking my unbelief. No matter how far I went,
he would be there. In fact, he would be in my own room, looking out for me.

I held on to my atheistic position for several months,
until finals loomed and I started to feel desperate about my

standing in my Princeton class. In that dark winter of my
first reading period—darker and colder that year because of
the oil crisis and the efforts by all to turn down the ther-
mostat and to turn off the lights—I worried that too many
late nights in the lounge trying to solve the problems in
the Middle East in heated discussions had taken their toll.
While my roommate had gone to bed punctually at 10:30
every night, I had reveled in the freedom of a dormitory
without parents and with few parietals. I had slept late a few
too many mornings, missing classes. I hadn't studied hard
enough. Now that I had to face finals, I didn't know how I
would manage without help.

One January afternoon I wandered into Princeton's monu-
mental chapel. The bright midwinter sun pierced the multicolored windows and bathed the pews with bright patterns—an
effect like autumn leaves on a forest floor. No energy crisis
here. I seated myself in the back. Someone was practicing Bach
on the organ up in front, the reeds and trumpets echoing off
the gray stone walls, rattling plaques that memorialized the
war dead.

I didn't kneel. I didn't open a prayer book or Bible. I simply closed my eyes and said silently, *Lord, I need help.* I spoke
as directly as I had when, at one of our church's annual youth
services while I was in high school, I had led the congregation in prayer with the self-conscious opener "Hi, God." Now,
however, I wasn't trying to shock my elders or shake anyone
out of a comfortable, complacent pew.

Hi, God. I need help. I need to pass my finals.

So there it was. I had asked God. I wanted something.
I needed it from him. And I wasn't greedy. I didn't expect

an A or a B on my finals. A C would do—what was wryly called a "gentleman's C" back then. I just wanted to pass Shakespeare and French 202 and the artfully named Physics for Poets.

Having asked God for help, I clearly believed there was a God to speak to. I wasn't just addressing the stained-glass windows or the bronze plaques or the wood carvings of apostles on the choir stalls. I hadn't even bothered to reintroduce myself. It didn't occur to me that I needed to. My behavior puts the lie to that old standby that "God helps those who help themselves." On the contrary, God is there for people who can't figure out how to help themselves.

Did I believe he really would help me? I must have. That's what desperation can do. It's the reason poor, bewildered inner-city dwellers often know more about the Lord than rich and well-insured suburbanites with blue-chip portfolios. The poor have to trust. They have to believe. So do the poor in spirit—like me. Back then I believed that any two camels could push themselves through the eye of a needle if God could help me squeeze out a passing grade.

"You were a foxhole Christian," my spiritual director observed.

"I was in a foxhole," I agreed.

"You needed help, so you prayed to God. That's the most basic aspect of prayer."

"But I still wonder...wouldn't God have helped me anyway? Did I really have to *ask* to be helped?"

"I refer you to a story in the Bible—one of the parables of Jesus. You should remember it—the parable of the importunate widow."

This is really one of the oddest parables of all. It opens with this preamble (as sobering as the surgeon general's warning on a pack of cigarettes): "And he spake a parable unto them to this end, that men ought always to pray, and not to faint."

The story goes, as Jesus tells it, that there was a certain widow who kept applying to a judge again and again, asking for justice against her opponent, until the judge, weary from her repeated visits, finally gave in. The point is this: Would God not do better than the unjust judge? "Won't God provide justice to his chosen people who cry out to him day and night?"

Where did that put me? Where was I meant to be? Clearly in the role of the pestering, importunate widow, badgering the judge until he gives in. The thought irritated me. Okay, so God is more merciful than any corrupt judge, but does that mean he tacitly approves of pestering? Day and night. Without ceasing. And if God knows what's in our hearts anyway, why should we ask? Why go to all that effort over and over, again and again? I had rather hoped God could be more direct. Ask and it shall be done. Your word, master. But no. Who was master here? God seemed to delight in my importunity, my servanthood.

"Asking is an important part of believing," my spiritual director said—and he was so wise here, so helpful. "Maybe God likes us to be repetitive in our requests. It's an exercise we need to go through. It's his way of preparing us for what he wants to give freely.

"Look again at another passage I've mentioned to you before: 'Ask for whatever you want and it will be done for you.' Believe. That's hard for a skeptic like you."

Once again he had read me clearly. When I asked, it was with the full knowledge of God's refusal. It was as though I had secretly supplied the Almighty an out. "Dear Lord, give me a job that I'll find fulfilling," I prayed, while muttering under my breath, "It's really a lot more than you can do. It's more than anyone can do. You don't realize how rough it is out there. When did you ever look for a job? It's a dog-eat-dog, swim-with-the-sharks world. I need to look out for number one. I'm afraid you can't help."

My sophisticated self worked overtime telling God what he couldn't do. Did I believe? Well, no.

So ask, ask, ask. Be importunate. Be insistent. Do something about what you're asking. Is it possible that you can become so tired of wishing that God would make something come true that you'll start believing it yourself?

"He wants us to be importunate because it helps us," my spiritual director said. "It helps us believe. 'Believe that you receive it and you will.'"

"I'll try."

He broke off a piece of toast. "By the way, did you pass all your finals that year?"

"Yes. I worked hard. I crammed. I stayed up late. I went to the library. I dropped by the chapel. I was willing to do anything, even believe in God, to pass."

"Did you believe he would help you?"

"I must have."

"Why?"

"It was finals, my freshman year. He wouldn't have wanted to see me flunk out. Everybody would have been disappointed."

"Good." He put his long fingertips together, gracefully forming a Gothic arch with his hands. "Do you believe he'll answer any of your prayers now?"

I shrugged. "I don't know."

"Do you remember what it says in the Bible about Jesus in Galilee after he'd been preaching to the people for a while and performing miracles? Suddenly he stopped. His work came to a standstill. No more healing. No more preaching to the people. The Bible has this telling phrase to explain it: *'He was unable to do many miracles there because of their disbelief.'"*

CHAPTER ELEVEN

After my first freshman finals, God and I were at a stand-off. I was willing to acknowledge his existence, showing him the greatest tolerance, like a teenage girl including her little brother on a date (with a guy she probably doesn't like much anyway). I was ready to believe God existed. I was not so ready to believe in his powers.

When finals came around again, I was a little more confident of my own ability. That can happen in the aftermath of an answered prayer. If your faith isn't strong, if you're still too proud to be thankful, you can easily convince yourself that you succeeded by your own merits. Or you can convince yourself that your knowing all the right stuff for the test was a mere coincidence. You start thinking that you would have done fine anyway. No need for divine help. Nice to have, but not necessary. An added frill.

I wasn't willing to make God a part of my daily life at Princeton, but during those four years I discovered him in other places. Outside of chapel, outside of the Bible study I visited once and hurriedly left (Christian folk songs ringing in my ears). Closed out of Sunday mornings, God crept into my weekdays. He made unexpected appearances on the syllabus.

I was an English major. And I had professors—intellectual, well-respected, recognized authorities in their field—who actually mentioned the Bible in the classroom. They had a way of smiling when they did it, enjoying the irony that Chaucer, Spenser, Milton, and Donne would have better luck at getting us to turn to the Scriptures than any well-meaning preacher or pamphleteer.

"Of course, you know," a professor would say, drawing us in with his flattering air of familiarity, "what Chaucer is referring to is the biblical passage in Genesis when God promises that he will never, ever punish man with an all-destructive flood again."

We nodded our heads. Our professors appealed to us where we were weakest, the academic's Achilles' heel: intellectual snobbery. No one dared admit that he or she hadn't opened a Bible since distant Sunday school days—but when our professors talked, we nodded. We understood. Of course, we knew.

God forgive me, I'm still an intellectual snob. When I applied to Princeton, I was told my chances weren't very good. "A weak possible," the admissions office said. I'm still overcompensating for that premature appraisal; still trying to prove I'm worthy.

The subtle and unsubtle references to Christianity in many of my English classes, especially when it came to anything written before the nineteenth century, had a cumulative effect on me. I decided it was all right for some people to believe. It was okay to ask the difficult faith questions. I saw that Christianity could come in palatable doses of good taste, which was even more appealing to my aesthetic snobbery. It could inspire the most profound literature, music, art. Bach cantatas weren't only formal experiments in music theory; they were also fervent expressions of faith. George Herbert wasn't just writing pretty poems; he was writing about something essential to his whole being. Flannery O'Connor's dark tales were comprehensible only when you applied to them her deep-seated Catholicism.

At this age I made an unusual choice for my senior thesis. I decided to write on the Victorian man of letters John Ruskin. At the time I explained it by saying I was interested in Ruskin's love of art and Italy, but now, upon reflection, I think I was also attracted to the dilemma of a man who was trying to reconcile his strict Calvinistic faith with his visceral attraction to the visual arts. He failed in the end, miserably—as anyone must fail who tries to make a direct correlation between good faith and good taste. It can't be done. The most sublime art can come from the most dreadful people, and the loveliest of modern saints can be satisfied with the most saccharine, cast-plaster statues and painted-velvet scenes. "God is not always choosy about the vessels of his grace," the writer Robertson Davies once said, and it's true, from overweight opera divas to debauched painters. Arresting beauty doesn't necessarily reflect religious truth, but I appreciated Ruskin's stubborn efforts to prove it did because I wanted someone to prove it for me, to codify in some reasonable way the connection between faith and art.

As I wavered in my faith, I wavered in my belief in myself. I was half confident and cocky and half scared to death. I couldn't figure out why. I liked to believe that God was a crutch only for the weak. I liked to think I could do very well on my own, thank you very much. And then huge doubts would assail me.

It was a time in my life when people said nice things to me about my talents and congratulated me on my achievements, and I couldn't believe a word they said. They're flattering me, I thought. I had an inferiority and superiority complex all in one.

As a natural charmer, I knew how easy it was to put someone on your side by a gracious word of praise. How was I to believe that my flatterers weren't as insincere as I was? I dismissed kind words as the balm of snake-oil salesmen. It takes one to know one.

One night at dinner, at the wide refectory table draped in linen beneath the flickering candles in the silver candelabra at my college eating club, I sat next to a psychology major who was attacking a fiercely individualistic, highly intelligent biology major from India.

"You cling to your faith because it's comfortable," said the psychology major. "You go to church and believe in God because it's the way you were raised. It's a mindless habit."

"On the contrary," the Indian fellow said, "I was born and raised a Hindu."

The comment rattled me. I identified with the psychology major, the learned skeptic, the independent thinker. And yet, who proved to be going against the grain? Who was the unique one? Who had taken the road less traveled? For the moment I wished I were more like the Indian fellow. He believed in something. Every Sunday morning he got up early to teach Sunday school, wearing his blue blazer with the crest of some old school in India. While pursuing a rigorous scientific field, he had still chosen to assert his faith. The unshaven, jeans-wearing skeptic barely rolled out of bed in time for Sunday brunch.

Another one who shattered my preconceived notions was the university chaplain, a fervent, Christ-believing World War II hero who had somewhat outlived his campus welcome. With a rich Scottish accent and a high Presbyterian style (the concept seemed an oxymoron), he delivered withering jeremiads Sunday after Sunday on the college's worldly ways. From my vantage point in the choir, I could listen to him remind us of the work of the devil, singling out the exclusionary practices of the eating club where I belonged. I could smile at his histrionics, honing my own imitation of his preaching, "It's Satanic! It's demonic! It's wrong, wrong, wrong, wrong!" But I admired his independence. I liked his commitment. I loved him for being unpopular. Nothing mealymouthed about him, nothing lukewarm. He wore Christianity with style. He even showed a sense of humor when I congratulated him on a sermon one Monday morning. "Well, at least you weren't asleep!" he said with the thick burr that had gotten only thicker the longer he'd lived away from Scotland.

If I were to become a Christian, I thought then, I would want to become a Christian like him. I would wish to be outrageous, anachronistic, a tightrope-walker. But I was a fence-sitter, and fence-sitters can stay stuck for a long time. It's amazing how long such indecision can last, even when you're searching, looking, reading, praying, sometimes landing right in the lap of God, then retreating back to your post on the sidelines out of the way. What did I believe? I didn't believe much in God. And I didn't believe much in myself.

CHAPTER TWELVE

H ave you ever heard of negative prayer?" my spiritual director asked me.

"Negative prayer?" It seemed a contradiction in terms. After all, wasn't prayer by its very definition an affirmation? When you prayed, you told God, "I want," "I desire," or "I need." The very act of praying seemed to be a means of saying, "I am," "I think," or "I believe." And all those usual sign-offs were affirmations: "Amen," "Let it be so," "Selah." How could prayer be a negative?

"Sometimes what we say to ourselves, what we think we want so badly, is destructive—even if we don't say it outright to God."

"But as a prayer?"

"Yes, prayer can also be negative. Look at the biblical evidence," he said. And then he began to pull biblical examples out of the air like a magician pulling rabbits out of a hat. He referred to the incident in Acts (I had to look it up) when Paul comes across a sorcerer, "a false prophet," who was trying to turn the new converts away from their belief. Paul, filled with the Holy Spirit, zaps the man and makes him blind—"only for a season" (which must have been a kind afterthought for the overzealous Paul). That was a sort of negative prayer.

"Remember how Jesus takes offense at a fig tree that bears no fruit?" he asked. This one I remembered. Jesus was walking along the road with the disciples and saw a fig tree with nothing but leaves on it. He cursed the tree and it withered before their eyes, as in a scene from one of those nature films of blooming flowers now suddenly run in reverse.

"Or there's the time when Jesus casts out the demons from a man and throws them into a herd of pigs. Do you remember what happens to the pigs?" Sure I did. The possessed pigs charged off a cliff in an act of mass suicide worthy of a modern apocalyptic cult. Maybe this was meant as a joke for kosher-keeping Jews, but I've always wondered if the owner of the pigs got recompense for Jesus' miracle. The healing was a positive act, but what of the fate of the pigs?

"There's tremendous power in a negative wish," my spiritual director went on. "If you repeat it over and over to yourself, it can become a prayer. All the kind, good, positive things you hope for can be obliterated by those negative, self-destructive thoughts. Think about it. If the Holy Spirit could be used by Paul to blind someone, or Jesus could wither a fig tree with a simple curse, what damage can we inflict on ourselves by our withering, crippling thoughts?"

Sermon finished, point made.

Then, in his usual distracted manner, he looked at his watch and opened the sliding mahogany doors of his study. The sunlight poured in, illuminating a shaft of dust raised on the old Oriental rug as I walked past. He fumbled at the series of locks on his front door, rang for the elevator, and bid me good-bye, giving me a hug, leaving me to think. How impatient I became with him, but I think there was a genius to his ways. He made me do the mental footwork. I had to connect the dots.

Negative prayer. Back in college we used phrases such as "He hosed himself," "He shot himself in the foot," or "He flushed himself" when a person did himself in. I suppose that was a kind of negative prayer at work.

In college I was in a small, tight-knit, all-male singing group. Twice a year we'd audition new members. In a campus lounge we'd listen to singers try to sight-read a few bars of close harmony and sing a couple phrases from the national anthem. Most guys were pretty good, but once in a while we'd hear a fellow who was so shy, so uncertain, so lacking in confidence that we knew before he opened his mouth that he would fail. Maybe he could sing, maybe he had a nice voice, but you could never tell from the way he handled himself. It was torture to listen to his intervals and watch him blush as he warbled through a few measures of "Oh, say, can you see" while backing up to the corner of the Steinway. You wondered why he put himself through it. You could see the poor fellow thinking, "I'm not very good at this. I can sing in the shower, but not here. I can't even carry a tune. What in heaven's name inspired me to sign up for this audition anyway? I can't take it anymore. I've got to get out of here. Help!"

Finally the misery would be over—misery as great for us as it was for the would-be singer. And after the door was closed and the singer out of earshot, we shook our heads and repeated the obvious: "He flushed himself. He hosed himself. Did himself in."

You could tell the moment the auditioner came into the room how he thought he would do. His attitude became a self-fulfilling prophecy. The losers looked like losers. I remember seeing some of those guys around campus later. They weren't losers elsewhere. They walked with confidence in the campus dining hall, swaggered as they carried their trays, certain that they had friends waiting for them. Or they were quick thinkers in seminars, leaning back in their chairs, listening to the discussion warily before contributing an incisive observation, making a clever connection no one else had made. But when they were out of their realm, even before they sang, their bodies shook.

I knew how they felt. When I was out of my element, I acted the same way. As a kid playing baseball or football or soccer, I always went where the ball was least likely to go. And when I came up to bat, I repeated this mantra: "I'm never going to hit this. I'm never going to hit this. I'm never going to hit this." I never did.

By the time I went to college I had learned how to protect myself. I had gathered a whole arsenal to save myself from the inner voices that wished for my failure, to guard myself against futile collapses of my fragile confidence. Believing that a man is what he thinks about all day, I found ways to make my thoughts as complicated as possible. Sophisticated, I thought. Witty, cynical, self-deprecating. But where do you draw the line between self-deprecation and self-hatred?

Don't get your hopes up too high. This was one of my self-protective devices. I think it's a common parental warning, because parents are afraid to see their children disappointed. They prepare the child for disappointment even before it comes. "Don't be overconfident about making the team," they warn. "After all, you're younger than the other kids and you don't have as much experience. Don't get your hopes up too high." Or they say, "I'm glad to see that you're trying out for the lead in the senior class play, but there's a lot of competition and it's a very hard part. Don't get your hopes up too high. I don't want to see you disappointed."

A wise child soon learns the message. You repeat it to yourself, turning it into a magical incantation. You decide that if you don't wish for a thing to happen, then you won't be let down. If you don't want something too much, you'll be happy with whatever comes. Pessimism masquerades as pragmatism. "If I don't hope this will happen, if I don't expect it, then maybe things will turn out all right. I'll be pleasantly surprised."

What a contrast this is to the faith, the optimism, even the blind belief of those who were healed by Jesus! Take the woman with "an issue of blood," who believed that she needed only to touch the hem of Jesus' garment to be healed. Or take the centurion, who believed that he needed only to have Jesus say the word and his ailing servant would be healed. Jesus didn't even need to go to the centurion's home; Christ's distant healing would be enough for the faithful soldier. *It will happen for you just as you have believed.* That's all anyone needed—a little faith.

I distrusted faith like that because it seemed to stem from ignorance. Blind faith, like blind confidence. Cocky people, I told myself, acted that way because they didn't know any better. They weren't sensitive enough to perceive their own faults. They couldn't be stymied by doubts because they didn't have any doubts. And yet what good did my religious doubts and self-doubts do for me?

As I walked away from my spiritual director's place and headed for the subway, I lingered over his words. *There's tremendous power in a negative wish. It can become a prayer.* I recalled auditions and interviews where I had disqualified myself quickly. While working as an actor, I had once told a prospective agent, "I'm not really a very good actor. I haven't had enough experience." Disarming candor? Hardly. I had hosed myself, flushed myself; I had done myself in. The agent must have wondered what I was doing in her office. She must have wondered how I had talked myself through the door.

I remembered doing an audition for a Shakespearean troupe, reciting Prince Hal's speech from *Henry IV*, part 1: "I know you all, and will a while uphold / The unyok'd humor of your idleness:/ Yet herein will I imitate the sun...." I identified with Hal. I liked to think that so far all I had done was a mere prelude to who I would become. *Herein will I imitate the sun*. Staring out from the stage at the empty red-velvet seats, I believed my glorious dawn wasn't far away. So I shouldn't have been surprised when the director said to me, "That was very nice."

Immediately I had my doubts. Quickly I explained that I didn't know how to do Shakespeare, had never been in a Shakespearean production, hadn't really studied him much.

"I liked what you did," the director reiterated. "You have a nice lyrical quality."

Amazed that I hadn't been asked to leave yet, astounded that I had repeated the entire monologue without being interrupted, stunned by the man's appreciative comments, I rambled on, digging myself a deeper hole. "I don't think I really have the voice for Shakespeare. My voice is too high. It would be nicer to be a baritone. And I've never done any stage combat."

The director became irritated. Almost red in the face, he insisted, "I liked it. You did a nice job."

I backed off the stage like a lowly servant retreating from a throne room. Outside I felt sick. Why didn't I believe in myself? Why couldn't I accept a simple compliment with grace and courtesy?

Cynically I decided it was because I never gave an honest compliment. I was a manipulator. I used flattery to make people like me. It was my stock in trade, a verbal tic. Usually there was an element of truth to what I said, but truth-telling wasn't my real purpose. Compliments were a way to please people, to make people enjoy me. So why would I believe anything nice that was said to me?

Several years later, when I was no longer acting for a living, I thought of the new job I was starting. Riding the subway to the office, jammed in the rush-hour train, I recalled the negative prayers I must have said as I began other new jobs. Not "Lord, let me succeed," but "Lord, don't let me be a miserable failure so that I attract attention." *Don't let me catch this ball. Don't let it even come my way.* It was one of those minor miracles of human stamina and stubbornness that I had succeeded at anything. So I was a good faker. But why fake out God?

And then it came to me, the point the good minister was driving at: you can't lie in a prayer. You can't fool God. He doesn't hear just the words; he knows the real wish of the heart. *What fills the heart comes out of the mouth* (Matt. 12:34). God had heard the prayers of my heart, no matter what words had come out of my mouth.

I thought of all the prayers I had written in my journal, prayers God had been kind enough not to answer: "God, make me a famous, sexy soap-opera star." "God, make me a Wagnerian tenor." "Lord, make me the author of a runaway best-seller that makes so much money I'll never have to work hard at anything again." "Jesus, give me a better body than the one I've got." (A few trips to the gym could have helped.) "Christ, why can't I dance like Fred Astaire?" (The countless dance classes I'd taken should have answered that question.) Had I really believed any of my prayers? What had been the prayers of my heart? Did I really want to succeed?

As I was traveling uptown to take on a writing assignment for a magazine, I wondered if I was doing what God wanted me to do. That was the help I wanted from my spiritual director. That was why I had gone to him in the first place. I wanted to know my vocation. I wanted to settle an issue that had plagued me for years. And now he was asking me if it wasn't my own limited faith at fault. Was that the advice I needed to hear? Was this the word meant for me?

I was right where I'd been ever since I graduated from college. I was still struggling with the same issue.

CHAPTER THIRTEEN

P erhaps, until one starts at the age of seventy to live on borrowed time," Graham Greene writes in his autobiography, "no year will seem again quite so ominous as the one when formal education ends and the moment arrives to find employment and bear personal responsibility for the whole future." Graduating from college, I concurred.

I wasn't ready to leave a world where everything was planned for me and enter one where I had to take responsibility for myself. What would I do? Where would I go? How would I live? I dreamed I could do a thousand different things, from running a Fortune 500 company to becoming a monk, and yet I didn't believe I was capable of anything.

At the time, I wished for a pair of parents who thought very little of what I did. Then I could prove myself or defy their wishes. But my parents' only declared wish was for me to be happy. Their all-embracing, all-forgiving, unconditional love embarrassed me, partly because it seemed so undiscriminating. I wanted to be told to enter the family business—if there was such a thing. I wanted to be ordered to do something patently practical, like writing advertising copy or giving piano lessons or selling encyclopedias door to door. I hated to be told I was smart, clever, talented, and capable of deciding for myself what to do. I hated to be given the chance to pursue whatever I chanced to dream.

The height of my misery came on graduation day. After wearing my cap and gown and receiving my sheepskin, I came back to my dorm room to do some final packing. Tears tumbled down my cheeks as I put old textbooks in boxes, rolled up old posters, folded blankets, and packed pillows in a steamer trunk to be sent ahead to California. In my self-dramatizing way, I was sure life was coming to an end. I would never discuss the fate of the modern novel again, never harmonize at midnight under a neo-Gothic arch, never swim in a fountain, never dance in a moonlit courtyard beneath blooming wisteria, never have so many friends in one place again.

Everyone else on campus seemed to be moving toward a promising future. But all my summer plans had fallen through. I'd lost a job, messed up a relationship, given up a summer sublet. I wouldn't be going to New York City, where half my class planned to converge. Instead, I was headed home. With my diploma shoved into a manila envelope, I would be driving across the United States with Mom and Dad. The only plan I had for my future was to paint the outside of my sister's house.

That hot summer, as we drove along the interstate, the plains had never looked so flat or the desert so desolate, the Joshua trees like prophets foretelling my despair. "The pathetic fallacy," my mentor Mr. Ruskin would have called it. My emotional state determined how I saw the landscape. When Mom and Dad and I came over the Cajon Pass into the hazy Los Angeles Basin, I felt I was staring at the quintessential paradise lost. The orange groves were shrouded by June smog, the vineyards were being squeezed out by flimsy housing developments. Gray palm trees nodded their heads behind dusty billboards. Ribbons of concrete freeway cut through the hills. I breathed in the stench of diesel exhaust, and the familiar sight of Forest Lawn with its phony statue of David with a fig leaf struck me as a tragic blight on the mountainside.

I wanted to turn back; I didn't want to go home. That night, as I lay in a bed I had long outgrown, my feet sticking out at the bottom, I felt like a scared child. With only the slightest effort, I could imagine I was a mental patient recently released from an institution with no prospects for remedial job training. There was no future. This was the end of the line.

All through my growing up my father had a set of practiced phrases he used to shore me up. Before hanging up from a long-distance telephone call, he always signed off, "Love ya." Backstage after a high school performance, or when I was handing him an award-winning essay, or when I was catching my breath after a cross-country race, he always exclaimed, "Your mother and I are proud of you!" When I was discouraged or disheartened, he proclaimed, "I'm sure you'll do the right thing." Now I had to hear those phrases continually at short range, and they didn't make me feel good; indeed, they made me feel worse. I didn't feel worthy of my father's pride. I wasn't so sure I'd do the right thing.

As I painted the white stucco of my sister's house with painstaking slowness, taking ten times as long as a professional painter, I stared at emptiness, the white paint spreading over the sun-drenched white walls. A whole day would pass without my speaking to anyone or hearing anything but the radio. The wind rustled the bougainvillea; flies buzzed in and out of open windows; the neighbor's dog barked; the phone rang once or twice. The biggest challenge of my day came at lunchtime, when I had to decide whether to pick up some Mexican food from a nearby taco stand or drive to McDonald's for a burger. Lying in the grass for my lunchbreak, peeling patches of latex paint off my fingers as I listened to the fruity-voiced announcer on the classical radio station make foreign musicians' names sound even more foreign, I found I could be very happy doing nothing. Emptiness—the blank canvas, the clean tablet, the empty mind, the white wall—was a very good place to start.

"Schedule a daily time for prayer," my spiritual adviser would later say. "Put it on the agenda." "Schedule a time for nothingness," he might as well have said.

That summer of my twenty-second year, when I had decided my life was over, I found the healing power of nothingness. To my surprise, I enjoyed going nowhere, having no ambition, just painting white on white. It was as though my own palette needed to be rid of its muddied colors, as though my brushes had never been cleaned between dabs of fuchsia and burnt sienna. I was in too much of a hurry. I needed to slow down. I needed to catch up and consider all the colors I'd splashed on the ground and spilled on my smock. For a change I needed a new canvas—pure, empty, flat white to take the new clean colors. No, I didn't pray while I was painting. I didn't even meditate. But maybe the experience helped me years later when I did pray.

I could visualize the pure white, the emptiness, and then the dripping rollers adding some cream on top, filling up the crevices of the stucco in a graceful pattern with no predetermined plan. I recalled how Dad, when I couldn't sleep at night as a kid, would come into my bedroom and massage my back, telling me, "Relax. Make your mind blank. You can see nothing but a blank wall. And behind it another blank wall. And behind that another blank wall. The white is soft, smooth, comforting. Your eyes are heavy. Your arms and legs are heavy. You feel yourself floating. You can think of nothing. You can see nothing but the blank, empty wall."

I still do that. I still meditate using those images. The blank wall, emptiness, nothingness. Nothing but God.

The summer days had no order to them. I painted when I wanted and stopped when I felt like it. My only vague deadline was sometime in September, when my sister would give birth to a baby and the mostly empty house would suddenly be filled with a family. September was the month when I needed to be moving on, to attach myself to some life goal. September was *always* when things started up again. It was a time to go to back-to-school sales and to buy fresh notebooks from the stationery store, to take up piano lessons again after the summer's hiatus. It was a time of soccer practice, school dances, football games, the new fall season of TV sitcoms. In September I'd give up nothingness for good.

I thought of the baccalaureate service back in the Princeton chapel the day before graduation. Trying to keep my own personal confusion at bay, I listened to one of America's great spiritual leaders give his speech to the assembled senior class and their parents. I sat in the choir, where we had sung the Randall Thompson "Alleluia," as inoffensive a piece of music as you could find for a nondenominational service: the only words were "alleluia" repeated over and over again. But the speaker himself had no compunction about being spiritually specific. He used biblical language and stressed the Christian concept of charity. Afterward I remember one parent complaining that his advice had been too parochial, that it was meaningless to those who didn't adhere to Christianity. Perhaps it was, but it inspired in me a goal for my life.

"I would like to be happy," I announced to a classmate after the service, as though I'd just discovered the secret for decoding Mayan hieroglyphics. No one is ever supposed to be changed by those long-winded springtime exhortations; no one is expected to follow their advice. Maybe I didn't, but meditating on the theme inspired a certain direction in me. After all, as Kurt Vonnegut once said, we don't go to church to hear a sermon but simply to daydream about God.

"I would like to be happy," I repeated to myself, holding on for dear life to the remote possibility.

So I daydreamed about being happy. To be happy—what did that mean? I began to define it almost in negatives. Happiness meant I wouldn't do the practical things urged on graduates by well-meaning advisers in the college placement office. I wouldn't listen when they shook their heads in those recession days and said, "Don't come to us ten months from now looking for a job. By then it will be too late." (Too late for what? I wondered.) Perhaps I was trying to affirm that the lucrative offers of New York City bank training programs wouldn't make me happy, nor would the Washington, D.C., internships. Even then the quandary of a classmate who claimed, "I'm trying to decide between twenty thousand dollars a year at Union Carbide and going to Union Seminary," struck me as faintly ludicrous. If you were spelling it out in dollar terms, you were probably going to take the money.

Happiness had to be something inside of me, not someone else's decision about what I should be. I wouldn't be rich or powerful or blindly ambitious. I would be happy. Maybe that doesn't sound like a noble decision—"to be happy," as though I were trying to stave off the near-certain misery I saw in most of my other options. But clinging to that thought kept me focused as I stared at my sister's stucco walls. Somehow, somewhere, I would be happy.

As the latex paint wrinkled in the sun, I hatched a plan. I would go to Florence, Italy. I would be a writer there, living a gloriously Bohemian life, eating only pasta and beans, having long, leisurely conversations with other expatriates about the quality of life, reading Dante and Ariosto in the original, owning nothing more than the clothes on my back. The money I earned from this endless painting job would get me there. When I found picturesque garret accommodations, I would survive by becoming an English teacher to wealthy contessas and nouveau riche industrialists (supplementing the meager earnings of pen). Surrounded by great art, I would soak up the sun, the language, the music, the refined aesthetic sensibility.

It was an outrageous dream, one I needed the boring hours of painting to indulge. I'm surprised no one laughed (did they even smirk?) when I shared it. "That sounds like a good idea," my ever-tolerant parents said. "To discover your vocation means following your dreams one step at a time," a wise older friend suggested. "Going to Italy sounds like the perfect next step."

Outrageous as it was, much of that dream came true. I arrived in Florence in October when the city was bathed in a diaphanous light that hung on the gray cypresses, reflected off the golden palazzos, spattered the rust-colored vineyards, and shone on the silver olive trees climbing the hills. Within a week I found a job teaching English. I found a viewless room to rent and volumes of Dante and Ariosto to read (with a well-thumbed Italian-English dictionary in hand). Within two weeks I went on a weekend excursion to the monastery in Vallombrosa, where the golden leaves had fallen just as they do in a simile from Milton ("Thick as autumnal leaves that strow the brooks in Vallombrosa"). There I met some expatriates who readily indulged my desire for long, leisurely conversation on the declining quality of life back in the States. We decided that no one else read the great books anymore. No one talked using the fine language we did. No one ate fine, elaborate meals. No one lived the good life as we did.

Lord, I still smell the fragrance of Italy in my dreams. The smell of rosemary cooked over an open fire, the scent of coffee sprinkled with cinnamon in the morning, the lovely crunch of the first basil of spring. I see the flowers: the geraniums falling from balcony grills, the purple iris multiplying under olive trees. I sing them a song as I pass that tells of the wonders of May when you're young and in love with life.

I could, if you like, paint a rich, vivid picture of the two romantic years I spent in Italy: the long dinner parties in lofty, dank apartments; the restaurant scenes with pasta, Chianti, and thin slices of veal; the palazzo I moved into, where in lieu of rent I walked an Italo-American contessa's overfed dachshund and practiced Italian with her aging retainer. I could describe the students of English who footed the bill for my two-year Florentine sojourn. I could introduce you to the soigné ladies in my afternoon class who made me blush with their flirtatious charm. You can imagine picnics, if you like, in the soft Tuscan countryside, and a rarefied aesthetic life of concerts, operas, plays, films, and rambles through the city's overstocked museums. A surfeit of riches, a dazzling array of choices, a once-in-a-lifetime opportunity. You could probably imagine a picture of me—I have a copy—looking long-haired and effete, staring out across the Arno River with the Ponte Vecchio behind me, bearing the weight of declining Western Civilization on my furrowed brow.

I sang too. Opera, lieder, art songs. I had a short Italian voice coach who greeted me at his palazzo in a black beret as he unlocked a row of double bolts on the front door. His wife had been a diva in the forties, and the apartment was filled with her portraits: Butterfly, Violetta, Mimi. "Sing to the pictures," he said. I sang with all my heart, believing that Italy was heaven on earth. "If you have a heart and a shirt, sell the shirt and move to Italy," went an old proverb. I agreed.

And yet, to be frank, the reality of those years was something different. I remember spending long hours chasing after orange buses, rushing unprepared to classes I was supposed to teach, going to music lessons and voice lessons and dance lessons, hurrying to the little American church where I was the most loyal of choristers. I went twice to the Uffizi in two years, visited the real David at the Accademia only once. I was too busy preparing American high schoolers for college entrance exams, tutoring a German-American in spelling and a Dutch boy in math, trying to earn enough money to pay for my rent (after the dog-walking stint)—and for the dinners, the concerts, the operas, and the music lessons.

How impatient I was with the American tourists who clogged up the streets of the town, drinking in its beauty, slowing me down on my busy errands and appointments. I remember running into one otherworldly California acquaintance who proposed that we linger over a cappuccino at some bar.

"Can't," I said with irritation. "Too busy. I've been up since five-thirty. I had to take the six o'clock bus to teach a group of Italian NATO officers at the War College. I taught housewives at two, college students at three. I've got to practice the piano for a lesson tomorrow, and I have two classes to teach tonight. I don't have time to relax."

I didn't write the Great American Novel when I was in Italy. I didn't even keep a diary most of the time. My greatest literary effort was poured into entertaining letters home. Was I happy? Most of the time I was worried about wasting my time. I was worried about not doing anything significant with my life. Stuck in a European backwater, I was going nowhere. I had no real definable purpose in life, no future. What was my goal? I tried to shrug off these worries as unnecessary appendages in my grand evolution—like adenoids that could be excised. But the anxiety was there. In this sunny, good-natured Catholic clime, I was full of Calvinistic guilt for enjoying myself. So I became busy, looking for a purpose in my busyness. "Feigning frenzy," a friend used to call it. Rushing here, rushing there, too hurried to look up at the golden light on the watermelon-shaped Duomo, too impatient to enjoy the long, leisurely conversations I insisted on having.

When I left Florence for the last time, my Italian friends gathered at the train station, waving white handkerchiefs with good-natured Florentine self-irony. *Ciao, hello. Ciao, Rick. Addio.* As the train moved down the platform around a corner and they disappeared out of sight, I knew that one chapter of my life had come to an end. My two-year *Wanderjahr* was over. Now I would do something serious. But what?

CHAPTER FOURTEEN

Y ou're so dismissive of your Italian experience."

"I don't mean to be. It was great. It was the first time I went off and did something on my own. I made the agenda. I found my own apartment, own friends, own jobs. I went to a city where I didn't know a soul and discovered I could do all right. The experience gave me self-confidence."

"Good. I'm glad to hear that."

"But I guess I'm confused by it because it didn't have anything to do with moving me forward in any sort of career."

"Are you so sure?"

"It was an interlude," I said. "A slight break in the ordinary. A vacation, a retreat."

"Don't you believe God uses such experiences to show us the direction we're meant to be going?"

In Florence, one point in my compass had been the American Church, a curiously out-of-place northern neo-Gothic structure in a southern Renaissance town. Where every other church was cavernous and grand, here was something quaint and twee. Built at the turn of the century, it had tan brick walls, fake travertine marble arches, a wheezing Victorian organ, and walls of brass plaques memorializing the donors. It was as though the American expatriates, incapable of making their mark on the old stones of Florence, had shipped over a suburban confection to wear their graffiti.

After I arrived in Italy, the rector was one of the first people I looked up. In my search for work and a place to live, he proved helpful. Out of more than just gratitude I promised I would come back to worship the next Sunday. The church was Episcopal, and the service proved more liturgical than any I had experienced—almost as foreign as the one in the Duomo. I stumbled from program to prayer book to hymnal, trying to follow the American rite, but something about the theatricality of it appealed to me. I returned. In time I used the basement for practicing my singing and the choir loft for showing off. I came to attend services regularly, convincing myself that the choir-singing was good for a musician like me. If anyone asked me why I went—particularly my left-leaning anticlerical Italian friends—I apologetically explained that it was "for the social life." Indeed, I counted many of the other churchgoing expatriates as friends, and I was relieved to be in a place that celebrated great American holidays such as Thanksgiving and Halloween. I lingered at coffee hours to chat with academics and art historians on sabbatical. But saying I was there to meet people was a white lie. I was also there because I was looking for something spiritual.

I found words in that hallowed space, words about God. They particularly stood out in this worship context because everywhere else Italian words were being spoken. Coming from the crowded streets and buses where I struggled to eavesdrop on Italian, I stepped into a world of bold, Elizabethan, majestic *Book of Common Prayer* words. They seemed both familiar and strange. We presented ourselves "to be a reasonable, holy, and living sacrifice." Why "reasonable"? "We have followed too much the devices and desires of our own hearts." What were those mysterious devices? That word made me think of Machiavelli. And then there was this very sweeping statement: "We are not worthy so much as to gather up the crumbs from under thy table"—a phrase that I quickly associated with Italian *trattorie* and dried crumbs of tasteless Tuscan bread on the white linen tablecloths.

At every service we sang or chanted psalms. When I was feeling self-conscious, I couldn't decide where to put the emphasis in singing about, say, going down into the pit and being rescued from my adversaries and saved from my transgressions. At an Easter Eve service the pastor asked me to sing the longest psalm imaginable—one about "fire and hail, snow and fog" and "wild beasts and all cattle, creeping things and winged birds." I chanted for an eternity, trying desperately not to lose my pitch or my place as I squinted at bars of music in the dimly lit sanctuary. I must have gone on for fifteen minutes, with incense billowing and candles flickering. "Praise God for all these things indeed," I thought, wondering what my Puritan forefathers would have made of this mock popery. "Praise God if I can finish this list."

But oh, there was something tantalizing about the cumulative effect of those liturgical words week after week. I could never concentrate on them all at once; it was too much, like a heavy diet of creamed sauces and red meat. Only one or two passages would stick in my mind, and then often because of some odd association—the way one turns "for which it stands" into "for witches' stands." My thoughts wandered during worship, but I liked hearing those words. Part of me couldn't believe they were repeated year after year in the same manner.

I wanted to ask the impertinent schoolboy's question, "But what does this have to do with me in the twentieth century?" Another part of me, a deeper part, found comfort in the mere ritual. I would stop asking "Why?" or "Who?" and let the timeless words wash over me like the light streaming down from the stained-glass windows. It was a pleasant feeling that stayed with me, like the faint aroma of incense that stuck to my tweed jacket for days after Easter Eve.

Among the people I met at the American Church was a Harvard history professor on sabbatical, the sort of woman who intimidated me in my college days. Smart, articulate, and not one to suffer fools gladly. In ultrachic Florence, where women took pains with their fashionable (and presumably uncomfortable) footwear, she looked startlingly out of place with her sensible "earth shoes" and no-nonsense corduroys. But she had a wry way of smiling when she talked that I liked, whether she was describing the impossible-to-follow political conflicts of Renaissance Florence or her local fruit and vege-table man. At a church coffee hour in the rector's study, as I nibbled on my Styrofoam cup, she said something that I was to ponder over for many months. "Whenever anyone asked Jesus a question or tried to stump him, he would simply tell them a story. Pin him down, and he tells you a story."

Stories I could deal with. Indeed, the stories of Jesus appealed to me. They were unlikely, unexpected. There was the parable of the talents: the lowly servant who carefully preserved the one coin he was given was scorned in favor of the lordly servant who took his five coins and doubled them with investments. Caution wasn't rewarded; good fortune came to the servant who took a risk. I liked the parable of the lost sheep: the one lost lamb was worth as much as the whole flock. The message of the brides seemed a striking contrast to the usual browbeaten Christian humility: "Is a candle brought to be put under a bushel or under a bed and not to be set on a candlestick?" The story of the good Samaritan seemed a little obvious, and it easily became confused in my mind with the name of a dozen hospitals, but the parable of the prodigal son was good enough to be irritating. How would you feel if you were the older son? After you've done everything right (probably feeling self-righteous in the bargain), your black sheep of a brother suddenly comes home, having squandered his inheritance, and is not only welcomed with open arms but given the fatted calf you were counting on eating yourself? Who would set *this* up as a paradigm for behavior? What sort of justice is it? Only a first-rate storyteller would try it on his audience. Only someone who wanted to shake up the play-it-by-the-rules caution of nature's unprodigal sons.

Influenced by the parables, I debated my choices for the future. "I won't be overly cautious. I'll try something different, squander my inheritance perhaps—chance a risky investment of my talents." My mom and dad came to visit me in Italy that spring. After they had been in Florence for several days, I told them with some trepidation that I was trying to decide what I would do with the rest of my life. We were walking down one of Florence's narrow streets, only wide enough for us to proceed single file. Without direct eye contact it was easier to talk, as it is when you're riding in a car. I told them that I had been offered a job as a high school teacher at a fancy Swiss boarding school—a bird in the hand, really. And then I wondered aloud whether I should maybe pursue my singing, "…or do something different like that."

As Dad followed me down the narrow, lightless alley, I waited for his response, his benediction.

"I don't know," he said in that agonizing way he had of turning over important decisions to his own children. "You should do what you want to do. Take a risk. Do what you enjoy." *I don't know*, he'd said. Never ordering, never forcing, never commanding, trusting me to be able to make my own wise plan. As I walked ahead of him, sidestepping a parked motorcycle, I knew what I would have to do.

"You should give your father more credit," my spiritual director said to me.

"You think so?" What son ever gives his father enough credit?

"Yes. He guided you. He was enlightening you spiritually. He wanted you to follow the dreams you had. To do what you wanted."

"Well, you should see what I did next."

CHAPTER FIFTEEN

Why not become a teacher instead?" my old friend Patti said to me. "Why an actor?"

For two years she had lived the life of a New York actress, waiting on tables, hustling for interviews and auditions, making the rounds from agent's office to ratty rented rehearsal rooms in the Ansonia Hotel to pay phones (where she checked on her answering service with the roll of dimes she kept on hand). She had impressive printed cards with her name and picture on them, and she'd explored the exercise classes, dance classes, voice classes, movement classes, and acting classes that keep actors and actresses busy at their craft in the long fallow periods "between jobs." She knew the New York rental-housing market and where to look for a reasonable sublet. She knew how much to pay for a room in a shabby apartment building filled with actors roving from summer stock to regional repertory to waiting on tables while hoping for a commercial that might air on the networks nationwide. She knew what I should do to be a New York actor, and she wasn't encouraging.

"Teaching seems a lot saner," she said.

"It doesn't make a good story," I explained. "Consider the schoolteacher who wishes he were an actor and inflicts on his students dramatic readings of Shakespeare with him in a starring role. The teacher with pear-shaped tones who uses the classroom to prove he could have been Olivier's successor." I'd seen enough of frustrated ambition and thwarted creativity. I didn't want to be the kind of person who exclaims, "If there'd been a bit more money, I would have been fabulous on the stage."

"Compare that," I said, "with the talented actor and singer who later gives up a promising career on the stage for the love of teaching. That makes a better story."

"A much better story," she agreed.

So went the discussions I had in Patti's large Upper West Side apartment. I couldn't quite explain to her what an impression the prodigal son had made on me. Not that I would descend to the prodigal son's level of riotous living, filling my belly with the husks meant for swine. I just wanted to do what seemed unexpected. I wanted to shake things up. To myself I looked starchy, straitlaced, stiff, and conventional. I could have been one of the subway riders in a sacklike Brooks Brothers suit reading the *Wall Street Journal* folded vertically. Instead, I bought the actor's uniform: black pants and white shirt for busing tables, sweats for exercise and dance classes, and a lot of denim for in between. With the help of friends like Patti I had a résumé put together, exaggerating what few stage credits I had earned, and I had my picture taken—two glossies: one of me with a stiff, insincere-looking smile and the other with a blank, empty-headed expression that I hoped was very sexy.

My first job was in a summer stock production of *South Pacific*. The theater's locale, a Victorian dance pavilion on the edge of a lake in upstate New York, was idyllic. All summer long we watched the corn rise, the apples ripen, the day lilies bloom and die. At night we listened for approaching thunderstorms coming out of the hills, waiting for them to interrupt the theatrical proceedings with hailstones on the dance pavilion's tin roof.

With vigor I threw myself into the enthusiastic "Let's put on a play" atmosphere of the company. I hammered nails in the sets, glued costumes together, coaxed props out of theater patrons. I sang in fund-raisers at the town's old folks' home and was part of a Rodgers and Hammerstein Fourth of July festival on the village green. I was interviewed by the local paper and entertained by the local citizenry. Backstage I shared in the opening-night jitters, hugs, and kisses. But on stage, in my romantic tenor role as Princeton-educated Lieutenant Cable from the Main Line, PA, I felt like a sham. I knew I could sing all the notes—my high G I was particularly proud of—but I didn't know a thing about acting, and from the awkward way I walked through my part, it must have been obvious to the last row in the bleachers. Even at the curtain call, when the applause was generous, I could only smile woodenly at the appreciation.

You see, I didn't "feel" my part; I wasn't "in touch with my emotions"; I hadn't "found" my character; I hadn't explored his motivation; I didn't know where his vulnerabilities lay. Back in New York I had enrolled in a Greenwich Village acting class that met in the basement of a doctor's office, and when each class began we had to do exercises based on different emotions: anger, rage, love, jealousy, hostility, hate, despair, fear, joy, anguish, terror. Our teacher would call out the different emotions as we writhed on the indoor-outdoor carpeting (until the nurses from the doctor's office upstairs complained). When our teacher called out, "Anger!" "Rage!" many of my classmates dissolved into shrieking tears, while like the character from *A Chorus Line*, I felt nothing. I had no emotions. I believed I was an emotional midget. Now on stage at the Victorian dance pavilion they'd found me out.

In the afternoons before performances I tried to do some of the exercises I had learned in acting class. I stood many furrows out in the cornfield and acted to the budding ears of corn. "Tell us, Rick," I made the corn ask me, "who do you hate more than anyone else? Try to see that person. Show us how you feel." I closed my eyes and tried to dissolve into tears, but the person I hated more than anyone else was me, and I couldn't see pummeling myself in the cornfield. My performances on stage became an endurance test, and I couldn't wait to talk to my acting teacher when I got back to New York. I'd tell her what a failure I'd been.

"I didn't feel anything," I bravely proclaimed back in Greenwich Village. "I don't have an emotional life. I can't act."

My dear teacher must have resisted a strong impulse to say, "What utter rot!" Instead, she replied, "Rick, why don't you sing for us?" That I *could* do. I picked a very sentimental ballad. Not daring to look at any of my classmates, I sang to the spotlights burning down on me. I didn't have to conjure up images of conflicts with my parents or a crisis of personal inadequacy. The song itself spoke of love and loss and a melancholy I felt deeply. By the time I finished singing, I was visibly moved. I usually was when I sang. Why had I never noticed that before?

"See, you feel," my teacher told me. "I saw it in your face, and I felt it. Tell me the names for some of the emotions you felt."

"Love."

"What else?"

"Despair, maybe."

"And?"

"Anger, sorrow, hope."

"Yes, I think they were all there."

No, the class wasn't therapy. It wasn't meant to be. Still, it served a wonderful purpose in my life. I was asked to feel, and I was asked to find names for how I felt. This can be an incredibly frustrating process at first, just like closing your eyes in prayer and hearing nothing more than the hum of the air-conditioning unit and the buzz of the fluorescent lights. Gradually, though, it got a little easier and started making more sense. Because of my acting class I began paying more attention to how people said what they said, asking myself why they said it. I started to see how an answer such as "Nothing" to the question "What's wrong?" can mean a dozen things more complicated than "Nothing." I began to look for the feelings of characters in plays. And when I asked myself the actor's proverbial question, "What's my motivation?" I started to ask Rick Hamlin the same thing.

What *was* my motivation? Most of the time, I had to confess, it was to be loved, to be appreciated, to be needed, to be adored. I was pretty good at constructing defenses to shield that truth from most of the people I met, but there it was, on the indoor-outdoor carpeting, in the glare of the spotlights: I wanted to be loved.

I discovered what a bad liar I was. I suspect most of us are. How frustrating God must find it, listening to us get our wants all wrong, hearing us ask for the new house, the better car (if we can be that honest), the job with more prestige, the good tennis game, when what we really want is to be loved. I was no different. I thought I wanted things that would give me the power to impress. Instead, I just wanted to be loved.

"You wanted to be loved?" inquired my spiritual director.

"Yes."

"Had you ever realized that about yourself before?"

"Perhaps, but that was the first time I'd articulated it clearly. That was when I first discovered that the need for love was such a motivating factor in my life."

"So few people know that about themselves," he observed. "When I give speeches on the dinner-party circuit, it's the one theme I know will captivate any audience. It's the one thing everyone has in common, rich and poor alike."

I looked at him a little differently. He was just like me. *He* wanted to be loved. "I was scared to admit it," I said. "I still find it hard to acknowledge at times."

"What did you do about it back then?"

"It's not that I did anything; it's what it did for me."

CHAPTER SIXTEEN

In New York my "day job" was a night job at the now defunct Hotel Winslow. I was a desk clerk on the four-to-midnight shift. At that time the hotel had only thirty permanent residents, all of whom the owners were trying to relocate. The structure was being transformed into an office building. My job was mindless and boring. I sat for hours underneath a few bald lightbulbs, distributing packages and mail to a handful of elderly residents who believed against the evidence that they could stay on in the aging building, one tenant to a floor. I had long hours to myself, to study scripts, write letters, and chat on the phone to friends. The hotel residents, in threadbare coats and moth-eaten hats, would linger in the empty lobby, sitting on the rattling radiators and making polite conversation as though their world weren't crumbling around them.

As most actors' "money jobs" went, it could have been worse. I found plenty of time to memorize scenes for my acting class, learn music, and read through three different daily newspapers. From the front desk I watched the drama of everyday life pass through the shabby lobby: a Russian expatriate cinematographer looking in vain for some news from home, an impoverished French diplomat's wife waiting for an inheritance that never seemed to come, a middle-aged Belgian "nurse" who did more lucrative business at night as a call girl, a Cuban refugee always rushing to Saint Patrick's Cathedral with her rosary beads in hand, and friends of mine who stopped by on their way home from their more conventional nine-to-five jobs.

One of those friends was a college chum who worked in publishing. She was compiling a calendar of quotations—a provocative quote a day—and to earn some extra money I dutifully retyped the manuscript. She was at a transition point in her career and in her life. She knew she could get a job that earned her more than her publishing salary, or she could earn a lot less and take a risk by doing what she really wanted to do, which was to be a freelance writer. She'd recently forgone the Talbot sweaters and khaki skirts of college days; now, with hair flamboyantly hennaed red, she dressed in Bohemian black or outrageous purple. She rolled her eyes at the motley crew assembled in the lobby and issued sharp, opinionated views on the New York cultural scene. Of course, I advised her on her job quandary. "You should be a writer," I told her. Easy for me to say.

"How do I make money in the meantime?" she asked, ever practical.

"I'm sure I could get you a job here at the hotel," I said. So she left her publishing job and took over the 8:00 a.m. shift, working on her manuscripts at the front desk. I usually came early for my 4:00 p.m. shift, or she lingered, so that we could talk. She was great fun to talk to. Witty, clever, she had strong opinions about everything. Moreover, she gave me the feeling that the things I said were witty and clever too. In the gossip and banter, sometimes subjects of great seriousness would suddenly emerge. I thought it odd one afternoon when she bit her lip, avoided my gaze—perhaps afraid that I would be censorious—and announced, "You'll never know what a difference you've made in my life."

It seemed such a curious cliché from a woman who scorned anything that faintly resembled cheap sentiment. "No, I guess I won't," I mumbled then, not knowing what she was referring to. But the brave acknowledgment of some feeling, some hidden depth of understanding between two people who pretended to be aloof to raw emotions, was an invitation. We were good friends, we had a good time together, we enjoyed each other's company, and now we were teetering on the edge of something that threatened to do in a good friendship. When we talked about books, we weren't really thinking about the books; when the movies came up, we weren't wholly analyzing their strengths and weaknesses; when we gossiped about friends, we had another scenario in mind.

Maybe I should have known from earlier signals. Once when she was away for two weeks on vacation I house-sat at her apartment. When I got restless at night, I'd search under her sink for ammonia and cleanser and take to the windows and walls, attacking hidden spots like the top of the refrigerator, the narrow area behind the john, and the smudges on the telephone. (I also untangled the phone cord by hanging it out the skyscraper window.) She blushed in embarrassment when she returned, shaking her head and muttering, "I can't believe you washed my phone!" as though I had scored a touchdown with only seconds left in the fourth quarter. And there was the Sunday brunch she arranged so that I could meet her best friend—a brunch at which she served a shad roe omelette that I didn't eat much of. Afterward she told me how much her best friend liked me, as if I were somebody who had to be inspected, my jawline checked out for any flaws, my teeth examined like a horse's. Did I count in some unexpected way?

Then there was the bright winter morning when we went to a piano warehouse downtown and I bought the cheapest instrument we could find, firewood that I would later pay someone to take away. As we walked side by side in the bitter cold, our breath blowing behind us as if we were two steamships climbing the Hudson, everything seemed magnified: my delight in the day, the rashness of spending several hundred dollars in one fell swoop, the crush of her parka when she brushed against my wool overcoat. My perceptions were heightened, and something as mundane as the steam billowing through the holes in a manhole cover seemed as magnificent as Old Faithful. What did this mean?

Growing often involves giving up what's familiar for the unknown. It can mean going from what's comfortable and reassuring into a dark and forbidding void. After all, you don't know if happiness lies beyond where you are until you've traveled there. For both of us the risks were enormous. It would have been easier if we were strangers drawn to each other, but proven and time-tested "affection" and "warmth" were such risky things to give up for an unknown quantity like love. I used to tell myself, "I can imagine us being great friends when we're old and retired, but I can't fathom our relationship when we're grown-up thirty-year-olds." We could visualize a future together of comfortable fondness— like gray-haired siblings at an old folks' home—but it was too threatening to imagine being together boyfriend and girlfriend, committed, in love.

Conveniently enough, or inconveniently, I decided to try my luck as an actor in California. I was feeling only half-committed to the profession, and half-committed is even less than half of what it takes to survive the hustling, the penury, the hassles, and the rejection that always feels personal even though you repeatedly try to convince yourself that it isn't. As an actor you're supposed to be sensitive and vulnerable, but after enough of "Thanks—don't call us, we'll call you," you realize a greater asset would be a thick hide. So professionally and emotionally, I was ready to try the geographic cure. I could still call myself an actor in California and probably get some work, but I would also be a few thousand miles away from someone I wanted to see more than reason allowed.

The night before I was to leave New York, she invited me to her place for dinner. There, far above the traffic noise, with nothing but a view of midtown Manhattan lights (no room to put a picture on the wall), she cooked liver in onions—it was cheap—and I munched on potato chips. The winter wind blew through the cracks in the uneven casement windows, she sneezed again and again from a terrible cold, and we kept conversation going rapidly about everything but us. It was as though we were cartoon figures stepping off a cliff, suspended in midair without knowing it. If either of us had looked down, we would have plummeted—a free fall. Falling in love can be made to sound so romantic afterward, but it can be utter torture when it's happening. Neither of us could bring ourselves to say that maybe…perhaps…it was possible…

"You need to get up early tomorrow," I said, trying to excuse myself with the convenient cover of politeness.

"And you probably have to do Christmas shopping, or something like that."

"Something like that." I gave her a friendly kiss—a kiss on the cheek. There was some hesitation, a momentary fluster, an awful awkwardness.

"We'll talk," I said, trying to recover.

"Yes. Okay. We'll talk."

CHAPTER SEVENTEEN

Sometimes it's awful to contemplate what might have happened, terrible to imagine what could have resulted if I had not or she had not done this or that. It makes for agonizing daydreams. How right the sentimental soul who declared, "'What might have been'—the four saddest words in the English language." When I look on this moment in my life, I squirm uncomfortably. I can barely read the letters I wrote to Carol back then, because they're filled with the hidden fear that things would not work out all right. All my tentative, hesitant, self-conscious yearnings are there beneath the arch, meandering.

What if she hadn't written that first brave letter making the first courageous declaration that we were falling in love? What if I hadn't responded to her letter with a paragraph (rewritten countless times) conceding that maybe, perhaps, she was right? Yes, we were falling in love, and doing it in the best, time-honored Victorian fashion. We joked on the page about publishing the whole lurid correspondence—a limited edition with lavender endpapers—but I can't imagine that anyone would find a romantic, inspiring word in it. There certainly was never a spontaneous thought. Every feeling, every emotion, every whim went down on paper only after it had been analyzed and edited to death. Sometimes whole paragraphs were rewritten and copied onto a new sheet of stationery. We took risks by baby steps, revealing ourselves in asides and then backing up and saying, "Of course, that might not be true."

For months we lived for those letters, sometimes three or four a week, single-spaced, several pages long. I could hardly wait for the letter carrier to call. Whenever I came home, I looked for those typed letters with the address written in a southpaw's backward scrawl, in a fountain pen's blue ink. I opened them and read them slowly, savoring each sentence, my heart beating rapidly in case she had changed her mind over something she had previously said. We were always two or three letters behind in our responses, giving us time to catch up with our thoughts as the mail crossed the continent. We enjoyed discovering who we were on the page, because even if we were ever so careful, we were also honest. We were open in a guarded way. We learned to read each other's minds between the lines. We allowed ourselves to love a little. All the while we made but a few long-distance calls for fear that the immediacy of the voice would send us both back to our clever, aloof, distanced selves.

Did I pray to God for any of this to happen? Hardly. I was too afraid. I couldn't allow myself even to fantasize that the love I was being offered could be real and long-lasting. I could accept it only from letter to letter, from tentative step to tentative step. For four months I stayed in California and we wrote to each other. She talked about religion. She described a sermon she had heard that had touched her. It was about Mary, the mother of Christ, and how this young, inexperienced girl could be chosen for such an enormous role. The minister took the occasion to talk about God's calling—and how God calls each of us and can help us do far more than we think we're capable of if we only accept what we're asked to do. God can help us even if we make mistakes. He's helpless only if we do nothing—which Carol and I were both quite aware was the danger we faced with this fierce love we had discovered. God could never help us if we did nothing, if we let apathy and the two thousand miles of distance separating us take their course.

In another letter Carol talked about going into a Manhattan church at midday to pray after she had been severely tempted to start up a relationship with someone else. She didn't say whether the prayer had helped. She didn't mention if the temptation had been successfully squelched—but there it was, as backhanded an acknowledgment of commitment as ever there was. She was telling me how important I was to her. What would I do about it?

I ask myself now (and I wondered then), Why should it be so hard to accept love? I'd already admitted to myself that love was what I wanted more than anything else, and now that it was being offered, I could barely bring myself to say yes.

At the time I was doing children's theater. Driving from one elementary school to another, our troupe put on a forty-five-minute-long play for squirming, squealing kids. Sometimes we did three or four performances a day, putting up the set and taking it down at each auditorium, gym, or sloppy-joe-stained cafeteria. At the end of a long day my voice would be hoarse and my back weary from carrying the set. My fellow cast members were a good-natured bunch, but they couldn't understand what attraction New York held for me. Why live in that stinking hole when, living in Southern California, you could drive to Hollywood in the morning for an audition and surf that afternoon? I was beginning to wonder if they were right. After one hundred performances, we were given Easter week off. This was my time to find out.

"I can't really afford it," I told a friend, "but I probably should fly back to New York for the week to visit a girl I might be in love with."

My friend didn't hesitate. "I'll give you the money for the trip," he said, though at the time he didn't have any money to throw around. With that I knew I had to go. Friends have a way of forcing you to do the things you want to do anyway, giving you the courage to do them.

I took the red-eye flight on Saturday night, arriving at Kennedy Airport on Palm Sunday morning. The grass was that pale-green color that's called "spring green" on children's crayons. The blossoms on the tulip trees looked like limp toilet paper, and the daffodils leaned against a cold wind. Before anyone else was awake, Carol and I sat near the rowing pond in Central Park and watched the ducks waddle through the mud and the sun break out behind pink clouds above a limestone-sheathed apartment building. We both managed to say, "I missed you." It was much harder to say, "I love you."

For a week—Holy Week, no less—we did all those frivolous, romantic, two-on-the-town things New York offers young lovers in the spring. We walked through museums hand in hand, went to movies in the middle of the day, sat in Central Park in the fuzzy sun, ate hearty breakfasts at Greek delis. I bought a pair of overpriced linen pants at a Madison Avenue boutique and was coaxed into paying for a jaunty Panama hat, wearing it even though it was out of season. We lingered in bookstores, window-shopped when the money ran out, took cover in hotel lobbies from the occasional shower, and drank big mugs of hot tea.

We went to visit her mother in Connecticut one day, I guess so I could be inspected. Afterward I wrote the obligatory thank-you note. I said something to the effect that I looked forward to seeing her again "when my ship comes in." Carol's mother wrote me back, a thank-you note for a thank-you note, saying, "Don't wait too long. Ships are notoriously late coming in."

All the while in New York, we hid from our friends. We both sensed that for our love to grow it needed to be kept a secret; it was too young, too delicate, too tender, a seed germinating in the dark. In the Sermon on the Mount, Jesus told his listeners to pray in isolation, literally in a closet. Perhaps that was meant as an exhortation against flamboyant demonstrations of holiness—but it also must have had something to do with the fragile nature of our deepest longings. There comes a time when our dreams can be exposed and they blossom before a crowd, but at first they find power and strength in privacy. Some prayers are meant only for God's ears, even after they've been answered.

No, there was no need to pray that week. Love letters and love poems are never written when you're with the object of your desires; impassioned pleas for happiness don't need to be made when indescribable bliss has made an unexpected appearance. It was rare enough for two usually self-conscious people to give up analyzing and articulating their every feeling. The future was confusing enough. For a week we just enjoyed the present. Finally, though, on a rainy Easter Sunday, the week came to an end and I had to return to California and resume performances for loud, jaded schoolchildren in Orange County. When would we see each other again? Whose turn was it to make the next move? Who would visit whom, and where?

This is the worst part to remember. This is when I squirm most. This is the part my memory would rather glide right past. I was so craven, so timid. I can torture myself even now by wondering, What if it hadn't turned out all right? What might have been? Pride is a strong emotion and doubly powerful when coupled with fear. Pride justifies fear, wraps it up in excuses that sound legitimate. I could have quit the exhausting children's show and returned to New York, where I knew I was meant to be. But I told myself I wasn't going to alter my career for a girl. That would be a bad start to things. Maybe I wanted to see how much I counted. Maybe I was testing her. Maybe we did indeed need to wait for "the fullness of time."

At any rate, there was a miserable year of phone calls, letters, transcontinental flights, and interminable waiting as we tried to decide who we were to each other. That summer I was singing the lead in *West Side Story* in Santa Barbara, and Carol came out to visit at the end of the run. In August the water off Santa Barbara's coast was unusually clear, with visibility of thirty or forty feet. You could see the rocks, the purple kelp, and the white sandy bottom. But Carol swam in the ocean with trepidation. She said she preferred the murky water of Long Island Sound, where in waist-high water she couldn't see her toes. I saw that as a metaphor for where we stood. I didn't like clarity; I preferred murkiness; I didn't want to see as far as a clear future.

I wasn't unoccupied while I waited—waited, that is, for my actions to catch up with my emotions. I formally gave up being an actor and decided to call myself something else. I would be a writer—as though giving myself the title were enough. I got a part-time job with a Hollywood production office as a Boy Friday and all-around "gofer," starting my shift at two in the afternoon so that I could write in the morning. At least it was a way of taking time for myself, almost like painting my sister's house. I drove in the morning to one of the parks in the arroyo and sat at a picnic table under syca- mores and eucalyptus trees, watching the dew lift and the fog turn into smog.

Those mornings in the local parks brought back my boy- hood, the fragrance of eucalyptus, the merry-go-rounds that made me throw up, the carob seedpods and live oak acorns I had collected, the sandbox castles I'd built. As I wrote, I tried to trust the images of my imagination. I wrote a novel, some- thing I've never reread and have never asked another soul to look at. When I finished it, I was ready to give up whatever prevented me from doing what I wanted to do. I was ready to love and be loved. I was ready to stop waiting.

I should have got down on bended knee by the time I returned to New York. I should have scripted a long, dramatic, romantic proposal. But in fact the marriage proposal had to be coaxed or embarrassed out of me by another friend. *O Lord, was I that passive? Was I so craven?*

Carol and I were out at her mother's house in Connecticut with our mutual friend Steve. We took him on a tour through the picturesque New England town where she'd grown up, passing the school she'd attended, the library where she'd read for endless summer afternoons, the village green, the main street, and finally the church where she'd worshiped.

As we passed it, Steve, who has a gift for being blessedly blunt, said, "If you two were to get married—say, to each other—would you get married there?"

"Not in that church," Carol said, and we both blushed. "I'd prefer to get married in New York."

Later, when we were treading water in my future mother-in-law's pool, I said, "Well, what about it?"

She said, "Well?"

"Well, what? Do you want to get married?"

"Of course. I wondered when you were finally going to ask me."

"I was waiting for you to say you were ready."

"I was waiting for you to *be* ready."

Well, we were ready.

CHAPTER EIGHTEEN

S o you wrote love letters," observed my spiritual director. "That's how we courted. Yes."

"What a help for you in your prayer life."

"How's that?"

"They taught you how to wait. You knew what it was to express yourself when all you had to go on was hope. You learned how to take big risks when you couldn't see the face of the one you loved and couldn't know what her reaction was. You had to trust. You had to accept her response on faith. A prayer can be a love letter to God, pouring out your soul."

I could see his point, all those letters back and forth where we had to accept each other's word on faith. But I had to disagree in part. My prayers were never as tentative and canned as those letters to Carol. My prayers were never so wordy. In fact, they often didn't include words, just inchoate thoughts and deep feelings that I would never have been able to express if I had had to. "I've been more honest in prayer than I ever was writing love letters," I said.

"But look at the resolution of all that letter writing. You learned what it is to be loved and to love in return. You gave of yourself and you gained a partner for life. No one can develop fully without being understood and appreciated by one other person. You found a relationship, an earthly version of the great spiritual one. That's why we use the term 'relationship with God' or 'relationship with Jesus Christ'; that's what we're thinking about."

And yet being married to Carol didn't seem to help me in my struggle with my work. I wasn't instantly led to my vocation. I still wasn't certain what I was meant to be doing. I feared that I was floundering.

That first year of marriage other young married couples often came up to us and asked, in grave tones (as though we were recovering from a serious illness), "How's it going? How is it to be married? You know, the first year is the hardest."

Hard? It was as easy as falling off a log. Being married seemed the only logical, sensible thing I'd done since graduating from college. Sure, you can act like you're giving up everything, making a sacrifice greater than any saint's, willing to live as a committee the rest of your days. You can pretend to be a martyr because you had to give up your own private identity for the sake of a shared one. But if it's the right person, you find that you're not really giving up anything after all. I was never very good at being a bachelor anyway.

I loved saying the word *wife* to myself. It amused me no end to refer to Carol as "my wife." I couldn't get over the novelty of wearing a wedding ring, the gold clanking against any hard object I picked up with my left hand, reminding me of my new status. In Italy on our honeymoon, I thought we could pass as any normal couple. Instead, every time we checked into a new hotel or *pensione*, someone at the front desk would smile coyly and ask, *"Sposini? Luna di miele?"* "Newlyweds? On your honeymoon?" I was a member of the club, this not-so-secret society that made everyone smile, everyone wink, everyone laugh.

I was happy. I delighted in this new identity, this unexpected pleasure of belonging.

But with this new responsibility, what I found hard was facing the perception others had of me (and I had of myself) that I wasn't...well...doing anything important.

"Mr. Hamlin," the society reporter from the *New York Times* who was writing up our marriage announcement had asked, "Mr. Hamlin, are you still a...writer?" I could hear the snotty scorn in his voice. How dare I presume so much about myself? "Are you working for anyone? Have you published any books yet?"

No, I hadn't. But it wasn't for want of trying.

That first year of marriage I sat at my typewriter in the living room and she sat at hers in the office/bedroom of our tiny apartment. Every day we wrote. I could hear her typewriter go clickety-clack at an intimidating pace—eleven pages before lunch—while I hunted and pecked my way through another turgid manuscript, another piece deserving of the form rejection slip that came back in the stamped, self-addressed envelope. That first year, I earned a couple of thousand dollars from my pen, but it didn't compensate for my low self-esteem. I wondered if I should go back to being an actor/singer again. Maybe I could earn some money. Heck, a woman on the subway, seeing me study a Gilbert and Sullivan score for an amateur production, gave me her card, said she was an agent, and asked me to come by her office. That had never happened when I was knocking on every agent's door from Fifty-seventh Street to Forty-second.

What made things so hard was that I felt surrounded by confidence. When I used the research library in midtown

Manhattan, I could see young men and women who looked like my friends walking purposefully from subway to office, briefcase in hand, their faces strained with thoughts of meetings, presentations, legal briefs, documents, and fleeting arguments with managers and colleagues. I called my old college chums at their offices, and women old enough to be their mothers referred to them by their surnames: Mr. Rich, Mr. Hilboldt, Mr. Byrns. When did we grow up? Or were we just faking it? Had I missed the boat?

Eating lunch by myself, I could sit on the library steps and watch the yuppie procession pass—the coats left back at the office, the windblown ties flying over one shoulder like would-be scarves. I eavesdropped on conversations about public offerings, marketing strategies, and ad campaigns. Over lunch with my friends I would try to make the budding lawyers tell me about cases they couldn't talk about, hearing them refer to clients anonymously as "a well-known international corporation headquartered in Cleveland" or "a Third World country that needs to refinance its massive debt." Sometimes their faces became curiously rigid and their expressions unanimated, as though I were the boss or the managing partner. I marveled at their sangfroid in office disputes, their political machinations, their ambition and determination, but I didn't envy them their work. I didn't want to market toothpaste or stay up all night at the printer's to proof a public offering.

One evening, as I listened to my wife talk about publishing a book of hers, I felt hopelessly out of it. I had no direction. I was a failure. She had all the smooth self-assurance that I lacked. That night on our futon, after she had fallen asleep, I scribbled furiously in my journal and I cried in my pillow. I was at the end of my rope. *Lord,* I prayed, *what do you want me to do?*

That night I had a dream, as mixed up and muddled as most of my dreams. I was at church in the choir loft, wearing my choir robe, and down in the pulpit preaching was a young female assistant, a woman not much older than I was. I knew her well. Her husband had been trained as a pastor too, but he'd gone on to become a pastoral counselor, then a professional therapist. Susan was speaking from the pulpit in my dream, and as I listened to her, I heard a Godlike voice inside me say, "Be like Susan's husband."

I woke up in the dark on our futon, the dream as vivid as a movie just seen. I sat up for a few minutes, alert, so I'd be sure to remember it in the daylight. "Be like Susan's husband" was the important message. I wouldn't forget it. And I returned to sleep, rested, calm, not certain what the dream meant but confident of a path to follow to figure it out.

The next day I made an appointment with Susan to talk. My wife seemed pleased: I was doing something that seemed practical. When I met with Susan she served me some herbal tea and fed her five-month-old infant as I recounted the dream. Between burping the baby and warming the bottle, Susan asked me, with an enigmatic smile, "Was this dream a...mystical experience?"

What a flattering question! Oh, to think that the gods might be so generous with me! How I would have loved to be shown a simple, direct path, as in one of the visions of prophets and saints. Had I experienced something mystical? I stared up at the high ceiling in the overheated room and wondered.

Then reality intruded, as mundane as the beep of the microwave announcing that the baby's formula was warm. No, the heavens hadn't opened up. The dream wasn't a godly recipe. It felt like all my other dreams: pieces of half-baked thoughts and images gathering in a confused narrative of my subconscious mind. Just as my father had graciously never told me exactly what profession to follow or what job to take, God wasn't dictating to me. It wasn't a cosmic order. But there was something persuasive about the dream, as though one of God's angels had tapped me on the shoulder.

"No, it wasn't mystical. But it was important enough not to dismiss. It made me think. That's why I'm here." And then I asked the big question on my mind: "How do we know what God wants us to do?"

"There are many ways." We talked then a lot about spiritual things, interrupted only by the cooing baby on the couch. And it dawned on me that this was the first time I'd told Susan or anyone that I somehow believed God wanted me to be someone special or do something special and that I wanted to figure out what it was.

Susan, never one for quick, pat answers, suggested prayer and study and talking to other people. I took the least intimidating approach—talking to other people.

First I talked to Susan's husband. He told me what a therapist did and how one became a psychologist, and neither the necessary education nor the profession appealed to me. Next I talked to a minister who had been a college classmate. He mentioned prayer and Bible study too. Then he handed me a thin devotional book as I was leaving his office. I shelved it back at home. I talked to other friends as well. I asked them how they had settled on a vocation and whether God had had anything to do with it. They pursed their lips, shook their wise heads, and said, in effect, "I figured I could find something on my own." More followers of the doctrine that God helps those who help themselves.

I was grateful for the advice. I wanted someone else to be right about my life. I wanted to find the one fortune-teller who would give me a forecast I agreed upon. If only the decision making could be taken out of my hands. If only the secret plot with the satisfying denouement could be found in a word, a book, a fortune cookie.

Finally a friend suggested his godfather, who also happened to be a minister. He had been very kind to my friend, so I was disposed to like him. "He'll help you sort things out."

That man, that minister, that godfather became my spiritual director. And he did that odd thing: he didn't dismiss the vocational question. He heard what I said and brought it back to something more central. "Do you know God?" he had said.

"Why is that important?" I finally asked after several sessions.

"Because if you're concerned about doing what God wants you to do, you should at least start out by knowing God. Do you know God?"

The television in the next room kept blaring, children nearby continued their boisterous playing, cars outside honked, a clock on the mantelpiece ticked. The question embarrassed me. I would have preferred to be cavalier, offhand, slightly sarcastic in my response, but it was too serious a question to duck. I paused. I started to ramble. Then I went back to pausing.

The pause went on for many months, and many visits, when we talked about prayer and I reported on my progress. You've read about that time already. I've tried to describe it both as I remember it now and as I remembered it while it was happening.

During one of our visits, when I had sunk into some sort of profound silence about the ineffable, the minister told me *his* story.

"For fifteen years I read Scripture, I delivered sermons, I prayed, I organized rummage sales, I ran parish meetings, I taught, I studied—and for those fifteen years I didn't really know God. And then I faced a personal crisis."

(I smiled at that—"personal crisis" was such minister language.)

"And in that personal crisis, I prayed, I doubted, I felt lost. I was almost ready to give up being a minister; I felt like an impostor. And then one morning, when I was reading Psalms and came across the passage in the forty-sixth psalm that talks about the city of God and how God is in the midst of her, I felt deeply moved. Maybe because I was in the midst of the city and that's where I had made my ministry. At that moment I experienced a strange calm. I knew that God existed, that Jesus was his son, and that he loved me."

He could have been talking about Paul on the road to Damascus, or John Wesley feeling his heart "strangely warmed" while listening to a reading of Martin Luther's preface to Romans, or even the testimony of some TV evangelist who could name the exact date and time—down to the illuminated seconds on the clock-radio dial—when "the Lord Jesus Christ entered my life." It was a phenomenon as old as time, and the boldness of it, the shopworn vocabulary, the prepack-aged glory made me uncomfortable.

"What do you suggest I do?" I asked timidly.

He'd stopped looking at me. He was fishing around in his desk for something and probably glancing sideways at his watch to see if it was time for his next appointment, his next searching soul. Then he looked up, almost surprised to see me still there.

"Open up your heart. Look. Listen. God will find anyone who looks hard for him."

CHAPTER NINETEEN

I did what I usually do. I went searching for stories, this time from friends, to understand something of the divine.

For a long time Jim didn't believe in God. He'd grown up in a "rationalistic" household. His parents were both scientists, brilliant Ph.D.'s. On Sunday mornings they drove him to the nearby Unitarian Church and dropped him off at Sunday school so that he'd know something about religion, but they didn't believe in anything more than a deistic concept of God, a mathematical construct that must have been hard to pray to.

"The only way I knew anything about faith was through the Bible my grandmother gave me," Jim said.

That Bible sat for a long time on a shelf full of economic textbooks, business law journals, and his wife's novels. Only as a young father did Jim take down the Bible and start reading the Gospels. They filled him with a desire to believe. He longed to have faith like that of the woman who was cured by touching the hem of Christ's cloak, or faith like that of Thomas, who in the end didn't have to touch the wounds in Jesus' hands to believe that he was the risen Christ, or even faith like that of the bumbling Peter, whose zeal continually got him in trouble. For over a year Jim's work took him to a small, bleak Iowa city during the week, away from his wife and children. On long lonely nights in his rented apartment close to the train tracks, where he could hear the mournful howl of freight trains rumbling past, he turned to that Bible.

"But I still didn't believe," he said. "I read the Bible and went to church on Sundays with my family, but I couldn't quite accept something I couldn't see or feel or touch. Intellectually I came to a point where I could acknowledge God's existence, but emotionally I didn't know God at all." (He sounded like me.)

Then came the night of the dream. He'd been on the phone that evening, planning a church trip to the ballpark, lining up people, trying to get enough names to fill a block of seats. That night when he fell asleep, he dreamed about the ballpark. The group from church was in a lounge skybox, one of those expensive corporate clubhouses that provide tax-deductible perks for business entertainment, with a wet bar and a television and a great view of the game. Jim's church group sat on sofas, looking down at the green field.

Suddenly Jim felt the urge to leave. He had to go on some vague errand. He promised the group that he would be back. Next thing he knew he was running along a tree-shaded street near his church. He was moving very fast, almost at the speed of a car. He turned a sharp, gravelly corner and his legs slipped out from under him. As he started to fall, he feared that because of his high speed he would be killed on the hard asphalt. Just then he was picked up and carried, borne above the ground by strong arms. He felt safe. He was loved and cared for. He was protected.

"I understood even while the dream was happening that this was God rescuing me. He cared about me, loved me, knew me," Jim said. "I was left with such an intimate feeling of comfort, warmth, and protection. It was a sense of well-being. I was absolutely at peace. I knew that if I died, no harm would come to me. I was in God's arms."

When he told me this story, I asked if it was the only time he had had such a mystical feeling. Was once enough? Yes, once was indeed enough. But there had been another occasion. Smaller, a fleeting feeling, like a wave passing over a sandy beach and quickly retreating, changing the landscape nevertheless. It happened one evening when he was lying in bed with his wife, both of them reading. Suddenly he felt vulnerable and exposed. He realized how helpless he was on his own. He leaned over and held on to his wife, embracing her. *I know that feeling too*, I thought. *I've felt that sureness, that closeness, that holy satisfaction.*

"But the weird thing was," he said, "I knew I was embracing more than her. I sensed that at that moment I was also, in a weird, mystical way, holding my arms around God."

He shrugged his shoulders and smiled as he said it, like one who knows that well-constructed, intellectual arguments can never explain what the heart believes. He was embarrassed because before he'd had the experience and the dream, he wouldn't have believed such stories from someone else. Logical, careful with words, practical, the kind of man who saves for his daughters' college education when they're barely out of the womb, he'd suddenly embraced the absurd.

Then there was Claire.

I knew about Claire in college because she was older and glamorous, a campus star. After graduation she made her way out to Hollywood and quickly became a studio vice president. When I was a struggling actor in California and going through the misery of no one returning my telephone calls, I sent my photo and résumé to Claire's office, explaining that I was a friend of a friend. After leaving a couple of messages, I received a call from her secretary, who promised that Claire would receive me at 2:05 the next Thursday. She was doing this supreme favor "not because of Princeton," I was told, but because of our mutual friend (oh, the power in the right name).

The office reeked of Hollywood, with thick green carpets, bamboo print wallpaper, a white upholstered sofa, framed film posters, and a small refrigerator from which the secretary took out a bottle of fizzy mineral water, pouring me some in a crystal glass. But Claire herself didn't seem very Hollywood. Pretty, vulnerable, and absolutely sincere. She set up an appointment for me with the studio's casting department and was honest about my limited chances. (This was one instance where I refrained from volunteering all my potential failings as an actor.)

We ran into each other again a year later in California at a church gathering when I was no longer an actor and she was about to leave the studio. Sunday morning's guest speaker, she spoke candidly about the failure of Hollywood to deliver films that improved people's lives or addressed inner needs, and she described the beginnings of her own spiritual search. That search ultimately took her along a torturous path that veered off into half a dozen religions, not to mention several health therapies (this *was* Southern California). Fiercely intelligent, intellectually adroit, she left making movies to be able to read, meditate, study, and pray while living a more precarious hand-to-mouth life. She stoutly maintained that while all religions seemed to reflect aspects of the godly light—as the moon reflects the sun—she was searching to know the light itself.

And then one day she had an experience that changed her forever. She had been praying and fasting, following a Native

American rite that involved long periods in a steam hut. (As I write this, I'm aware of my inability to understand and describe the nuances of the ritual.) She had the day to wander through the fragrant, arid California foothills, and in the heightened awareness that often comes with prayer, she sat down on a granite boulder, staring at an ant.

The ant seemed confused. As if trapped in a shallow depression in the rock, it wandered around in circles, back and forth, down and across, marking but never leaving its circumscribed fortress. It could easily have escaped the warming granite, but it couldn't choose one path. It searched for a route but wouldn't follow any of the choices available. It baked on the rock as though surrounded by concrete walls.

"That's me," Claire thought. *That's me too*, I thought when I heard the story. Exploring all the options, she couldn't commit to one religion. She remained a prisoner of her own intellect. She couldn't take the necessary leap of faith, catapulting over those walls. And because of it, she was circling in her own path, like Winnie the Pooh and Piglet wandering around the same tree again and again, more frightened every time they saw their own footsteps. *God can help you if you make a mistake, but he can do nothing for you if you're indecisive.*

Claire made a decision that day. She made a commitment. She chose one path—a path that took her out of her intellectual self. She finally gave herself to faith. And that's what I was finding it very difficult to do.

Here I was, Sunday morning's star tenor, warbling the Doxology in the choir loft, reciting every word of the creeds. I loved the stories Jesus told; I loved the feeling I got when I prayed; I loved the glorious music of a Sunday morning worship service and the communion of saints in the liturgy. I liked church potluck suppers and stewardship campaigns. God forgive me, I even liked church committee meetings. But I didn't really believe half of what I heard, recited, or sang.

One day after church I was standing in the sun on the steps, amid the noise of the honking cabs and screeching buses, and I turned to my friend Jeffrey, as worldly and wise as any friend I've got. He buys his suits at Paul Stuart and writes elegant stories for glossy magazines. He's an expert at things I don't know how to handle, like getting a good table at a restaurant and returning telephone calls to publicists. A regular churchgoer, he's no starry-eyed, Bible-thumping, Spirit-moved Christian, but altogether sensible and practical. I figured he would have the straight goods on Jesus. So that day on the church steps I asked him if he really bought it all, hook, line, and sinker.

"Frederick," he said—the only one of my friends to call me by my christened name—"Frederick, you believe it or you don't. But if you don't, you might as well not be here."

I was there and he was there (and he wasn't even being paid to be there, as I was).

When I listened to Jim or Claire or even Jeffrey, I distrusted the *neatness* of believing. I was reminded of those long, drawn-out narratives of people who had sinned on drugs and drink and sex and then suddenly found God and everything was okay. The instant turnaround, the quick change of direction, the crystal-clear insight—those plot devices bothered me. Oh, the new believer might start with a disclaimer such as this: "Things didn't get better overnight. I struggled, yet now I had God on my side." But such people's stories were notoriously void of details about the postconversion struggle.

The dramatic turnaround was the climax. That and maybe two more getting-high-on-God paragraphs.

And then something happened to me...

(I wish I could say this to you in person, for you would see the smile on my face and note the way I express myself with bemused wonderment about what I don't understand. Perhaps it's just as well that we do this in print instead. I would make a horrible evangelist, a miserable soul-saver. I can't let go of the slight cynicism for long enough to take the smile off my face. Even when I tell the most bold-faced truth, I laugh as though it were a small white lie. I wear the shrug of the shoulders and crooked grin of the fabricator. So here, now, when I'm talking about the gravest mystery, you'll just have to take my word for it.)

A very sincere Christian friend wrote a letter asking me to pray for him. I wrote back, saying that yes indeed I would pray for him, although I wasn't sure about all this Jesus business or the workings of intercessory prayer.

"Boy, I thought *I* had problems," my friend wrote back. "But you've really got 'em! I'm going to be praying for you every day from now on."

My halting prayers for my friend probably laid the groundwork. When we pray for someone else, we're made vulnerable and compassionate. We become raw and broken; and when we're broken, we can finally be remade. Something extraordinary happens when we allow ourselves to be broken for someone else. I suspect a sort of spiritual energy passes through us; although I don't have the faintest idea how it does it, it can travel hundreds of miles through phone wires and the postal system and the atmosphere we breathe.

And then there was my friend's promise to pray for me. I was impressed, touched, warmed. My friend's prayers helped make me listen to what I needed to hear. They opened me up to the possibilities. A business consultant once told me that the hardest thing to do with his clients is to get them to listen and hear, *really hear*, the solutions his company can offer. Pinpointing the problem is relatively easy. Convincing a stuck-in-the-mud, slow-moving, bureaucratic corporation to turn on a dime is next to impossible. It takes hours of showing charts and pulling out graphs and looking at figures—all to get a person to listen. A single remark can change your whole life if you're tuned into it. If you're listening.

I wasn't listening very carefully that day at church. I was up in the choir loft, as usual, turning from leaflet to hymnal to anthem to psalm. I gave my ear to a fellow tenor whispering about his hangover from a party the night before and to another chorister excoriating the performance of a new diva at the Met. A visiting nun gave the sermon that day, and she had a small voice that didn't travel very well to the back of the chancel. I tuned in, began really *listening*, only when she came to her final prayer. (It would be about time to turn to a new hymn and then another anthem.)

Then she said these shocking (to me) words: "In Jesus' name, our Creator, Redeemer, and Lover." *Creator, Redeemer, and Lover.* Creator, yes, of course; that referred to the creation story in Genesis. And Redeemer, that was about death on the cross, the rolled-away rock, and the empty tomb. Predictable enough. But Lover! That was about God alive and with me in such an intimate way, it embarrassed me.

A dozen images went through my mind in the briefest second, a whole host of associations with the word *lover* (lowercase). I slept with my lover. I happened to be married to her. She cooked most of my meals—and I did the dishes. I gave her chocolate on Valentine's Day, took her to dinner for our anniversary, bought her nightgowns for her birthday that usually turned out to be the wrong size. She was the one who worried more than I did when I was sick and dreaded the day when I might die. She was the person whose approval mattered so much that I refrained from asking for it, and yet I drank it up like nectar when it came with sweet thank-yous if I took out the trash or polished the silver or balanced the checkbook without even being asked. She was why I rushed home at night and what made me happiest to roll out of bed in the morning.

Lover was a word for someone who met my deepest needs. My lover (lowercase again) was someone who knew me inside and out. My lover was the inspiration for all the songs I sang. What a metaphor for God! It seemed so right. It shocked me, amazed me, startled me, delighted me. That sort of companionship, that kind of partner, that Other who took greater delight in me than I took in myself: Lover.

My spiritual advisor might have explained to me that this notion of God as Lover was as old as the Song of Solomon ("O that you would kiss me with the kisses of your mouth") and was beautifully used by Saint John of the Cross in his explicit love poem to Christ ("One dark night, fired with love's urgent longings..."). But I didn't need any explanations.

The word sank into my subconscious mind and transformed my understanding. Maybe the next day, maybe two weeks later, I realized I was praying to this man, this Lover (uppercase), this mystery bigger than any name can hold, Son of God, Word Incarnate, Jesus. I hate the exclusiveness of the Jesus club, those who claim no prayer can be made without the closing "In Jesus' name," but I understand their enthusiasm. His whole life was a prayer.

Like the Russian peasant pilgrim who prayed over and over again, *Jesus Christ, have mercy on me, a miserable sinner*, I could repeat, "Jesus Christ, have mercy on me..." Jesus, Jesus, Jesus. Those were words that led me to forget myself and enter into a prayer that transcended all my petty needs. On the subway, if I closed my eyes and repeated those words, I wasn't praying out of want. No desires needed to be mentioned. *He knows the desires of the heart.* What a prayer! What a lover!

CHAPTER TWENTY

For our last meeting my spiritual director took me to his club for lunch. This felt right, just the kind of place for the society minister I had taken him to be. Through the unmarked doors with their polished brass handles we went, up the marble steps with the red carpet held flush by brass rods, stopping for drinks in a paneled room hung with Hudson River school landscapes. Mr. Spiritual Director, dwarfed in a wing chair that rose above his dark head like bat's ears, had a beer and I had some mineral water, popping peanuts into my mouth in between sips. Like a favorite high school teacher you visit after you've had a taste of "the real world," he suddenly seemed smaller, less clever, more ordinary, hardly insightful at all. He could have been an accountant in a bespoke suit, an auditor on an expense-account lunch. No clerical collar, no Buddha aura. This was my guru? This was the man who was my spiritual guide?

He listened to my latest spiritual revelations with his usual combination of intense concentration and impatience. Gazing about the room to see if any cronies had arrived, congregation-cruising, he turned to me. "Jesus will help you in your prayer life. Give you something to focus on."

I was reminded of a classic Rotary introduction. The guest speaker is sitting on the dais, and the club president steps up to the lectern to make a long-winded introduction. "I'd like to tell you about the most important, fascinating, earth-shattering person who ever existed. He's changed the shape of history.

He's influenced kings, princes, popes, and czars. He's made his mark in literature, music, art, philosophy, theology. And here to talk about him is my good friend Joe." Yuck, yuck, big laugh. *Here to talk about Jesus was my good friend, Mr. Spiritual Director.*

"So what have you decided to do about your career?" he asked.

"I'm feeling better about what I do," I said.

"Really? I thought you weren't happy. I thought you wondered what God wanted you to do."

"I did. But I really like this job now." For the time being, I *was* happier. I'd found a writing job at a magazine. "I get to write. I get to read a lot about God. I get to talk to interesting people. Sometimes I daydream about God."

"Glad to hear it. Have you ever seen that movie *Chariots of Fire?*"

I nodded my head, chomping on a peanut.

"There's a scene in it where the young man who's going to be a missionary, Eric Liddall, I think"—the minister was back—"is walking with his sister in the hills of Scotland. And yes, he tells her, he does plan on going to China and doing what God calls him to do, but first he's going to run in the Olympics, because, he says—and this is a wonderful phrase—'When I run, I feel God's pleasure.'"

"I remember that."

"Whatever you do, look for that. You're doing the Lord's work if you feel God's pleasure."

We went into the dining room, where he had pasta and I ordered shepherd's pie. We spoke of architecture, art, and the rotting beams in his church's apse. We talked about the books that lined the club's walls and a few of the paintings. (I was

struck with an acute case of lust for a New England landscape.)
And then he became very sincere. He looked at me straight on
with his lapis lazuli eyes. "You will be very successful," he said.

How did he know?

"People like you are successful," he added, which made me
wonder what kind of people I was.

After dessert we stood up. I brushed away the bread crumbs
that always fell on my lap and set my crumpled napkin beside
my plate like a trophy. We walked to the red-carpeted landing
and shook hands. His parting words were, "Never stop praying. Each day you'll learn something new."

That was that. He sent me on my way. I almost wished he'd
patted me on the head, like the Grinch patting Cindy Lou
Who ("who was only two") on her nearly hairless Dr. Seuss
head. I felt unprepared to meet the world. What about therapists? What about shrinks? What about twelve-step support
groups? Weren't you supposed to need them forever? Weren't
you in perpetual recovery? Wouldn't I always need a spiritual
director?

I took the carpeted stairs two by two, pushed the polished
brass handle of the front door, and walked out into the din of
midtown. What now? What about all the unresolved problems in my life? Where would guidance come from now? Who
would hear about my prayers? Who would interpret them?
Would I even say them if I knew no one was going to give me
a regular checkup?

The next morning I was standing as usual on the subway
platform. I had a brand-new copy of *Vanity Fair* in my briefcase, wafting waves of fragrance from the perfume ads I hadn't
yet ripped out. I had the urge to coddle myself with the current

events of life's vanity fairs, as forgettable as the lyrics to last year's hit song. I could start out the day by catching up on a scandal, indulging my envy of the rich and famous, searching for details to support my moral superiority. Or I could take out the small green-bound Gideon volume of the New Testament and Psalms.

Three psalms, that had been my recipe. Then silence. Listening for God.

I hesitated for a moment; then, giving in to some internal prompting, I turned to the Psalms. I was into the meditative habit. It was too late. I was hooked on morning prayer. *Vanity Fair* would have to wait. (And don't think for a moment that I didn't read it later.)

It's the same way a college student goes to the library with his textbook, knowing that the place itself with its quiet, books, and other students will inspire him to study. Or the way a salesman who could never gather the pluck and charisma to make aggressive calls from home finds inspiration at his desk, not far from the water-cooler gossip. A place and time can trigger the desire to pray. I've trained myself to use the subway like that.

The distant rumble of the approaching train, the rustle of my neighbors' newspapers, the sight of someone look-ing at a Bible or fingering a rosary—these are my signals to resume my own spiritual journey. I've worked at making this place sacred for me. That means overlooking the smell of urine, the bum with his plastic bag of cans, the rowdy high school kids, the neighbor who wants to banter about the weather. Like the mental distractions that constantly intrude when I'm focusing on the divine, they are banished. When I'm finished and I open my eyes, I might just see the beauty behind the nasty headlines or the homeless man. Right now I need to pray.

I close my eyes and I'm jogging on my weekend loop, up along the rows of art deco buildings with old ladies sitting in the sun in aluminum chairs, their Caribbean caretakers next to them. Up through the park past picnickers who've decorated a copper beech in pink and blue crepe paper for a child's birthday party. "Quiet Zone" says a sign, and beneath it music on a boombox blares. I leap over a six-pack of empty beer bottles and run around a pile of trash that's been picked out of a can by a beggar in search of booty. On top of the hill is the Cloisters museum, filled with stones from crumbling medieval monasteries, the hewn blocks taken down, marked, boxed, and shipped from Europe, reassembled above the Hudson in a simulacrum of holiness. Somehow, even in the antiseptic environment, real holiness can be felt. The prayers repeated behind those stones for hundreds of years seem to echo in my ears whenever I pass. Sometimes I think of Thomas Merton, who spent boyhood years in France not far from the original site of one stripped cloister.

Now this subway train is my cloister, hallowed by the prayers I've said here as I stand with my hand around a cold metal pole or sit in a warm orange seat. The closing doors are my call to worship, the conductor's voice on the loudspeaker calling out the stops like the announcement of Sunday morning hymns.

I've been amazed at how prayer can transform a place, even a place as uninviting as a subway. I've seen the same thing happen on the fifteen blocks that go from my apartment to the teeming, overcrowded city hospital where my two sons were born. Both boys were born in late winter, when the streets had none of the promise of early spring, only the gray, grungy, garbagey stench of unchanging damp days and diesel exhaust from city buses hanging in the air. The route winds past neat bodegas, plantain vendors, rap-screaming radios, greasy pizzerias, laundromats, discount clothing stores, and check-cashing outfits with bullet-proof windows. Drug dealers linger on corners, and the down-and-out try to coax coins from suburbanite drivers by threatening to wash their car windows with filthy rags (blackmail, really). And yet that stretch of Broadway reminds me of the prayers of thanks I said in passing, rushing to hold a newborn, filled with the joy of new life. Prayer has made it sacred.

On the subway I say the same prayers over and over again. Even now I say them. *God, I wish you'd give me a little bit more money. God, I'd give you such pride if I had just a little bit more cash. Think of all that I could do for the poor.* (My own transparent attempts at blackmail.) *Dear Lord, I'm tired of behaving like a jerk all the time. Why can't I be a little nicer? Why can't I be kinder? Okay, okay, I'll forgive the bastard, but you've got to forgive me. Okay?*

How I must bore God to tears with my repetition. He's heard it all before. He's heard it from people worthier than I. He's heard it from me before. But all this talk, all this vain banter, all this praying with words is just a prelude so that I can go beyond words. So that it will simply be my needs doing the praying. That's where I really need help. You can try very hard at expressing just what you think God wants to hear from you, but your jealous, angry, or hurt self will speak up very quickly and show that you're not a saint.

The first crisis I had to handle without my spiritual director came when a friend let me down in a big way. Whether through flakiness or malicious intent or maybe jealousy, he messed up.

(I feel odd putting it down on paper, even in general terms, because to forgive is to forget, and to write about what has been forgiven is to pick at old wounds. Worse yet, cloaking the ill deed in a veil of secrecy—alluding to it without giving the details—makes it seem so unforgivable it can't be named. It *could* be named. It could be described in intimate detail in a family magazine without exciting any censors. But I choose not to name it. I'd rather not go into it, thank you very much.)

When my friend did me this disfavor, I wanted to forgive. I wanted to forgive very badly. I wrote a note masking my hurt with good humor, making my anger look charming so that he could still approach me without embarrassment. I made a few telephone calls, speaking into his answering machine, keeping up the jocular, jovial attitude. I knew about therapy. I knew I needed to express my anger openly, lest it turn against me and attack me like a worm eating the insides of an apple, making it rotten to the core; so I expressed my anger in a disarming way. But really, I wanted painfully, desperately to forgive. And I was never given the chance. I was never allowed to communicate the magnanimous words I had rehearsed to myself. All those short tries into a telephone answering machine were useless. My calls went unreturned, my letters unanswered.

When I walked by my friend's apartment, I was tempted to drop in unexpectedly. I imagined running into him in the street. His eyes would look away. Given enough warning, he would cross the avenue and hide in an ATM line at a bank.

"Don't worry," I'd say, seeking him out. "It was nothing. I've gotten over it. I forgive you." I'd be the star of the colloquy, Lady Bountiful passing out indulgences. (There's nothing so damned self-righteous as goodness that hasn't said its prayers.)

For weeks I continued to rehearse the fantasy I'd been acting out. Eyes closed, I practiced to myself the right expression of forgiveness. How kind I would be, how accepting.

As the months passed, my playacting diminished. The initial sting of the wrong done was gone, leaving behind only bewilderment. Then I began to see myself more clearly. I was a phony. Had I forgiven my friend? Had I *really?* No. In fact, I hadn't done a darn thing. Instead, I had only tortured him (in my imagination) with my bigheartedness. I had wished for him to squirm in the presence of my wonderful kindness. I had made myself the star of the scene, both the victim and the hero.

This is the key to one of Christ's crucial messages. Pride is a deadly sin, and the pride of self-righteousness is the very worst, because it doesn't see itself for what it is. That's what I had found in that frustrating tale of the prodigal son. I had identified with the stay-at-home brother. He's the helpless one. He's the one most in need of God's forgiveness and love. I knew I couldn't get beyond the wrongs done me, except through prayer. "Forgive us our trespasses as we forgive those who trespass against us." It *is* a two-way street.

Strolling down that two-way street on the subway, I could finally forgive. And really forget. Get on with it. If by some golden chance I were to run into my friend, I would be able to greet him with unaffected honesty and delight.

He *did* eventually get in touch with me. Maybe God worked through him. At a moment of distress he called. First he spoke to Carol, addressing himself to the matter at hand. And then he spoke to me. I didn't have any trouble saying, "I've missed you. It's been a long time. I'm glad you called." There was no rancor. I didn't have to be self-conscious about my voice, wondering how it sounded, wondering if it wavered. I meant what I said. That's a miracle of prayer, the work of God reaffirming who we are, giving us authenticity, making our words true.

Here on the subway I repeat the same prayer over and over again until I can get it right. *Forgive us our trespasses as we forgive those who trespass against us*, except that I usually say it in the Presbyterian version of my childhood, using the word *debts* instead of *trespasses. Forgive us our debts as we forgive our debtors.* I'll probably never get it right, but I try. Prayer is the only earthly endeavor where trying is enough.

My eyes are closed, and the train shakes as it rounds a curve. I clutch the green-bound Bible in my hands. The man next to me falls asleep. Suddenly his head falls on my shoulders. I open my eyes as he jerks his head up and apologizes.

"That's okay," I say, thinking, *I forgive you.*

CHAPTER TWENTY-ONE

I'm back on the subway on a warm spring evening, riding home on the crowded rush-hour train. I picture my wife at home cooking dinner—peeling the carrots or punching soda crackers into the meatloaf—and I'm filled with thankfulness for all the good things God has given me. I can imagine my children sprawled on the floor, plotting elaborate battles with their plastic knights and castles. Soon I'll get home and take them to the park to toss a ball or climb the jungle gym, and later I'll read to them the exploits of the children in the Narnia chronicles or the myths of the Greek gods. I'll sing them their goodnight song and hear their prayers; then Carol and I will have adult conversation about the book she's writing and what happened at the office today and what movies were reviewed today.

Overwhelmed with the goodness of life, intoxicated by the spring air (even in the A train), delighted by the murky shape of my life, I can barely concentrate on the paperback book I'm reading. I'm hardly aware of the surge of commuters around me, the doors slamming open and shut, the conductor calling out the station stops. I close my eyes in a deep satisfaction that's like prayer.

The next thing I know, someone is slugging me in the face, a cold fist hitting my nose and cheek. I duck my head; the fist comes again. My fellow passengers scramble to get away from the guy who's hitting me, and someone shouts, "What the...?" Echoing that thought, I stagger to my feet, still hiding my head, and dart out the opened door in the company of several others. My nose is sore and bloody; I'm in a daze. The doors close, separating me from whoever it was, and the train disappears from the platform.

"It looked like a Hispanic guy," one man tells me on the platform. "You should make a report."

"He's still on the train," another observer says.

"There's a police station right here," an undercover straphanger says, and I stagger past a glossily painted orange concrete-block wall into an unmarked underground office right out of Perry Mason, radios crackling, phones ringing. A couple of uniformed cops, their extra bulk hanging over their black belts, ask me questions, and a prim secretary types my answers on a manual typewriter (a typewriter!). Was there any motive? Did you see who hit you? Had he been drinking? What was he wearing? What did he look like? What time was this? Are you in shock? Then one of the guys, taking my measured answers in stride, tells me off the record that I look like a prosecutor. Am I an attorney? No, I'm not. Well, at any rate, they decide to get an ambulance for me. "We'll have them take you to Presbyterian. You'll feel more comfortable there than at Harlem Hospital." (They're trying to tell me it was a racially motivated incident.)

First I call Carol. "Don't worry," I say. "I'm all right. Somebody hit me on the subway."

"Are you really all right?" she asks.

"I think so. Maybe my nose is broken." I can hear her take a deep breath. "Start dinner without me. It'll probably be a while."

I'm whisked away by ambulance, sirens blaring, from 145th Street to 168th Street, and I sit for hours on the hard plastic seats in the emergency waiting room with mostly Dominican immigrants, their feverish children sleeping in their laps, older siblings playing portable video games beneath the fluorescent glare. Nurses look up from clipboards; cashiers behind bullet-proof glass take money and promises to pay; a beefy security guard fiddles with the handcuffs jangling on his thigh.

By now I feel no anger, only bewilderment. Maybe the cops were right. Maybe I had the wrong shade of skin that day on a multicolored train (though I wasn't the only male with lighter skin). Maybe I reminded my crazed attacker of some teacher who had flunked him. Maybe the guy just wanted my seat. If he wanted my jacket, he could have asked. I started to feel a little proud. A certifiable victim of crime, I had the marks of the twentieth century on me—plus a first-rate shiner and a slightly modified nose. I sailed through triage, was X-rayed, then waited some more. Finally, at about 10:00 p.m., a doctor told me that my nose wasn't broken but would probably swell up before it went down. Released, I was back on the streets. I walked the fifteen blocks home.

"Rick, you've got to be more careful than you are in the city," a friend warned. "You've got to guard your flank and keep your wits about you at all times." *Thanks all the same*, I thought—and I still think. I'd rather not. Life is too short to live in fear. *Perfect love casteth out fear.* I'm careful, I'm not foolhardy, but there are certain blows you can't shield yourself from. Fists can come out of anywhere. You can't hide all the time. You can only live the best you know how and trust that your faith will help you through the dark tunnels and unexpected knockouts.

The bruises bloomed like a Christmas poinsettia and then faded. Life went on. A kid at work volunteered to track down my assailant and beat him up. I said I'd pass. My prayer life went on. I'm a little less oblivious on subway trains, but I'm not afraid of taking the A train at 11:00 p.m. after going to the theater or the rush-hour local past 145th Street. I suppose the only real casualty was Tolkien. I've never had the urge to finish volume two of the trilogy (the drops of dried blood dissuade me). The prayerful state I was in at the time of the attack was interrupted, but prayers are always interrupted. And then they resume. They can continue even when the rest of life is going on about them.

There's a Henry James story about two well-known artists, one a painter and the other a writer. They're vacationing in Switzerland, going on picnics, hiking, and talking—mostly talking interminably, as people do in Henry James stories—when the narrator notices something odd about the writer. Wherever he might be—on the veranda, in the hotel lobby, at the dining room table, back in his room—his real self is working furiously on his writing. On the other hand, the painter, a brilliant conversationalist, doesn't really exist unless someone is around to hear him speak. He's like the moon, incapable of generating his own light, able only to bask in another's glow.

When I first read this story, my greatest fear was that I would end up like the brilliant conversationalist, that I wouldn't really exist unless I was providing company for others. I wouldn't exist on my own. I could never be alone. I thought that maybe I'd have to become a great artist to savor solitude.

I don't feel that way anymore. My work on prayer has given me that quiet room in the back of my head (or maybe at the bottom of my soul)—that space where I'm furiously working at growing in spite of life's interruptions and setbacks. In the midst of making phone calls, filling out forms for the PTA, taking cash out of the ATM, or being beaten up on the subway, my best self can be back home in my prayer closet. (A closet case!) If I can give God a good ten minutes of my morning, he'll give me the rest of the day. *Watch me with the very pupil of your eye! Hide me in the protection of your wings.* I don't mind losing myself in busywork as long as my real self, my deepest self, is concentrated in the regenerating pleasures of the soul. *The Lord is close to everyone who calls out to him, to all who call out to him sincerely.*

So where is *your* prayer closet? Where is *your* quiet place? Don't look for the mountaintop with a magnificent view. You want a spot where you'll be encouraged to look inward. I read once in a handbook of advice for writers that a writer should choose a room in the house where she won't be distracted. She should look for a place with a limited vista—a garden wall, a corner of sky, a few trees, a bush in the backyard. A dramatic view of snow-topped mountains and singing pines can be too much. Just a bit of foreground is enough. So too in prayer: look to the blades of grass or the lichen on a rock. Observe the pill bug hiding under a leaf or the impatiens dripping out of the redwood planter; then close your eyes. Look inward.

I love the beach for praying. You can lie on the sand near the ocean and close your eyes, and even if you're on Coney Island in August you can feel quite alone; the sound of the waves on the shore drowns out all other noise. You can't hear the couple arguing next to you, and the radio blasting near the lifeguard station seems miles away. All sounds are smothered by the ocean's white noise. On a busy, blanketed beach I've often felt utterly alone—in the world but not of the world. It's almost like being on a crowded rush-hour subway train.

Here I am, back on the A train, thankful for the click-clack of the wheels on the track, the rumble of the car in a dark tunnel, the roar of the accelerating train. There's the old lady praying with her rosary and the young Orthodox Jewish man with his beard and prayer book. Out of the corner of my eye I can tell that the black girl sitting next to me is looking at my Bible and me. I try to ignore her, fearful that she will interrupt to tell me about her Wednesday night Bible study group and her church...perhaps I'd like to come? *No, I wouldn't*, I tell myself even before I've been invited. I want this precious time alone, that's all.

"Is that your Bible?" she asks. A ridiculous question. Who else's would it be?

"Yes," I say tentatively.

"I forgot mine. I usually read it on my way to work."

"Would you like to borrow mine?"

"Thank you."

I close my eyes, knowing that I'm with a silent minority of people at work.

CHRISTMAS GREETINGS
TO THE HASTINGS

FROM THE HAMLINS:
THORNTON, PEGGY, HOWARD, RICK & GIOIA

RICK (CENTER) POSES
WITH BROTHER,
HOWARD, AND SISTER,
GIOIA FOR THE FAMILY
CHRISTMAS CARD
(1956)

THE HAMLIN
FAMILY
CELEBRATES
CHRISTMAS AT
HOME IN SAN
GABRIEL, CA
(1957)

THE AUTHOR AS A
YOUNG MAN IN PARIS (1978)

BUDDING ACTOR RICK PERFORMS
IN A HIGH SCHOOL PRODUCTION OF
BRIGADOON (1971)

RICK IN 1984

PEGGY HAMLIN BEAMS AFTER
WATCHING HER SON IN A BLUE HILL
TROUPE PRODUCTION OF *PIRATES OF
PENZANCE* (1985)

NEWLYWEDS RICK HAMLIN AND CAROL
WALLACE AFTER THEIR WEDDING AT ST.
MICHAEL'S CHURCH IN NEW YORK CITY (1983)

AT THE COUPLE'S
WEDDING RECEPTION
IN FAIRFIELD, CT
(1983)

WITH HIS FATHER, THORNTON (1998

IN HIS OFFICE
AT *GUIDEPOSTS*
MAGAZINE (1998)

(L TO R) CAROL WALLACE, WILLIAM HAMLIN, RICK HAMLIN, AND TIM HAMLIN AT WILLIAM'S HOUSE IN SAN FRANCISCO, 2016.

RICK WITH WIFE CAROL AT THE HOLLYWOOD PREMIERE OF *BEN HUR* (2016). CAROL WROTE AN UPDATED VERSION OF THE CLASSIC BOOK, WHICH HER GREAT-GREAT GRANDFATHER, LEW WALLACE, PUBLISHED IN 1880.

RICK AT HIS DESK, BACK AT THE OFFICE, 2018

RICK AND CAROL WITH SONS TIM
AND WILL AT THE BEACH, 2017

WITH ROBERTA AT
CHOIR PRACTICE (2015)

Back to Work (2015)

Carol, William, and Rick at the Brooklyn Botanic Garden (2018)

PART TWO

CHAPTER ONE

The ER

Here's a leg on my journey of prayer that I need to put down, a time of the worst and the best all at once, an episode worth analyzing, although I dread doing it. I often write to get rid of fears or at least to shrink them into manageable size. There on paper they won't haunt me. They are simply words on a page. Once I asked a best-selling author, "Do you ever pray?" "When I write I pray," he said. I thought I understood what he meant. Anything that requires that level of trust as you gaze into the unknown is prayer. You can't go forward without it.

When I think about writing this, I start talking myself out of it: Don't write about that medical crisis. Don't go there. Who wants to know that you almost died? You're alive now, so it's ancient history. You don't want to relive it anyway. It's over, done with. Why wrestle with it? Why do you feel you must give it some meaning on the page? That's so tiresome. You're still processing it anyway. Let it rest. Give it another ten or twenty years. (Twenty years? Geez, I don't even know if I'll be around in twenty years.) Your readers don't know you all that well. Most of them don't know you at all. How is this going to help them?

Would that I could say like Jesus, "Satan, get behind me," because the dark passages of our lives, when shared, can become healing passages of our lives, for us and for others. I will tell it straight up, and you can decide yourself if it's one long organ recital, as in "Can you top this medical disaster story?" or if it was indeed a winding path of prayer. Forgive me for going into clinical details.

It began two years ago—or at least this part of the story began—with a boil on the back of my leg. It looked like some sort of ingrown hair. (Nice.) "That's looking pretty ugly," my wife, Carol, said, "you should go get that checked out." This being the Saturday of Labor Day weekend, the only place I could think of that would be open was the urgent care facility on 165th Street, around the corner from the Art Deco remains of the Audubon Ballroom (where Malcolm X was shot). The urgent-care place is affiliated with and across the street from the sprawling New York–Presbyterian/Columbia University Medical Center, where all my doctors work. If I could go any-where, I wanted to be in a spot where they could access my medical records at the click of a computer key.

We live about fifteen minutes away. I jogged down Broadway, past bodegas and Laundromats, a parking garage, and an Irish pub, people pushing strollers and shopping carts. I signed in. Didn't have to wait long. A young doctor checked me out, said that yes, it looked infected, and prescribed two antibiotics. I picked up the pills at Hilltop Pharmacy near our house and started taking them that day. I felt pretty good the rest of the weekend, and the boil looked like it was shrinking.

On Sunday we went to church and that afternoon I visited a homebound ninety-four-year-old parishioner, Wesley, who'd served with the Tuskegee Airmen during World War II. He was also a superb musician. We sang, as always, a few hymns together—he harmonized from his hospital bed. Too weak to sit up, he could still hold the baritone line. I headed home. Carol and I watched TV that night, an episode of *Broadchurch*, a creepy British mystery series. The next day, Labor Day, I ran some errands, did the laundry, went for a run, washed some windows, vacuumed. So much for a laborless holiday.

On Tuesday I went to work but found myself getting really chilly in the air-conditioned office. I just couldn't get myself warm. Wishing I'd brought a sweater, I wrapped my hands around a mug of tea. "Isn't it cold in here?" I asked my colleagues. "Aren't you freezing?" They humored me but nobody readily agreed. "You probably have a fever," I told myself, gritting my teeth to keep them from chattering, bouncing my legs at my desk to get them warm. Even so, I had no intention of heading home early. There was work to do, five days of it that had to be crammed into a four-day workweek. I'm an editor at *Guideposts* magazine and just because the world took off for Labor Day didn't mean that our deadlines disappeared. In some faintly puritanical stance, I hesitated about taking an ibuprofen because it seemed like doing that would simply mask the fever rather than make it go away.

I left work at the usual hour, shivering on the subway ride home, ate dinner, took my temperature, finally—yes, I had a fever—and went to bed. Carol's medical advice has always been to give in to whatever you've got sooner rather than later, because you'll get rid of it sooner rather than later. Don't soldier on. Go to bed immediately, take a sick day. Not that I always follow this good advice, but I did then.

I called in sick on Wednesday, the fever not diminishing despite the ibuprofen I was now popping every four hours. I went back to the urgent-care place. They said, "Keep taking the antibiotics." On Thursday I got an appointment with my internist, whose office is in the hospital complex. I like Seth a lot. He's warm, caring, wise, and wry. He's always overbooked, but it's never stopped him from giving his full attention to his patients or insisting, as he once did at the end of a session, on showing me a funny video clip on his computer that I watched over his shoulder while his ever-patient assistants were rolling their eyes and pointing to the clock. I try not to call him Seth but Doctor because I want him to know I respect him and esteem him, but I think of him as Seth.

"It's freezing in here," I said to his assistant when I checked in. The fever speaking.

"Sit in the waiting room," she said. "It's warm in there. The air conditioner isn't working."

"Give him my sweatshirt," Seth called from his office.

They gave me a big gray sweatshirt with New York–PRESBYTERIAN written on it in red, some swag from a medical conference, I figured. I took a selfie, the coddled patient, and texted it to Carol: "Look what Seth loaned me."

When Seth finally examined me, he listened to my lungs, switched me off one of the antibiotics, had me do some blood tests, and said I might have pneumonia. He sent me to the lab to get a chest X-ray, but all I really wanted to do was get home, get warm, and get in bed. Plenty of rest was the order of the day. He'd let me know if the blood tests showed anything.

"What shall I do with the sweatshirt?" I asked.

"Keep it," he said.

I nursed myself at home on Friday, piling blankets on top of blankets, sipping mugs of tea and broth, even in the warm September weather, and taking these big ibuprofen horse pills. But the fever only got worse. On Saturday morning it spiked at 104.2, with no sign of diminishing. "I should go to the ER," I said to Carol. It was around 11:00 a.m.

"I'm coming with you," she said. "We'll take a cab."

You know it's bad when a tightwad and public transportation junkie like me makes no objections to taking a cab, instead of a bus, the fifteen blocks to the hospital.

We got out at the wrong corner and had to walk half a block more—it felt like half a mile—to the entrance of the emergency room. I expected the usual long wait, like trying to flag down a salesperson at Macy's the week before Christmas, but we sat in the anteroom for less than fifteen minutes before I was admitted. I guess they could tell I was pretty bad off, every breath becoming a struggle, my body trembling to stay warm.

Half aware, half in a daze, I felt myself slipping down mortality's rabbit hole with no desire to reach out to the divine.

How can I explain this? How can I show it? It's at the crux of what I struggle to understand about prayer and the life of the spirit. When my body goes, my faith goes too, and long-practiced spiritual habits hardly count. I remembered this from open-heart surgery. When I'm really sick—and I was really sick then, sicker than I'd ever been—my spirit diminishes. The world becomes smaller, and all my internal anguish takes over. I am not a holy person at all but some poor soul caught in a trap. I want to be able to cry out to God but I can't. I monitor the downward spiral I'm being sucked into, and find no means of salvation. I've read about the saints who found pain and suffering a means for drawing closer to the Lord of sorrows, the one who died on a cross for us. But physical suffering isolates me from such love and solace. I am consumed with myself and forget about my Maker. When I think about dying, this is what worries me most. That I would become such a stranger to myself. Am I just a sunshine patriot and no winter soldier? Is not my faith bigger than this?

Did I think I was dying? Not then. My brain sank into a fog. The techs and nurses put me on oxygen and an IV drip. We were lodged in a cubicle with curtains at the sides, a pod with other patients across from me and Carol in a chair next to me. Everything was illuminated with bright lights whether we were awake or asleep. They hustled me off on a gurney or in a wheelchair for an echocardiogram—I think—and a lung X-ray. They took my temperature and drew blood. The nurses and doctors came and went. I dozed and stared and wondered how long I would have to stay in the ER. Surely they would admit me into the hospital. Maybe they would send me home. What time was it? Couldn't Carol go home? Much of this is fuzzy to me, but then there were moments I was acutely aware of.

I remember when the aides were decking me out in a gown and those non-slippery socks they give you in hospitals. "Not the yellow ones," one woman said to another. "Those are only for the violent ones." I looked at the multi-tattooed patient across from me, a kid who appeared to be strung out on a drug overdose, rattled and shaking. He had yellow socks. A violent one?

The woman next to me was ninety-nine years old—I heard her say that—and I hoped for her sake she could go home and die in her bed rather than this place. She was in a plain gown with brown socks. The woman across from us, in her mere seventies I supposed, resented being told that she was being sent to the hospital's uptown outpost. "I want to stay right here. I don't want to go to the Allen Pavilion," she said, as though she were being asked to shop at a suburban branch of Saks when she was at the Fifth Avenue store.

I must have been seen by more than one doctor, but the only one I remember was a young one with blondish-brown hair, a three-day beard, and a bad bedside manner. He talked to the nurse or Carol about what grave trouble I was in, as though I were too far gone to understand his words, like talking about a deaf person in front of them. I recall him saying my condition was critical, and I realized the adjective had a very specific meaning here, like when they say on the news, "The victim was taken to the hospital and remains in critical condition."

He took my blood pressure. "Ninety over fifty," he said.

"Wow, that's pretty good," I thought to myself. "I've been trying to get it down." Like an anorexic on deathwatch, congratulating herself for being a skeletal eighty-nine pounds.

The endless afternoon and evening wore on. Carol must have gone out to get some food. I don't remember eating, myself. Our twenty-five-year-old son, Timothy, was living with us at the time—and soon to leave on a tenmonth mission trip to South Africa. Carol let him know where we were. He texted or called from Brooklyn, where he was at a party with his girlfriend. "Should I come by the hospital?" he asked. "You don't need to," Carol texted back. He knew her and me better than that and showed up at the ER after midnight. I remember him being there. I remember him talking to Carol and me. And then he left.

At 2:00 a.m. they finally admitted me.

I was taken to the step-down unit of the ICU on the sixth floor. They pushed me in a wheelchair on the sky-bridge across

Fort Washington Avenue. I'd seen it from below many times but had never been on it. It was the middle of the night and the corridor was lit up like the inside of a refrigerator. I could see the lights of the hospital out the windows, and it seemed as enchanted as the Emerald City. I think of a friend's mother who, when given last rites, exclaimed in wonder, "I've never done this before!" Another friend tells the story of his ailing ninety-three-year-old mother being airlifted off of Martha's Vineyard to get emergency medical care, her last flight on earth, and all she could say about it was, "That was the first time I've ever been on a helicopter!"

Perhaps that's how the spirit speaks when you're not conscious of making any prayer and feel incapable of it. You can still see things to marvel at. I wanted to turn to the aide pushing my wheelchair and tell him, "Gosh, I've never been on this bridge before." But the mask blowing oxygen into my lungs didn't allow for talking.

On the other side of the bridge, in the step-down unit, I kissed Carol good-bye or, more likely, she kissed me because of my oxygen mask. "Go home. Get some sleep," I wanted to say, although I couldn't really speak.

The next morning, Sunday, September 13, Carol sent the first of her mass e-mails:

Dear ones, forgive the mass e-mail but this is the easy way to start this news moving around. Please feel free to forward this e-mail—I started with a bare-bones approach.

Rick has had pneumonia since Thursday and took a turn for the worse yesterday. We went to the emergency room at Columbia-Presbyterian, and at length he was admitted to a step-down unit—a slightly tamer version of the ICU. He is getting great care.

He is very sick. Sepsis was one diagnosis, along with pneumonia, but he was having trouble getting oxygen. When I left him a few hours ago he had on a device that blows oxygen into his lungs.

That's all I can tell you now, but I will keep you apprised, probably via a blast e-mail. Add names if you like.

He doesn't have a phone at his bed (retro!) but he will have access to his cell. Right now he's so sick I don't dare leave it there with him. Ditto computer. Tim is here and we will probably tag team for the next few days.

No visits or phone calls for now but I will pass along messages. E-mails to me might be best—I can print them out and take them to him.

I know you want to know what you can do. If you are praying people, do that. Otherwise, keep us in your thoughts.

Lots of love to you all.

Carol

P.S.: I am not really taking calls either but I am texting madly. Always assuming I remember to charge my phone!

CHAPTER TWO

Hospital, Day 1

When Timothy was four he broke his femur in a tricycle accident at nursery school. In those pre–cell phone days, Carol called work and left me an urgent message. I was at a dentist appointment and when I walked into the office the receptionist let me know Carol was trying to reach me. I listened to a few messages on my office phone, one telling me about the accident, one telling me how she had picked up William, our older son, from school, one telling me where she had taken Tim for an X-ray, one telling me where I should meet her and the boys.

I rushed uptown to an unfamiliar hospital building near Columbus Circle, not Columbia-Presbyterian, where both boys had been born. I struggled to find them, bouncing around from floor to floor, going up and down in the elevator. Finally I spoke to a person who told me Carol had taken Timothy down to the Hospital for Joint Diseases on East Seventeenth Street. I raced back downtown and at the hospital went up to what I thought was pediatrics. I got off the elevator to hear a doctor in green scrubs say to another doctor, "It's the worst break I've ever seen in a kid. Right through his femur. They said it was a tricycle-riding accident at nursery school, but it's hard to imagine any kid could get hurt that bad by a tricycle."

Some conversations you don't want to overhear.

I asked the doctors where I could find my son, the patient. I was sent back downstairs. Finally I found Carol and seven-year-old William sitting next to Tim in a crib with bars around it like a prison cell. He was lying on his back, his broken leg wrapped in bandages and held up in a swing-like device. He would have to be like that for twenty-six days, in traction. "It's a little like being trapped on an airplane with a toddler for twenty-six days," his babysitter Sharon later observed.

Carol was doing a good job of acting calm in the storm, wearing her best Florence Nightingale face—Nurse Barbie in action—but she was clearly frazzled. "I'll spend the night here with Tim," I said. "We'll be OK." We would have to alternate roles, one parent with the child at home, the other in the hospital with Tim.

That night Tim and I were in a double room, where the kid on the other side of the curtain was crying and his parents were watching a shoot-'em-up movie on TV, the sound blasting through the curtain. I sat in a chair that could be turned into a bed and tried to coax Tim to go to sleep. He and I dozed, on and off, but he woke up several times in the night, the TV still blaring on the other side of the room, the soundtrack in a minor key. I remember Tim grabbing the bars of his crib and clutching them like some prisoner. "Daddy," he said, "we're stuck."

"Yes, Tim-o," I said. "We're stuck."

That was how I felt now in my hospital room, stuck. I had a mask delivering oxygen to me, monitors connected to my heart, an IV drip filling me with pints of fluid. I couldn't go anywhere even if I wanted to. I was still feverish and whenever the fever spiked, I felt short of breath. I could barely talk. The first of many doctors began their procession by my bedside. Columbia-Presbyterian is a teaching hospital, and that meant an extensive cast of characters: residents, interns, physicians, plus the nurses, techs, and aides. This was the new routine.

That morning, like every morning, a beefy guy who looked like a truck driver came in with a big machine to give me a chest X-ray. I assumed the equipment was heavy. Three times a day a sweet-faced woman brought in a tray with breakfast, lunch, or dinner. The food was not very good, but I wanted to eat it because she was lovely and I didn't want to disappoint her, her voice musical with the inflection of some Caribbean island.

Then there were the doctors, interns, and residents. They asked the same questions over and over again. "Have you traveled lately?"

"We were in Southern California visiting my family in July."

"Have you been overseas?"

"We went to Budapest and Vienna in June." This was a dream trip that our sons gave us for Christmas, our anniversary, and our sixtieth birthdays combined, twenty-eight-year-old William cashing in thousands of frequent-flier miles he had garnered from business trips.

"Any other trips? Anything exotic?"

"We went to Kenya about three years ago." We have friends who have been working for several years on a water project in a small village outside Nairobi, building a well, which we got to see. We also took a safari to far-flung places.

"Do you have any pet birds?"

"No." We have a very large, very lazy cat, Fred, named for Frederick Douglass because he was rescued from the A-train platform in Harlem, near Frederick Douglass Boulevard. He's also hirsute like Douglass, with a combination of black, gray, and white hair.

"Have you ever worked in a shipyard?"

"No."

"Have you worked on a ship?"

"No," I said to this, although a good friend with whom I'd performed in a half-dozen amateur Gilbert and Sullivan productions later insisted I should have said, "I've served on the *H.M.S. Pinafore.*"

I wanted to be helpful. I wanted to give them answers that would lead to a diagnosis, but it was hard to keep my head clear and to speak when I was struggling for breath. The mask went over my nose so I could still get oxygen and speak but it made me claustrophobic.

In between the diagnostic Q and A's I slept fitfully. You never sleep well in a hospital, and yet sleep is what you long for. There are too many interruptions, too much noise, too much discomfort, too much light.

It was Sunday, my first day. Carol appeared after church. "Everyone asked about you," she said. Word had spread. She'd put my name on the prayer list and maybe hers too. She is usually loath to admit to needing help—aren't we all?—but she unloaded to the first person she saw at church, someone who'd shown up early for the service, not even a close friend. Is there ever a time when you need church more? Complete strangers are the closest intimates when you worship together week after week. They know you, you know them, you will be with them in times of need, they will be with you. You have known their prayers.

After lunch Kate, our rector, appeared. Two services in the morning and another service in the evening, not to mention coffee hours, forums, and meetings, but she managed to come.

I think of the son of a friend who had his first day of high school on 9/11 at a school not far from the World Trade Center. The students were sent home after the second plane crashed into the second tower. There was no public transportation, so they just kept walking north, the conflagration behind them. The minute the disaster happened the boy's father, our friend, headed for the school, determined to find his son. They met on the West Side Highway, father and son, one walking south, one walking north. "I knew you'd come," the boy said to his dad.

I knew you'd come. That's what I wanted to say to Kate. Not that there was any mystery about where she'd find me, but she was the connection to my church, to all those people who looked out for me as I looked out for them. She glanced at me in her clerical collar, her worried face telling me exactly how bad I looked. She'd brought her black-leather-bound *Book of Common Prayer* and was ready to pray.

Between halting breaths of air I told her, "I'm in despair. That's what I need…hope. Despair is the enemy."

I was at rock bottom, no shred of optimism left in me, no faith. This was far worse than the breaths I couldn't take or the oxygen that didn't seem to saturate me or the fever that sent my body into chills or my inability to complete a sentence without wheezing or the doctors' mystified stares and their inability to come up with a diagnosis. I had no hope. I remembered a college classmate who had a malignant brain tumor in his early forties and had countless miniseizures a day. "I have to hold on to hope," he said to me, a short seizure interrupting our conversation, his eyes glazing over for a few seconds. "As long as I have hope, I'm OK." I thought of my aunt, a life-long smoker, dying of lung cancer at sixty-three. There she was coughing up a storm, then taking a drag on a cigarette, while we pretended she was going to get through this. "I have to hope," she said.

That morning, before church let out, before Kate showed up, I remember thinking, "You're at the bottom, Rick. You're sicker than you've ever been before. You can't get any lower than this."

Then I had an even scarier thought: in a hospital, they dropped the bottom down even lower than where I already was. They would put patients in induced comas or give them a tracheotomy or put them on ventilators or feed them through tubes in their stomachs. They could make despair last for days or weeks or months by simply keeping you alive. What would be the point?

Here I was, a so-called person of faith, a man with a spiritual practice, and I was drowning in despair, over-whelmed with it, benumbed. They could blow oxygen into my lungs all they liked but what I yearned for was the breath of the Spirit. The things I normally did, closing my eyes to meditate, wiping my mind of all its anxieties and worries—putting on the mind of Christ, if you will—taking in a deep breath, listening to God by becoming very still, were impossible. Maybe if I'd had my Kindle with me, with its Bible that I read on the subway to work, highlighting favorite passages...but it was still at home, and even if I'd had it, I couldn't have concentrated. It would have been like searching for meaning in the classified ads.

I needed Kate to be there. I needed to vent, revealing my struggle. She listened, she prayed. Oh, how grateful I was for her prayers, although I didn't feel any relief. Not then. Not yet.

She left. More doctors came and went. Food trays came, and I tried to eat but had no appetite—not that the beef Stroganoff or the chicken cutlet or the fruit salad or the chocolate pudding in a plastic cup or the grayish beans and brownish peas were that appetizing. Taking the plastic wrapping off a roll or trying to get the butter out of its metallic wrap was an exercise in occupational therapy. It took all my strength. (I write this here, but I don't think I could eat much of anything yet. Not Sunday. I wasn't well enough.)

The day nurse had appeared after seven that morning, writing her name down in red marker on the white board opposite my bed, erasing the name of the night nurse who had been on duty. I wanted to talk to the nurses and aides and techs, ask them where they were from, where they lived, where they had gone to school, find some way of connecting that wasn't just caregiver/patient. A question or two could take me out of myself and my misery, but conversation between breaths was almost impossible.

"You live...in New Jersey...very far away?"

"Do you...have...children?"

"Where did you...go to...nursing school?"

"Do you...like...being a...nurse?"

They took my blood pressure, my temperature, dispensed pills, took my blood, changed whatever was in the IV drip, adjusted the tubes giving me oxygen, brought me bedpans and took them away. They checked out whatever the machines said, recording the numbers, but not once did I feel they were just looking at the machines above my head. They were looking at me.

"I have to get out of here soon," I thought, absurdly enough. "I've got a big conference in California to attend in two weeks. I have to be there."

I hated to put Carol through this, hated to drag her away from the repose of a Sunday nap or the Sunday *Times*, or a football game on TV—and it was she who followed the NFL, not me, she who watched the games with the boys. Now she was running interference for me in a drab hospital room. She could ask the doctors questions and understand their answers. She could respond to the litany of their queries: no, we had no wild birds; no, I had never worked in a shipyard; no, we hadn't been to any exotic locale recently; no, I had never served on a ship. I wanted to talk but I was too tired to talk. I wished she could get lost in a good book, but she was too worried for that. And the interruptions were constant. Here we were, two people whose love for each other was greater than words, and there were no words to describe the mess I was in, not even a diagnosis.

Timothy was there that day, and at one point when no one else was in the room, he sat in the chair in the corner and read a psalm in that careful way he reads aloud, not overdramatic, his voice comfortable with each phrase, like he's really talking to you, not reading. I don't remember which psalm he read, I wasn't even sure it really happened, my brain in a fog, my memory faulty, my faith habits nil. If I couldn't manage to read a psalm, had I imagined someone else doing it for me? Was it all a fantasy?

A couple of weeks later I e-mailed him in South Africa. "That first day I was in the hospital, did you sit by my bed and read a psalm to me?"

"Yes," he replied. He couldn't remember which psalm either.

This is when I picture some underground system like the pneumatic tube network that ran under the streets of Paris, delivering packets of information and documents from one building to another. I can see the pipes racing out in one direction, carrying their disturbing news, urging others to send spiritual sustenance and healing—urgent healing—back my way. I can imagine some wan signal or message, a dim bulb, a faint flickering, coming from me, and a blinding flood of warmth and light returning, people caring and praying and hoping and believing what I couldn't possibly have believed on my own. It's all completely unscientific and unprovable and vague in my *Charlie and the Chocolate Factory* imagining. "Can't you come up with a better metaphor?" I ask myself. Can't you come up with something more gracious and elegant, or at least something that holds together? Why do you see all of this as plumbing?

As soon as I had any sort of voice and could talk, I would call my eighty-nine-year-old mother, who lives out in California. I wanted her to hear my voice from the hospital so that, despite her fears, she could know I lived and spoke and was sentient. Over the phone for a few minutes I hoped to fake good cheer for her, just to make her feel better. Maybe I would fake hope, too, talk myself out of despair.

But I don't think you can talk yourself out of despair. You need something coming back to you, you need something filling you up from the inside, you have to have something big to hold on to, you can't just clutch at air.

I didn't know when Carol sent out her first group e-mail. It might have been from the hospital or during the limited time she had at home, when she wasn't by my bedside. I had no idea who was on her list. The whole idea of putting together a list like that would be daunting even if I was in the best of health.

"I've let everybody know where you are," she said on Sunday. "I told them they can text me or e-mail me back. And you're on the prayer list at church." She promised to read me what people said but if she had done that with every e-mail, she would have wept. Some she eventually printed out. Some she showed me on her laptop. Some I never saw until I was quite well. I was glad she said no phone calls. I wouldn't have been able to handle that. It was hard enough for her to keep track as her e-mails went viral, people sharing them with other people who knew me or knew of me or didn't know me from Adam but somebody had told them to add me to their prayer list and they wanted to let her or me know. I still meet friends of friends who say, "We were praying for you."

The prayers reached for me down in my pit of despair. Think of how your brain can leap and jive and plummet off a cliff to the worries and fears of "what might happen" and "how things can go wrong," or maybe, possibly, with a little help, "how things can go right," and then imagine a mental state where you can't even set your mind into any future-thinking at all because your present feels so dreary, so dark, so sepulchral. You feel too stuck to even be anxious, too rotten to be depressed.

Love was headed my way, if I could only fathom it, an onslaught to do battle with my despair. I was already upheld by Carol's presence, Tim's psalms, the nurses darting in and out, the doctors' concerns, the lovely lady bringing the food trays, hugging Carol and promising to pray, the minister from our church coming to me in the midst of her busiest day. That I even thought "I knew you'd come" was surely a sign of hope when I couldn't recognize it. I wasn't up for visitors or phone calls. "I got the nicest e-mail from...," Carol could say.

September 14, 5:39 p.m.

Forgive me, dear friends, for silence. I got tangled in multiple e-mail chains so some of you are getting double info and some have e-mailed Rick and not heard back and that's the state of play right now. He still doesn't have enough energy to read e-mail so there's a stack of lovely messages in his inbox (I forwarded rather than printing) that will delight him when he can read them. And again, keep up the forwarding. I know I'm missing people.

Not much to report. He's a little stronger today—can sit in the chair for a little while, say a sentence or two. Still getting oxygen, still often very short of breath. Docs are stumped. Keep asking probing questions like, "Have you ever kept birds as pets?"

Just pause and imagine that: the NYC Hamlins with pet birds. Um, no.

But best, this morning, from the pulmonology team, to RICK HAMLIN: "Have you ever worked in a shipyard?" They both looked at him as if they understood what a foolish question it was, but had to ask it anyway.

So obviously we have turned into an episode of "House" and we need to have Hugh Laurie turn up at the door. Which would be kind of cool.

Still believe the care is excellent. Rick is still in step-down and not going anywhere soon, it seems. The extensive monitoring is important. Problem is that they can't treat until they know *what* to treat.

Nothing you guys can do yet. I'm sure a time will come when he gets better and then gets bored and we'll invite you to visit or call, but he's far from that stage for now. Let it be said that he has an angelic temperament and is enduring this with patience. We are literally supported by your concern and your prayers.

Lots of love, Carol

CHAPTER THREE

ICU, Day 2

W hen I came home after spending that first night with four-year-old Tim in traction, I was completely rattled. "I don't know how we're going to do this," I said to Carol. "I can't imagine having to stay with him in that hospital for twenty-six days and nights." I still had to go to the office during the day. Carol worked at home so she had more flexibility than I did. But there was also seven-year-old William at home. Someone had to watch him. How would we take care of the kids and how would we take care of each other? How would any of us get any sleep? At least Will would be off at school, and there was the babysitter, who came in the afternoons.

It was a Friday, Good Friday, so I had the day off from work. But I was expected to sing in choir at the Good Friday service at church that day. I hustled off for rehearsal and the noonday service.

I came home that afternoon to more bad news. William, it seemed, had chicken pox, red splotches all over his skin. He needed to be quarantined for ten days. A bath of milk was supposed to be soothing.

Will lay in bed, reading. I kissed him on his head, the place my father would kiss me, and rejoined Carol in the living room.

Now we had two sick children on our hands, two parents with not enough hands. How were we going to manage? It was struggle enough to keep all the balls in the air on a good day: work, school, children, shopping. Friday night was my night

229

at the supermarket. I would gather all the empty cans and bottles—five cents a pop—and put them in the fold-up cart, then head up to the pathetically understocked A&P at 187th Street. I cruised the aisles with the list, Cap'n Crunch for Will, frozen waffles for Tim (he liked to eat them just like that, frozen), Progresso beans and Campbell's corn chowder, boxes of mac and cheese, Rice-A-Roni, ramen noodles that were dubbed "Sharon noodles" in our house because they were our babysitter Sharon's favorite.

That was how we managed, divide and conquer, split up the parenting duties and we could get it all done, baths, bed, books, homework, laundry.

Throw one wrench into the works, and life would lurch and plunge. Throw two wrenches into the works, and it would spin out of control. The image that came to me was of being at the edge of a merry-go-round that was cranked up to top speed, and everything would start flying off, including us.

I sat on the futon and held my head in my hands. "I don't see how the center can hold," I said.

"We'll manage," Carol said. "We'll figure it out." She's usually the worrier, unless I become worried and then, alternating roles, she becomes the stronger one, ultracapable, organizing, planning, checking off lists, keeping her worries to herself. Divide and conquer again.

"We'll call Mom." Mom could come out and help. She'd done that when the children were born, devoting a week to us with one morning off to go to the Metropolitan Museum and indulge in art, a pretzel on the steps in the sun her lunch. Could she come out now? Then we'd be three adults for two kids, a better ratio.

First we let the hospital know that Timothy had been exposed to chicken pox.

"He'll need to be quarantined," they said. We'd have to put on masks and gowns when we visited him, we'd have to wash our hands and wear gloves. But, first things first, he'd have to be moved to a private room. That was the one silver lining: he'd be by himself. Easier to sleep at night.

I called Mom. She volunteered before I could ask. She appeared that Easter weekend, with a bottle of California wine for the parents (as though California wine was not available in New York) and Easter baskets for the boys. Tim was princely in his hospital bed, staring at that singing purple dinosaur on TV, his foot permanently aloft. He had adjusted, would adjust. I secretly resented that there was no Easter Bunny to visit him, nobody bringing jelly beans. Wasn't that the sort of thing that happened in children's wards?

Mom took the subway train to the hospital in the morning, the A train to Fourteenth Street, then the L train across town to Third Avenue. She would be with Timothy during the day, while I went to work and Carol was with Will, and then we'd switch around in the evening, one of us parents sleeping in the foldout bed next to Tim, in traction, every night.

Mom was the eternal good sport, good-natured, sunny-tempered. The only thing she really didn't like was the train ride.

"But it's the place I pray," I said. My morning commute on the A train was my prayer time, the rumble of the train on the tracks like some sort of call to worship. I'd read a psalm from my tattered pocket Bible and then close my eyes somewhere around 125th Street, checking out to check in. This time, this place, this connection to keep me going. Some days it was the only thing that made sense.

I bought Carol twenty-six chocolate truffles, so she could mark off the days, her Advent calendar of hope. Our friends came and visited Tim in his princely room, putting on masks and gowns because he had been exposed to chicken pox. Someone gave him a disposable camera, and he took pictures of them from his horizontal point of view—we still have a scrapbook of the results. "I can't believe it," our friends remarked, "two crises all at once. One sick child here, one at home."

What we refrained from saying but still thought was, "Don't these things come in threes?" What shoe would be next to drop? It's a sort of reverse faith, expecting the disaster begotten by a disaster begotten by a disaster, a glass-half-empty mentality, mumbo jumbo, and yet it was there.

The staff at the hospital was lovely. We always promised ourselves that we would go back when Timothy was well so we could thank them for their care.

But we never went back. When something like that is over, you don't want to revisit it at all. You want it to be over, completely over. Done with.

My second night in the ICU step-down unit was the worst. I hardly slept. I was being given oxygen, tubes running into my nose, the monitor ready to beep or scream or whatever it did when my oxygen levels sank to the danger level. Every half hour that night the monitor beeped, waiting for the nurse to come in and check it. All night I was awakened every time I dozed off because I wasn't getting enough oxygen. (Like I said, hospitals are terrible places for sleeping.) Finally I asked the night nurse, "Could you please lower the alarm...so it doesn't keep...waking me up?" Better a good night's sleep than not enough oxygen, better dead than harangued by beeping machines.

"A man who keeps death before his eyes will at all times overcome his cowardice," said one of the Desert Fathers.

But who wants to think about death all the time? Who wants an alarm alerting us to the continual truth, "You will die. You might already be dying. You could be getting close this time"?

I have a very loud heartbeat. I can hear it beating whenever I am still. In the audience during a concert, sitting before my computer, in a conference room during a meeting, in my bed when I'm waiting to fall asleep, on the sofa when I'm praying, in church when I'm singing (no, my heart rarely beats in time to the music). About the only time I can't hear it is when I'm running or when I'm on the subway, and the rumble of the train on the tracks is loud enough to bury the sound.

There are two ways to think about the sound of the beating heart, one upbeat and one not so cheery. It's a reminder—beat, beat, beat—that "You're still alive. Your heart is functioning. It's pumping blood through your system. You are on God's green earth. Enjoy it." Or the sound of the heart in your ears will say to you, "Your heart will stop someday. It can't always be working so hard, making all this noise. And didn't it just skip a beat? The light goes on and the light goes off. The beat goes on and the beat goes off. You won't hear it someday, because your heart won't be working. When that happens, you won't be."

To be conscious of your beating heart is a double-edged sword, a source of anxiety or a source of comfort. I'm most comfortable when distracted by work or writing or listening or caring or praying so that I don't hear it at all. It feels like the mark of a successful day. The less I hear my heart—the less self-conscious I am of it—the better I will have lived.

Does that sound judgmental?

I would like to think that to live with the knowledge of death is to see how precious each day is, how it is all that we're given and all that we have on this earth, every hour a chance to give and love until we return to our Maker. "Make each day your masterpiece," said legendary UCLA basketball coach John Wooden. Make each day your Rembrandt, your Van Gogh, your Sistine Chapel ceiling.

But that's so hard to do when you can barely move, can barely breathe.

The doctors came and went that day, all of them looking concerned, checking my vitals (that word *vitals*, an adjective turned into a noun through the addition of one letter). The only one who was a real crepe hanger was an older specialist in rheumatology. She arrived with a younger colleague in tow. The two of them checked me out, staring at the numbers on the monitors. She asked me a few questions and then she sat in the chair next to Carol and said, as though I were too sick to hear the news, "You need to prepare yourself for him to be intubated. He's not getting any better now and he's not getting enough oxygen."

Everyone else was holding out hope of some improvement, or pretending they were. Not she. Maybe she knew something the rest didn't know. Maybe she was the only realist in the bunch and was simply being honest. Whatever. I was appalled, frightened, and angry. "Get out of here!" I wanted to say, fighting the urge to pick something off the lunch tray and throw it at her, the uneaten fruit cocktail, the applesauce—as if I could throw anything. *Not getting any better?* What did she know? I usually have undying respect for doctors. Not for her.

The weirdest thing that happened to me that second day in the ICU step-down unit, when I was surely at my worst, was an internal change that didn't register on any monitor. Maybe it occurred before she visited or maybe after—I'm not at all sure which. I can't find the exact time for it. There was no come-to-Jesus moment or bolt of lightning. I didn't suddenly sit up in bed and shout, "Wow!" No, it was more subtle and subterranean, a rising tide pulling me out of my despair, a warm bath that was being made ready for me to submerge in. I could have hardly described it. All I knew was that somehow I was going to get better.

I should put a drumroll of prose in here or write it down in all caps: I KNEW I WAS GOING TO GET BETTER AND GET OUT OF THE HOSPITAL ALIVE.

Where did this come from? Was it my body telling me something that the doctors couldn't begin to see, my organs sending a message to my brain? Was it just wishful thinking? Was it faith?

"You might have to drag a can of oxygen around for the rest of your born days, Rick," I thought, "but you will get better." Perhaps I would never run again or sing again or give a talk at a retreat, but I would walk out of that hospital on my own two feet, no wheelchair, no special ambulance to take me home.

I didn't tell anyone this news. Didn't want to jinx it. It was too tender and fragile—*I* was too tender and fragile. People would have thought I was under some illusion. The machines were on their side. And anyway, my words could only come haltingly, each phrase punctuated by some deep intake of air, an intake that was never enough. I would try to suck in as much oxygen as possible through those tubes in my nose and breathe it out through my mouth. Every time my temperature rose, the breathing became harder. "More ibuprofen," I said. "I have a fever." They couldn't give it to me fast enough. It was the only thing that helped. I counted the hours between pills. When the fever went down I could breathe—mind you, only with the help of machines.

There was no immediate sign of improvement, nothing the doctors could tell me. Jay, the day nurse, one of my favorites, brought around one of those plastic boxes that you're supposed to blow into to make the balls in it rise and float; the longer you can keep them up, the better. They look like a children's toy and are meant to prevent you from getting pneumonia, keeping your breath flowing. Jay demonstrated how it worked, making the balls inside rise and float effortlessly. It was sort of like watching the strong man at the circus ring the bell on the first try.

"Here, you try," he said.

I blew into it, and the plastic balls hardly budged.

"Can't you do better than that?" he asked. He took it again and demonstrated. I took it back and blew with all my strength into the tube. Hardly any response.

"Keep trying," he said, and left it on my hospital table.

Carol looked to be at the end of her rope. No amount of sweetness could hide her worry. *Do I look that bad? Yes, that bad.*

And yet, and yet—how often can you write the words "and yet"?—I was going to get better. My body knew it or my spirit knew it and was telling my body this good news. There was no laying on of hands, no visit from a hospital chaplain (in the two weeks I was there I was never once visited by a hospital chaplain). But I knew I was being prayed for. That was clear from the e-mails Carol shared. Nobody prayed aloud in that hospital room except our hardworking rector and our son reading a psalm aloud in the corner. But people were praying.

I've always believed that when you can't pray for yourself, it's other people's prayers that sustain you. They do what you can't do. It was the sort of thing that motivated me to pray for others. Some of the writers I edited started a "Jog and Pray for Rick" campaign on Facebook because they knew I prayed when I ran, and now the prayers were going viral. After all, what do you do when you're desperate? What do you do when you can't do much else, beyond sending flowers or a box from Fresh Direct or fruit from Harry & David or a card or a note? What do you do when you want to make a difference? You pray hard and hope for the best.

Sept. 15, 10:00 p.m.

First, an apology: I know I'm not keeping perfect track of this list. Feel free to forward—and if you get this note AS a forward and want to be on the list, just let me know again.

Second, a request: no long-distance diagnosis or prescribing, please. I am listening to a lot of new information now and I want to focus on the stuff coming from the folks in the white coats.

OK, now the update. Drama in the morning: spike in temperature, funky O2 numbers, threats of move to ICU. Scary. But that resolved and I am now looking at a monitor that reads 100% oxygen saturation through the high-flow machine. (Feel free to let your eyes glaze over on details.) R looks a lot better and they are letting him eat but he has less energy than he did yesterday. Terrible night, monitor beeping the whole time, which may contribute.

Still no diagnosis. Most infections have been ruled out and a rheumatology team is now involved, looking at autoimmune issues.

Care continues fabulous. The cast of characters is huge and attentive and some of them are even charming.

Will arrives Thursday morning very early. He probably just wants to get in on all the fun Tim and I are having here with Rick.

Keep those prayers coming. He's still too sick for visitors or calls, and doesn't really have enough energy to read e-mail, but I have been telling him about your concern.

Lots of love from 6 Garden South, Carol

CHAPTER FOUR

ICU, Day 3

To love is to pray, anything that can take you out of yourself. Timothy recently reminded me of a verse from the first letter of John: "Those who do not love a brother or sister whom they have seen, cannot love God whom they have not seen." Lying in a hospital bed, the world of the unseen feels so close, even when it's many miles away.

It was earthly love that helped me grasp who God was, the hound of heaven racing after me as though I were some rabbit lure, and then coming around to meet me at the end of the race, me half out of breath, the everlasting arms ready to embrace me. God had been there all along. "Our Creator, Redeemer, Lover," the nun said in a benediction at our church, words that might have been of frequent usage for her, but they stunned me with newness. "Creator" and "Redeemer"—I'd heard all that before. But "Lover"? What a delicious shock. Yes, I knew what that was. Lover, like my wife.

Here Carol was, coming and going from my hospital room in the ICU, and I was being reminded of what love can do and will do beyond any power of its own.

That we became a couple and married some thirty years ago still seems like a miracle beyond our choosing. We were in the same class at Princeton, but she had all the patina of the East Coast—a private-school background, a bookish temperament, a sophisticated wit, a preppy wardrobe—and I was a public high-school kid from California in flared pants and tennis shoes, out of my depth. For a long while I felt

241

like an outsider looking in, trying to read the hidden clues. Breathless, I was determined to catch up, but I wouldn't have wanted any of my Princeton classmates to know how hard I worked at it. After all, effortlessness was supposed to count for something.

Secretly I went through *Time* magazine and circled words I didn't know, looking them up so I could use them, praying to God I got the pronunciation right. When any of my classmates wanted to play "You tell me your SAT scores, and I'll tell you mine," I kept my mouth shut. I figured it must have been some accident of the admissions office that let me in. Once, freshman year, playing a game of Dictionary, I picked the word *misogyny*, hoping I could stump my friends, having never heard the word before. "I see what you're doing," said one guy, "trying for a double fake out." "Sure," I said, figuring I could hide my ignorance by pretending I was way ahead of them. Maybe there was some third or fourth definition of "misogyny" that nobody knew.

I'd been pretty confident in high school, with a host of really good friends. We had a good time. ("Nobody should be deliriously happy in high school," Carol says. "It just goes against the grain.") Not that I was cool—I've never been cool—but I found a niche where I could be quirky and popular at the same time, the guy who mimicked Fred Astaire when hypnotized at a school assembly, the tenor crooner in the school production of *Brigadoon*. When I got the welcome packet from Princeton with the mystifying word "matriculation," I felt I was gearing up for the big leagues. My LA-born-and-bred grandmother assured me that people were much more formal "back East." I figured I knew what that meant, putting on a madras jacket like we did when we went to the Music Center for some show put on by the Los Angeles Civic Light Opera.

Dad took me to his favorite haberdasher to get suited up. "Rick will be going to Princeton, you know," Dad explained. Sizing up two suckers for an easy sale, the salesman took out a wool three-piece suit and threw in an orange dress shirt—"for Princeton, you know"—that would have appalled any dyed-in-the-wool preppy. And this was conservative Pasadena.

What did a Californian see when he showed up for Freshman Week? A bunch of kids acting prematurely old. Their madras shorts were faded and their loafers scuffed; at least mine were brand-new. They hung old hunting prints on their walls. Wouldn't a Beatles poster do? They dangled their father's or grandfather's class banners out their windows, claiming their place in Princeton's past, if not its Old-Fogeydom. They might have blasted Crosby Stills Nash & Young out those same leaded windows, but they were hosting each other at cocktail parties. Cocktail parties? Who ever heard of an eighteen-year-old throwing a cocktail party?

I'd spent the summer reading *Crime and Punishment*, thinking I could catch up with kids who'd floated through AP exams. There was one incredibly sophisticated girl in my freshman literature seminar at Princeton who wore horn-rimmed glasses and had blonde hair that fell over her eyes—she'd actually gone to school with Carol. She intimidated me with her references to things like "structuralism" and "deconstruction," more words I had to look up.

Fortunately I found my place on campus through singing: God's gift to me, a decent singing voice. Would that I would use it wisely and well. For many years that was my prayer, even at times when I didn't believe in God. That I wouldn't squander something that was beyond my own achieving, especially in a family where no one was particularly musical. No concert violinists or jazz pianists in the gene pool, not even a barbershop quartet singer.

At Princeton I discovered several groups that seemed glad to have an extra tenor. I sang in Freshman Singers, the Princeton Glee Club, the Chapel Choir, the student-written Triangle Show, and most important, one of the all-male a cappella groups. I was never a great sight-reader and could never get my line right until the third or fourth pass. "We'll call you Melody Hamlin," the guys in the a cappella group said. "All you're good for is the melody." "Melody Hamlin" became one of my nicknames (along with "Hambone" shortened to "Bones" which morphed into "Bonus" or just "Ness" in the happy absurdity of nicknames).

Through the group I became friends with some of the same people whose preppy behavior had seemed such a mystery. I learned that a threadbare tweed jacket with elbow patches was much better than anything brandnew from a department store, and that long-sleeve, button-down shirts were best worn when un-ironed. Ties should be narrow, the narrower the better. I'd learned the code so well that when my parents came to visit my junior year, I looked with alarm at my father's wide tie and his huge lapels that could have been fins on a '57 Cadillac. What would my prepster friends think of me?

Had I become as much of a snob as that? I cringe at the memory.

Carol and I ended up in the same circle of friends, a wry, tight, witty bunch. She was part of the gang that went for a midnight dip—in our bathing suits—in the Woodrow Wilson School fountain spring of senior year, a certain rite of passage. We danced to Lester Lanin playing Cole Porter tunes at my eating club, Princeton's homegrown version of a Greek frat. (How quickly I had adopted the preppy ways.) She was there that May day before graduation when some of us drove down to Winterthur in Delaware—she might even have driven us in her old Saab. After touring the museum, with its American antiques, we stopped at a farm stand and bought baskets of fresh asparagus and strawberries. We cooked up the former for dinner—did we add some meat?—and had a party on a friend's dorm-room rooftop, listening to his recordings of Edith Piaf singing "La Vie en Rose" and "Je Ne Regrette Rien," the host crooning along and raising his eyebrows in a Gallic shrug.

Carol and I were friends, just good friends. She had a boyfriend at Yale, and I had recently broken up with a woman at Harvard, not because I wasn't madly in love with her but because I didn't see how we could really make it as a couple when I had no idea what I was going to do with my life, and, in my heart of hearts, I believed that the next woman I went out with would be the woman I married, closet traditionalist that I was.

My entire family came out from California to witness my graduation. There is a snapshot someone took of that day with both Carol and me beneath the elms in front of Nassau Hall, gazing in different directions in our caps and gowns. She looks worried, her brow furrowed, and I look distracted, searching for family members in the crowd. I packed my suitcases that afternoon, sent a trunk home, and then drove across the country with my parents in their new Volvo, not sure I'd ever see my East Coast friends again. I had to come up with a plan for some sort of future, and so that summer, while painting my sister's house, I decided to go to Italy and live there as long as the money held out.

Indeed I did, living in Florence for two years, supporting myself by teaching English as a foreign language and tutoring kids in the expatriate community. I studied voice with an opera singer and nurtured secret hopes of writing a Great American Novel, at least a slim one. All I ever wrote were a few self-absorbed entries in my journal and lots of letters home—cramming those cheap blue aerograms with my tiny script.

Some of those letters were addressed to Carol. She was working in book publishing in New York City, following a more conventional career path. Maybe I'd move to New York after Italy. We'd see each other there. Good friends. We were just good friends.

Carol is a brave woman. She has a lot of emotional courage, more than she will ever admit to. She was the one to make the first move, to actually spell it out, admitting that possibly, frankly we were more than friends, that maybe we were falling in love. Brave? Well, brave enough. She was a writer. She declared herself by mail.

By then I had been living in New York for over a year, pursuing a career as an actor/singer. In between dance classes and voice lessons and acting classes and auditions I caught up with that circle of Princeton friends of which she was a vital part. We saw each other at parties, put on a wedding shower for some friends, went to see movies, dropped in at museums.

For a while I was homeless, sleeping on friends' living room couches. When she took a ten-day trip she asked me to house-sit her 300-square-foot aerie at the top of an Upper West Side Art Deco tower. Want to fall in love with someone? Live for a while in their space. I studied the books in her bookshelf, gazed at the photos on her bureau, listened to her records, and was baffled by the makeup she'd left behind in the medicine cabinet. I could picture her at her typewriter, the wind whistling through the windows, the music of the recorder players from downstairs wafting up through the floorboards. I cleaned her phone—she remembers this—scrubbing it of the grime that gets encrusted under the rotary dial, and bought her a colander so she could properly drain her pasta.

Later that year I found her a job as a desk clerk at an old residential hotel on Madison Avenue where I worked. She did the day shift, I did evenings. The place was closing down. There were only thirty residents left. All we had to do was give them their mail and buzz them in the front door. It left plenty of time for her to polish up manuscripts and me to memorize scenes for acting class.

She had left her full-time publishing job and was a free-lance writer. Her first book was called *Fabulous Nails*, a guide for doing your fingernails. She had also created a page-a-day calendar of quotations. "I wouldn't have had the courage to do this without your support," she said in an unguarded moment.

"It's a no-brainer," I said. If anybody could make it as a writer, it was she. Not only was she talented, with a distinctive voice that was both funny and authoritative, but she was also incredibly self-disciplined, never one to miss a deadline. At Princeton she'd managed to finish her senior thesis six weeks early.

In the three years since college she had taken on a new style, trendier, more urban. Her once-blonde hair was now reddish, thanks to henna, and she had a great purple plastic raincoat, which I could admire when we changed shifts at the hotel.

One of the things I missed from college was running into people, catching up between classes. With Carol I had a regular rendezvous five days a week. I could find out what she was doing, what she was writing. She was contributing to a satiric take on preppydom called *The Official Preppy Handbook*. She ended up writing about a third of the book, for which she got an author's credit on the front page but no royalty or copyright, just a flat fee, a mistake she would never make again. It has long been out of print, but I can turn to passages in the sole copy on our shelves and hear her voice, her barbed wit in essays like "Prep Sex: A Contradiction in Terms" and even see her picture, in which she is dressed, improbably enough, as the "Amazon" ("Don't worry, I have problems with my backhand, too"). The book was a huge best seller, more often studied as a sartorial guide than satire. For Carol, it launched her career as a writer, humorist, social historian, and novelist.

My own acting career moved forward in fits and starts. I was lucky to get work doing church choir jobs, singing the occasional memorial service, appearing in an off-off-Broadway musical, doing summer stock. But even when I was taking on a dream role—Lieutenant Cable in *South Pacific*, Hero in *A Funny Thing Happened on the Way to the Forum*, Tony in *West Side Story*—I felt like I was only faking it. This was not my calling.

The brave courtship letter came when I was out in California, trying my luck on the West Coast. "It was probably a good thing that you left New York for a while," she wrote, "because I think I was falling in love with you..."

I stared at the typewritten page for a long time, dumb-founded. There was only one way to answer the letter, the truth: "I think I was falling in love with you too..." How did I know? How do you ever know? Maybe it was a fleeting moment when we were putting on that wedding shower for our mutual friends and we were in the kitchen of the old rambling West End Avenue apartment, where I slept in the maid's room, my only view an airshaft. I was her sous-chef, enamored of her culinary skills and what she could make of a three-by-five recipe card with her illegible fountain pen script on it. Or maybe it was when she gave me a copy of the page-a-day calendar she had created and discovered the quote she had put on my birthday, "A strong response to art is like money in a Swiss bank. You can never go emotionally bankrupt," a line I'd treasured by Kenneth Clark.

It might have been when we went shopping on one of the coldest days of the year for the cheapest upright piano I could find, and as I watched her breath take form in the brilliant blue of a frigid New York sky, a blue that matched her eyes, I was seeing beauty I had mistakenly taken for granted. It went back to house-sitting in her apartment and wanting to know more about the books stacked next to her bed. She gave me the sense that somehow I counted with her, that I had made a differ-ence, that she wouldn't have taken this risk and called herself a writer if I hadn't believed in her. I did believe in her, some-times more than I believed in myself. Was this something we were meant to do together?

"Creator, Redeemer and Lover." To know God's love through the abiding affection of an earthly lover. To know that

God's love is that big and that immediate and that personal. God my Lover was moving in my life, making me change, turning me around, bringing me closer to the person I was called to be.

I lingered in California, getting a job as a spear-carrier in a production of *The Merchant of Venice* and then signing on to do children's theater, a couple of performances a day. I made enough to pay for the gas in the hand-me-down Toyota I drove. All the while, Carol and I kept up a torrid correspondence, letting our words do the difficult work of taking us from the comfort zone of good friends to the danger zone of lovers. Feeling freer because of distance, we shared everything on the page. We were hesitant about talking on the phone—would the sound of our voices separate us?—but kept up the writing.

Neither she nor I has ever dared reread all the letters we wrote back then. At the time we said that someday we'd collect and print them in a romantic volume for lovers only, a lavender-colored collection of purple prose. Falling in love can be thrilling and terrifying at once. And the most terrifying thought of all: What if it hadn't turned out all right? What if we hadn't forged this unbreakable bond? What if Carol hadn't sent that first letter? What if I hadn't responded?

And what now if I left her, making a premature exit from a hospital bed?

Faith mattered to both of us. That came through on the page. She didn't share my Presbyterian heritage— she'd grown up Episcopalian, and nothing was going to change that—but we were both inveterate churchgoers. We believed in worship, at the very least, as Kurt Vonnegut Jr. famously put it, for the chance to "daydream about God." Religion was a tool to help us find our place in the cosmos. In one letter she described seeing a documentary about an order of nuns that had left her weeping and wondering how she could find some holy calling. She took up a volunteering assignment through her church, visiting an old Irish woman in a walk-up in the East Eighties, Henrietta, who taught her how to knit.

After four months of writing back and forth we knew we had to see each other. I had spring break off from the children's theater gig and booked a flight to New York to see Carol and see if what we had was really all it had become on the page. I took the red-eye and arrived on Palm Sunday morning, when Central Park is just turning the light green that is called "spring green" in a box of crayons, the forsythia the bravest bit of color. We sat on a bench in the wan sun and watched the daffodils tremble in the breeze.

We had that week together, that perfect week when we dodged running into anyone we knew—at one point actually hiding behind a newsstand—for fear that what we had discovered between us wasn't quite ready for public consumption. We wanted to save it for ourselves.

Not for nothing did Jesus urge us to go into our closets and pray. "Go into your room and shut the door and pray to your Father who is in secret; and your Father who sees in secret will reward you." Sometimes our deepest yearnings are too fragile to share with anyone else but God.

There would be a long back-and-forth courtship, with a trying long-distance relationship until I moved back to New York for good and gave up all designs on an acting career. I joined the choir at the Episcopal church where she sang—where we still sing—and we got married there on the last day of April, but I still think of Palm Sunday as our anniversary.

CHAPTER FIVE

Hospital, Day 4

In between sleep and groggy wakefulness, in between a million doctor visits and nurses coming and going, I looked across the room, and Carol was still there, as constant as the IV drip in my arm and the blood pressure cuff that lurched into life at some unexplained signal, expanding and contracting on my bicep. *I'm sorry to be doing this to you. I'm sorry you have to be here. I'm sorry you have to worry and wonder and pray and send out all those e-mail messages and I'm grateful for them, sweetie.* "Sweetie," our word for each other, the one we use when no one is listening.

Don't apologize, her eyes tell me. *Don't go there. This is what I do. This is what I promised to do. This is what you would do.*

"For better for worse, for richer or poorer, in sickness and in health, to love and to cherish, till death us do part," we promised back then, when we couldn't possibly know what all that would entail. We were young, in our midtwenties. We knew enough about poorer. I became a freelance writer that first year of marriage and earned all of three thousand dollars. As for sickness, well, I was healthy. I still think of myself that way. On any questionnaire I've had to fill out where it says "health" I still check the box that says "excellent." Is that idle fantasy or faith at work? I remember being chided by my dermatologist for not checking the box that said "skin cancer."

"But that was just basal cell stuff you took off," I said. "Everybody has that. Anybody who grew up in the sun in California."

"It's carcinoma," he said, truth-teller that he is. "That's cancer. That's why I took it off."

Now I was not healthy, and Carol had to do this with me. In the hospital I was praying through her. She was my contact with the outer world and my contact with this inner world of doctors and nurses and aides and therapists. She had to ask the questions that I would never have thought to ask even if I could talk. She would understand the answers and their significance.

So much of marriage is this in-the-trenches work. Did you pay the Con Ed bill? What did Verizon say about our wonky signal? Are we free to go over to dinner at Scott and Katie's on Saturday? How is your mom? We're about to run out of toilet paper...OK, I'll put it on the marketing list. In a hospital the nuts-and-bolts of it is cranked up.

Note to self: may my loved ones always know they are loved.

Would you do it again, sweetie, if you knew how many times you would have to play the caregiver? In sickness and in health, indeed. When Frank Sinatra got married the last time, to his richest wife, he was said to have repeated the line "for richer" with glee. Would anyone say the same about "in sickness"?

She is horrified at the prospect that I will predecease her. Just on the basis of demographics, that's likely. Women outlive men. You see it every time you visit an old folks' home. "It just doesn't seem fair," she says. "Why would God bring two people together only to tear them apart?"

"Life is a gift," I want to say. "Right to life" is a phrase of faulty theological logic. Life is a gift, not a divine right.

If there's a spiritual lesson in sickness it must be that you can't make yourself well. You're out of control. You did all those things you were supposed to do to be healthy. You ate right (mostly), you got plenty of exercise (generally), you tried to get enough sleep, but what does all that matter when you're on your back in a hospital bed? You can't *do* anymore. You have to *be*. You have to let go and trust God and trust your doctors. You're at their mercy.

Day four, the routine had settled in. I would wake up after a bad night of sleep. Carol would walk down from our apartment. I would pretend to eat the food on my breakfast tray—the cereal, a roll with butter, juice, lukewarm tea—and we would greet whoever showed up. We might have been actors in a drama for them, the man in the bed with a mystery illness, the wife who wasn't sleeping or eating enough. But they were actors in a drama for us, too.

The day nurse arrived and scrawled his/her name on the whiteboard, erasing the name of the night nurse. Then they would take my vitals, recording them in some computer.

"What are you going...to do...tomorrow?" I asked Jay. He lived in New Jersey. Like most of the nurses, he worked twelve-hour shifts three or four days a week.

"Work around the house and ride my motorcycle."

"With...a helmet?"

"Never. I'm hoping to be a patient someday. So I can get treated like you."

We needed our jokes.

"When I come back, I'm giving you a shower."

"Can't...wait."

Dr. Chang, the attending, came at the beginning of the day and returned again at the end. She reminded me of a piano teacher, the sort who would listen to you play an entire piece all the way through, without interrupting, and then make a few salient points about your fingering or phrasing.

She could explain why a certain test was ordered and why some medicine was being administered or why a different specialist had appeared. I trusted her. I wanted stars and smiley faces on her report.

There was the newly minted resident who must have worked under her in internal medicine. Not much older than our twenty-eight-year-old son Will, he had a hipster beard and an easy bedside manner. A graduate of Middlebury, he'd grown up in Colorado and had doctors in his genes. I felt that I was collaborating on his education and advancement as a doctor, fully invested in his success.

I wanted to please all my doctors, to be at my best when they appeared no matter how rotten I felt, to be such a good patient that they would willingly come back as often as possible. The patient/doctor relationship is oddly symbiotic. Even with the younger doctors, like this one, I was glad to let them be the authority, the oracle, if they pleased. "I will get better for you," I would think, "thanks to all the prayers, and then I hope you can take credit for it." I would be the perfect pupil, wanting their achievements to reflect well on the teacher.

Some doctors *were* teachers. An older specialist would come by my bedside with a few medical students in tow. These visits confused the doctor/patient dynamic. Who was the student now? The specialist would look at me but at the same time he/she was performing for the fresh young minds who were taking in my situation. In the worst of these situations, the specialist would speak to his charges as though I weren't even there. I felt like a piece of meat. Chopped liver.

It was good that Carol had requested no visitors because these doctor visits were taxing enough. In each case I hoped to rise to the occasion. Patients can have performance anxiety too.

Seth the internist came by—dear Seth—more than once. I don't know how he found the time. I still had his Columbia-Presbyterian sweatshirt. I told him I'd give it back if he ever wanted it, although I couldn't imagine he'd take it with the new exotic germs I'd left on it.

The team of pulmonologists was confusing. There were a couple of residents who appeared, and an authoritative older doctor, but never the woman, Dr. DiMango, who was the specialist I went to. I liked her a lot. In fact, I credited her with saving my life eight years earlier. She'd ordered a CT scan for a persistent cough. When she got the results she called my home first—warning enough—and then got me at the office. "Your lungs are fine," she said in her no-nonsense way, "but you'd better do something about that aneurysm in your aorta." Aneurysm in my aorta? Talk about scary. Open-heart surgery came ten days later.

"We've talked to Dr. DiMango," the pulmonologists would say. "We've shared your test results with her." Keeping her in the loop.

I liked the infectious disease guy, although he was pretty dorky. Dorky can be reassuring in a hospital setting. Carol claimed that his lab coat wasn't very clean. There was an intern who visited almost every day, lingering in the room as though we were his parents, which we could easily have been. "Parents can die," I thought. "Parents can get sick and fall apart and land in hospitals where all the king's horses and all the king's men can't put them back together again. Beware."

The rheumatologists...well, I've mentioned them. There was the crepe hanger, a little stooped, pursing her lips and shaking her head, but the younger one was very thoughtful, engaging, hopeful. She reminded me of a really smart travel agent who can book a trip, recommend just the right hotel, and tell you about a garden or museum you should visit. As if I were going anywhere.

My beloved Italian cardiologist, Dr. Ravalli, appeared. He's Roman from Rome, *romano da Roma*, and he kindly tolerates my attempts at Italian. The first time I met him we talked about Italy for twenty minutes in the exam room before he delivered the bad news that I would indeed have to have open-heart surgery. That aneurysm needed to be fixed soon, right away, in fact. I've come to see that this chattiness is his healing touch, to take me away from my fears and remind me of the Piazza Navona, the Castel Sant'Angelo, the Pantheon, a plate of fresh pasta. He's also a runner, lean like a runner, and I consult him on things like plantar fasciitis and sore knees (he's tried acupuncture). I like to hear about what his kids are doing and how they've grown up, Italians in New York. We sometimes run into him at the supermarket down by the Hudson River on Sunday, shopping with his tan, coiffed, unmistakably Roman wife.

He looked concerned now.

That fourth day, Wednesday, Carol and Tim counted how many people checked on me between 9:00 in the morning and 5:00 in the evening. Fifty-four people, fifty-four people who wanted to help me as much as I wanted to be helped. I didn't tell any of them the secret holy plot that I was going to get better and get out of here. They were just supposed to keep me alive.

I couldn't always quite believe the message myself. That seems to be a spiritual quandary. You accept something as a divine truth, it has stirred in your soul, whether at a dark moment or light, and then, days later, although you still believe it, you wonder how it could possibly happen; faith surging, faith waning.

The underground pipeline was working. My spirit was being ministered to by more prayers than I could fathom. But part of me didn't want to fathom them. It would be too scary to have to take in all that love, to have to receive it. I preferred being the giver, not the receiver. A closeted control freak, I'd rather ask you how *you* are doing than have to tell you how *I* am. I find it hard to trust that others are all that interested in what I might say about myself. It's a wonder that I can receive God's love at all.

Sometime in the middle of that day, that Wednesday, some brief moment when it was just Carol and me, I brought up the trip we were supposed to make to California the next week. There was a big conference planned. We were both supposed to speak, and Carol would be one of the keynote speakers.

"You should...go...to California without me," I said.

She looked at me like I was crazy.

"I'll be OK here...There are people looking after me..."

"I'm not going to go," she said.

"You should... They need you... They're counting on you."

I felt guilty about being sick. It was a work thing, an obligation. At least I was clear-eyed enough to realize I wasn't going to make it. But Carol could go in my place.

261

"I have to stay here," she said, telling me that I was much more important than work, that love came first. I could hardly take it in. It would have been enough to say "Thank you," but I didn't. Not then.

You see what I mean about receiving.

When Timothy was four years old and in that hospital bed for twenty-six days, his leg in traction, I had my own medical problem that was wending its way through diagnosis. A tumor in my parotid gland, probably benign, as the doctor said, holding up one finger warningly to calm my nerves, but it would have to come out.

"This is not a very good time," I told him. "Our four-year-old son is in the hospital right now, twenty-six days in traction. He broke his femur."

"We need to do this surgery," he said. "You shouldn't wait."

"But my wife and I are scrambling. Our other son, the older one, has chicken pox and is at home recovering from that. Between the two of them and the two of us we're with one of them each night. We don't want to leave them alone."

"It'll be an out-patient procedure," he said, ever calmingly. "We can do it during the day, and you'll be free to be with him at night. What hospital is he at?"

"The Hospital for Joint Diseases on Seventeenth Street."

"We can do your surgery just a couple of blocks away."

Just as I'd feared, disasters coming in threes, an unholy trinity. We had our third now, in case we were looking for one. The surgeon, as surgeons do, I've come to see, played down the need for any recovery time and played up the routine nature of the operation. They'd take out the tumor in an afternoon, and that would be that. All the better that we had all these medical problems going on at once. We could take care of them all at once.

So in the middle of Tim's hospital sojourn I had surgery. The tumor came out, but I had no idea how awful you could feel coming out of anesthesia. Carol couldn't be there with me because she was with Tim—the babysitter was with Will at home. The operation went longer than expected, and the surgery was complicated. I woke up in the recovery room well after 6:00 p.m. to find a friend from church at my bedside. No telling how long she had been there.

"Rick," she said. "Rick, it's Auntie Margaret."

She had been a nurse with years of experience behind her at one of the top New York hospitals. Besides that, she was a diligent praying person, a pillar of the church, the woman at coffee hour who always made sure there were enough cookies and cheese and crackers and coffee stirrers to keep the post-worship crowd happy.

"*Ugggggggh*," I groaned. I had bandages wrapped around my face, like some wounded soldier in a Civil War drama.

"I have to go," she said.

"How long have you been here?" I tried to ask.

"The surgery went well. You're going to be fine. But you'll need to spend the night here to recover."

I nodded. What would Carol do? How would we manage?

"I've called Carol. She's got someone to stay with William."

We were loved—we *are* loved. Friends from church, friends from work, old friends from college, pitched in and helped out. Mom had already gone home, having done her stint. This time Dad came out, flying out on the red-eye, stepping out of the yellow cab in his red sweater vest.

All the nerves in my face were bruised. My smile was lop-sided, my face sagged. I needed to use my hand to help close one eye. "The nerves will come back," the doctor promised. "None have been damaged. They're just stunned."

He described enough of the operation that I had to admire how he'd done it, removing the tumor through the threadlike nerves without damaging any of them.

"But was the tumor cancerous?" I asked.

"It didn't look like it, but we'll find out." He held up his calming index finger, waving it up to heaven. "Don't worry."

Carol and I didn't see each other for a week. One of us would be at home, one of us would be at the hospital with Tim, and we traveled back and forth on the subway when our babysitter Sharon could spell us at home. The first time Carol saw me was at the hospital, and she was so horrified by the sight of my nerve-stunned face that she went out and bought a black dress, sure of her impending widowhood. In sickness or in health, indeed.

I remember sleeping in Timothy's hospital room at night, looking out at New York's never-dark sky from my cot by the window and thinking—praying—"You know, if I die, I will be glad that this is one of the last things I do. To be by my son at his bedside."

The tumor, I was finally told, was benign.

September 16, 5:16 p.m.
Well, we all knew Rick was special, right? How special? SO special that the best medical minds at Columbia-Presbyterian Hospital still can't figure out what the heck he has. At least there was no talk of birds today. The three

areas of focus are 1/reaction to antibiotics given for a boil last week (inglorious, that boil). 2/strange infection (really, really strange) or 3/autoimmune disorder. Many of the tests for the last take a long time to "cook." That's what they say, "cook."

More and more objects cluttering up this space. Oxygen machine, IV pole, device to squeeze his calf muscles since he can't get up, commode (why is it here if he can't get up?), spare tank of oxygen...not to mention the usual bed, table, and monitors.

And so busy! Tim and I have been keeping a tally of the individuals who cross the threshold to minister to Rick. Between 9:00 a.m. and 5:00 p.m. it's 54.

And I have to say, they've all been great.

He's still really sick. Didn't have a fever until late this afternoon, so that's good. On lots of drugs, lots of fluid, and most importantly, lots of oxygen.

Keep the prayers and good thoughts coming, dear friends.

CHAPTER SIX

Day 4, Evening

T hat night I had a roommate in the hospital, an older guy—maybe not that much older than me but old enough to seem older. He was on the other side of the curtain they pulled around my bed, but I could hear him wheezing. He'd had to wait in the ER for a long time before being admitted. On oxygen like me, he sounded like he was wearing a mask, not just tubes stuck in his nose. The oxygen machine hissed.

I wanted to talk to him through the curtain.

"Have you been here before?"

"Yeah, this happens to me a lot. I'm on oxygen at home. Carry around a tank with me, but sometimes that's not enough. I start wheezing and carrying on. I have to call for an ambulance, and they bring me here."

"Does it scare you?"

"Sure. But they've always been able to help me here. I get better and then I go home. That's what will happen this time."

I could see myself in some vague future, like this guy, carrying around a tank of oxygen everywhere I went, to the office, on the subway, a special pass allowing me to take it on the airplane. The bother of it, the comfort of it, the wonder of modern medicine, the pain of it, prolonging life, postponing death, the spirit struggling to catch up with the body. Compassion flooded me.

"Are you going to be OK?"

"Of course. It just takes time. I like this hospital."

"So do I. My kids were born here."

"You've got kids?"

"Two of them. Boys, twenty-eight and twenty-five. The twenty-eight-year-old is coming tomorrow to see me. He lives in San Francisco."

"Nice."

"He was the answer to prayer. Like all kids." I couldn't ever forget my blessings. Especially now. Count them at night like counting sheep when you can't sleep.

Those fifteen blocks from the hospital to our apartment had seemed like sacred ground back then. In the pre-dawn of a mild March morning I made that trip, barely able to contain myself. "My son is born," I would announce to the homeless guy in a refrigerator box near the Armory. "We just had a baby," I would tell the sanitation workers throwing trash into the garbage truck. The lady delivering a stack of morning papers was surely just waiting to hear: "It's a boy!"

It was too early to find a cab or catch a bus, and besides, I had to walk off the adrenaline. A miracle had happened. I'd just held our baby wrapped like a burrito in his blanket, pink-faced, wrinkly, tiny, brand-new and old-looking all at once. I had to sleep, but who could sleep now? How could you sleep when you were so full of hope? I was scared out of my wits and not at all sure I was up to the task the good Lord had given me, and yet certain that this was the best role I was ever meant to take on. Dad.

Courage is fear that has said its prayers, as the saying goes, and the prayers were being uttered with each footstep.

"There were two of us in that birthing room, and then there were three, and he's always going to be there. Forever, or as long as we live. He looks like he's smart, the way he turned his head, and he's got a pair of lungs, the way he cried. Do you think he'll be a singer? Or with those tiny arms, a slugger? Will I know enough to teach him how to play ball?"

William Sloane Coffin, senior minister at Riverside Church when I sang in the choir there, used to announce at every baptism that a newborn was God's way of telling the world that it was meant to go on. Then Coffin would look at the flushed faces of the proud parents, the two wreathed in smiles, and remark how these people were taking on the biggest responsibilities of their lives. Look how happy they were. Thrilled, ecstatic. "That's because," he would go on, "it's not our freedoms that give us the greatest pleasure. It's our responsibilities."

Lesson learned. All these responsibilities would make me happy. I can't imagine what life would have been like if we hadn't had children. But it was never a sure thing.

Carol and I gave our baby a name before he was born, before we knew we could even have a child. Truax, we called him. Truax, after some family name we found on an old genealogical chart. Truax, because we knew we'd never ever call a child by that name.

We refused to contemplate having a child until we had a place big enough to house a child, unlike the one-bedroom, third-floor walk-up we first called home. "This apartment isn't big enough to change your mind in," someone once said. So we began looking and came uptown to Washington Heights at the suggestion of a friend, wondering if we could raise a Truax here.

When we checked out apartments, I would go into the extra bedroom, the one that would be "the office" until it became "the nursery," and I'd make a lot of noise. I'd pretend to be Truax, jumping up and down, singing songs from some dreamed-up crib. "How noisy is it from the other bedroom?" I asked. "Can you hear Truax in there?"

We did it ostensibly to test the acoustics of our potential home, no doubt to the annoyance of the real-estate broker, but we were also testing ourselves, looking to the time when we would have children, when we would be parents awakened in the middle of the night by a real-life Truax crying at the end of the hall. Who would he or she be? Who would *we* be?

We remembered something, some good advice we'd received from the minister who'd married us. No, it wasn't Dr. Coffin, but the old bachelor rector of the Episcopal church where we worshipped and still worship today. Our premarital counseling was shortened into one cover-all-the-basics session over a glass of sherry in the living room of his down-at-the-heels rectory.

He circled back to the topic of children. What did he know about them? After all, he was a single man in his sixties, never married. We put down our sherry glasses and listened politely. "If you have children—and they are a blessing," he said as though to remind himself that it was true, "make sure you're happy. If you are happy, your children will be happy."

The message was clear: Be ready to sacrifice everything for your children, but don't sacrifice your marriage. The happiness you have as a couple, your love for each other, your care and concern for each other, will be the happiness your children

experience growing up. You could give them everything, every
material advantage, but if you don't give them that, the home
they have will not be happy.

We chose a two-bedroom apartment in an aging complex fifteen blocks north of the hospital. It was of mock-
Tudor design, reddish brick and half-timbering covered by
ivy, with an overgrown garden of roses and hydrangeas and a
small playground for kids. By the time we moved in Carol was
pregnant—*we* were pregnant—and she needed to be careful.
Our one mover and I carried most of our boxes of books, our
greatest treasures, up the flight of stairs. We looked out the
casement windows to a sliver of the Hudson, framed between
two taller apartment buildings.

Two out-of-work actors painted the kitchen and living
room. One of them, the less prepossessing of the pair, went
on to become famous, appearing in dozens of movies, and
for years afterward we regretted throwing out the sun-dried
tomatoes he had left in our fridge. We could have said, "Those
are Stanley Tucci's sun-dried tomatoes."

Everything we saw now was colored by our expecting, our
waiting, our hoping, our dreaming, our praying. Dreaming is
praying—hard to do in a hospital bed when your oxygen numbers are sliding and your fever is rising. But back then, could I
remember how it was, how I saw the world?

Would our baby—would Truax—slide on the slide in
that playground or climb the jungle gym? Would I push him
on that swing? Would the baby in that stroller become one
of his friends someday? The neighborhood was full of older
German-Jewish residents who had moved here before and
after World War II, finding sanctuary in the New World.

They lined the park benches, reading the *Frankfurter Zeitung* or the Yiddish *Forward*, and I readily cast a half dozen of them as surrogate grandparents.

We were happy without children and told ourselves that if we didn't get pregnant we would still be happy, and that if we did, it was meant to be, God's idea as much as ours. But as the days ticked by, the prospect became scarier and scarier. Everybody asked Carol how she was feeling. Did she have morning sickness? Did she get tired? Could she feel the baby moving inside? Nobody asked what I was going through. If they had, I would have exploded.

"I'm scared to death," I would have said. "How are we ever going to afford a new baby? How are we going to feed it, clothe it, send it to nursery school and kindergarten? How will we pay for piano lessons and ballet classes and gymnastic classes, let alone college?" I didn't mind economizing for myself. I could take homemade salami sandwiches to the office for the rest of my life and buy my jackets and sweaters at the church rummage sale, but I couldn't do that for Truax. He'd need new shoes and a Happy Meal.

One Saturday I went to Woolworth's and bought a plastic trash basket for Truax's room. THE VERY CHEAPEST ONE I COULD FIND. I saved a dollar and ninety-nine cents. I brought it back and put it in his room and realized how ridiculous I was being. The money wasn't the issue. It was the fear of not measuring up, not being patient enough or loving or caring enough to be a parent. A friend visited with his toddler, and the kid pulled every book within reach off the bookshelves. I watched the man calmly put all the books back. "I'll never be able to do that," I thought.

We bought the baby furniture: a crib, a chest of drawers, a toy chest, and a changing table. The latter was the most intimidating, with its drawers for diapers, baby powder, and wipes. It was hard to believe I'd ever know how to use them. But the dreaming part of expecting caught up with us when Carol painted the chest of drawers and toy chest with white enamel, stenciling letters in primary colors across it: "A, B, C, D, E, F, G, H…" I could imagine the day when I would point to them and ask Truax, "What letter is that?" and he would say, "Daddy, that's *A … B … C.*" I would take him to Disney movies. I would show Truax how to ride a bicycle in the little park. He would play in the sandbox. He would squeal with delight when I caught him at the bottom of the slide.

I would be called Daddy or Dad or Pop or the old man. Suddenly I would belong to someone else, the way I belonged to Carol. She joked about how she would be able to refer to me in the third person, talking to Truax, about "your father." As in "Your father will change your diapers this time" or "Your father will take you to the park this morning." This new triangulation: my husband, my son…your father. In families we claim each other and remind each other of how we're connected, just like Jesus saying to the disciples, "The Father and I are one."

The weather turned warm. Truax was late. It was early March, and suddenly there was a premature burst of spring. The kids in the neighborhood played their boom boxes in the park, the Latino strains of salsa echoed against the buildings near the hospital. The oldsters took their aluminum chairs outside, set up tables, and played dominoes. The medical students jogged in shorts up the hill. The weather wouldn't hold, we all knew that, but while it was spring it should be enjoyed.

At dawn on the seventh of March, with sunshine streaming in the windows, Carol got up early and lingered in bed, propped up against the pillows.

"Is this it?" I asked.

"I think so," she said.

Is this it? Like me asking the same question years later, sick in bed, wondering if I was dying, wondering if now was the time to rush to the hospital.

Truax was ten days overdue. Were we ready? Of course not, but we were tired of waiting.

I tried to remember all that we'd learned from the birthing classes. I was supposed to be Carol's coach, timing the contractions and helping her through the pain with breathing and relaxation techniques. For a moment I envied the dads of our parents' generation who didn't have to enter birthing rooms but paced hospital halls instead, cigars in their pocket.

"Can I get you anything?" I asked, hoping to sound solicitous.

"Maybe some videos to watch." We could hang out at home and make sure these contractions were the real ones. One hated to sound a false alarm. You didn't want to look like a fool, like going to the ER with a chest infection and being told it was nothing. On the other hand, maybe this was just the moment to look like a fool—part of the cosmic preparation of parenthood, part of life.

"What about some exercise?" I asked.

The teacher of the birthing classes, a big cheerful Irish woman with ruddy cheeks and a nurse's frankness about body parts, had said it was good to walk during those early stages of labor. Exercise could move things along.

"It's only seven in the morning," Carol said.

"It's supposed to be good for you," I said, taking on my coach role.

"OK."

I put on my jeans and a jacket, Carol wore her down overcoat, but to my mind's eye we looked like a pair auditioning for a Christmas pageant: Woman about to give birth to child, helpless husband standing by. All we lacked was a donkey and a manger. Every now and then we'd stop on the sidewalk and check our watches. Were the contractions coming quicker? Was today going to be the day?

The crocuses in the park were blooming, the azaleas were budding with pink crepe paper colors. I wondered if we would bring our kid—our Truax—here in another week or two. Would we be the proud couple pushing our newborn along the graveled walk?

A neighbor jogged past and stopped. "Carol," she asked, "are you in labor?"

How did she know? "Yes," Carol said.

Squeals of delight. "I won't tell anyone, I promise," our friend said. She'd been through it all herself, had a two-year-old daughter down the street. We walked back to the apartment, feeling like all eyes were on us. Our cover was blown. Would everybody in the neighborhood be looking out their windows to see when we would head off to the hospital? Were they timing our contractions too? Carol likes to believe that she is inconspicuous in any crowd. All at once she felt stared at. So did I, Mr. Soon-to-be-Dad.

That's part of it. You're having a baby. Branded before anyone can even see your offspring. You're entering a great unselective club that will give you instant rapport with more than half the world. Your heart will go out to the parent with the wailing child on the airplane because you know what it's like. You will feel nothing but pity for the mom or dad comforting the kid with spilled ice cream at the amusement park. No baby sounds exactly like another, but every parent's anguish is something you know.

Labor lasted all day, with videos and walks around the apartment, ice chips and phone calls to the doctor's office. By early evening we figured it was time to go. I picked up the bag that had been packed for weeks, and we called a cab to take us to the ER—quicker at finding it back then than twenty-eight years later.

We were taken up to the labor rooms in Babies Hospital. The efficient nurse checked Carol out. Only two centimeters dilated. "It'll be a while," she said, looking at us as though we were amateurs, which, let's face it, we were. Parents are all amateurs. "You live in the neighborhood," she observed. "You're better off waiting at home." It was like studying for an exam for weeks and being told you've flunked on the first question. Sent home.

We watched more videos and clocked the time between contractions, Carol's misery increasing, but every time I suggested we go back to the hospital she rejected the idea. No more humiliation. She wasn't going to be sent home twice. We watched a 1950s movie that I couldn't begin to follow. "Now?" I kept asking Carol. No, not yet, not now. It was well after 10:00 p.m. when we headed back to the hospital, and we had to take the bus—couldn't even find a cab. The bus ride, my moment of humiliation.

"At least I'll be able to get something at the hospital for the pain," Carol said between contractions. She has always welcomed every official opportunity for pain relief.

"I'm afraid you're too far along," said the nurse when we arrived. "It's too late to do an epidural."

There were shouts in Spanish from the woman in the birthing room next door. Carol and I looked at each other with concern. Soon the shouts were coming from Carol. I couldn't for a moment remember what we were supposed to do with the breathing exercises. Wasn't she supposed to blow out and count when it came time for the pushing? Some coach I was.

The obstetrician on call waltzed in from a Saturday night dinner party, took off his jacket, and loosened his bow tie. With a few more pushes, suddenly the baby was born. Our boy. Our baby. Born early on a Sunday morning, Sunday's child. What we had waited for and wished for and prayed for was now more real than we could imagine. He cried right away, his face red from the unpleasantness of having to come out from that place where he had everything taken care of to this world where he'd have to work to get it. That happy, lusty, painful, joyful, miserable shout. He was here. Not Truax. The fake name disappeared in an instant. This baby was for real.

Carol took him in her arms. "He's beautiful," she said, and he was, in his blotchy, scrawny way. All these years later when I look at him, I can still see in his grown face that baby he was in the birthing room. Better than any dreams we ever had for him, how incomplete our hopes had been.

The nurse wrapped him up in a blanket, whisked him away, and then brought him back so we could admire him, and we still do. Finally I kissed Carol good-bye and walked back through the darkened neighborhood, buoyed by hopes, by love, by the magnitude of what had happened. I was full of thankfulness at every block, wreathed in smiles like the parents at baptisms who are told that every child is God's way of telling the world that it should go on. I would call his grandparents, waking them up as they would want to be awakened, letting them know they had a new grandchild, this one named after both his grandfathers, William and Thornton. William Thornton Hamlin.

Chapter Seven

Hospital, Day 5

September 17, 4:51 p.m.

Will arrived from SF this morning with his hipster haircut and his math-oriented brain, and he was the one who got the rheumatologists' report, which he saw as a "mapping" approach to problem-solving. Basically, the infectious-disease guys tested tons of viral and bacterial infections and came up with nothing, so autoimmune disorders seem more likely. As we know, their tests take longer. (And by the way, they don't really cook the results, so disappointing. That Was a Metaphor.) They expect information in the next couple of days, some of which won't be as clear-cut as the yes/no info from infections. So if your mind works like Will's, maybe you see this graphically.

Short version: still no diagnosis.

So, yes, this is like living in an episode of "House," but a really boring one with uniformly nice characters and no drug addiction and nobody having sex in the supply closet, which I know because it's right outside our door.

However—Rick walked today.

That, my friends, is epic. Walked twice around the nurses' station. And twice today docs have nudged down the oxygen flow in his machine, and his absorption has remained steady. He is also eating like a starving man. Best of all, we aren't very interesting anymore. Docs come in, look at his color, look at his numbers, ask how he feels, and with a cheerful smile, leave for a sicker patient. Being boring has never felt so good.

So you see, all those prayers and good wishes? They seem to be working. Not that you should stop: there's still a long way to go. Stay tuned!

Lots of love to all of you from the step-down unit.—Carol

Normally if our grown boys are coming home we want to put the best face on it, at least for that first night's homecoming. I wash their bedroom windows, I vacuum, I clean out a shelf in the medicine cabinet, I scrub the sink and wipe down the tile in the shower. We want to look our best for our kids. We roast the fatted calf, we buy a box of their favorite cereal. Will, for one, always asks me about my work. I tell him, putting the best spin on things.

But there is no spin you can put on for a hospital visit. You can't shield your child from a scary fact: you are going to check out someday and, chances are, it'll be through a series of medical setbacks, demanding a series of hospital visits. "No, don't come," you might want to say, but you yearn to see them, to hear from them, to have one more conversation with them.

"Hey, Will," I said wanly. Did I ever truly believe that courage is fear that has said its prayers?

"Hi, Dad," he said, giving me a hug through the spaghetti of wires coming out of my chest and the tubes attached to my nose, giving me air.

Most of all I wanted to shield him from the fear. "This is the hospital where you were born, Will," I wanted to say. "Think of what a joyful place it was for us then. It can still be that way. Not the way it is or feels now. This is only

284

temporary, a little setback. I'm going to get better. It's ordained. You'll see."

Tim's way of dealing with the fear was to pray from the Book of Psalms in one corner. For Will it was using his quantitative skills, cataloging what the doctors were saying, creating in his head some Excel spreadsheet. Carol and I and Tim still wanted to see this as a narrative with an unwieldy cast of characters and a fuzzy plotline; Will would make sense of it the way he made sense of challenges at work, gathering information, categorizing it, asking questions, creating lists.

The first doctor of the day came in, started asking me some questions, then looked over at William and asked, "Is it OK to talk about this in front of him?"

"Of course," I said. "This is William, my oldest son."

William took down what the doctor said, his fingers flying across his computer. He would share with Carol everything. No secrets needed to be hid from my children.

My sons, my sons, you are my legacy. No book I ever write, no speech I ever give, no meeting I lead, no class I teach, will ever mean as much to me. You are what I leave behind, and I pour my love into you. At my sixtieth birthday party, only months before, both William and Timothy had roasted me royally in witty toasts. But then Tim said, "I'm not sure what I'm going to do with my life but the one thing I know I want to be is a dad, and that's a mark of how good a dad my dad was." What more could you want? Might as well kiss it good-bye and leave it there. Go out on a high note.

Not here, not in this hospital bed.

"How was your flight?" I asked Will.

"Good, Dad."

"You sleep...on the red-eye?"

"I got in a couple of hours."

"Easier than...in a hospital."

William can't really hide it from us. Tough and cerebral in a business setting, he is a softie at the core, much more likely than Tim to burst into tears.

He picks his moments, and they bust you up. He did it the day of my dad's funeral.

Dad had died after a long, slow decline. "He gave us the luxury of saying good-bye," was how Mom put it.

The service was at a packed church, the place they had worshipped for years. All four of us kids spoke. We could look down from the chancel, where we were seated, to the front pew, where he had always sat, bellowing the hymns at top volume in his out-of-tune voice. "He had a few good notes," I said, "and sometimes they were the right notes." Mom beamed at us from the same pew. We all wore his trademark bow ties, raiding his closet, everyone taking their favorite ones. He had served in the submarine corps in World War II, and a few of the surviving crew members showed up with a wreath. I sang that day for him, choosing Rodgers & Hammerstein's "No Other Love" because the tune was used in the TV documentary *Victory at Sea*, and to Dad, any good piece of music sounded "just like *Victory at Sea*." This time it *was Victory at Sea*.

After the service we hosted a reception for 350 people and, at day's end, we returned to Mom and Dad's house, the modern one they had built after we kids flew the coop. That evening, at what was now Mom's house, William burst into tears. I was downstairs getting ready for bed, but I could hear him in the kitchen, a twenty-something crying like a kid who has struck out at bat. The grandfather he loved was gone and nothing would be the same again. "Oh, Will," I heard Carol say, "it's all right, honey."

I didn't want him to cry now at the hospital. Didn't want him to cry ever. How lousy of me to rattle his world. Parents die, parents get sick, security gets shaken. Every time I attempt to reconcile myself to the concept of death and its inevitability—how necessary it is, how essential—I circle back to this: what a terrible thing to do to the ones you leave behind.

I wanted to be strong for Will. Somehow being the Rock of Gibraltar mattered more to me with him than it did with Tim—maybe because William was the oldest and I felt more responsibility. He was my firstborn, the first one I learned how to rock and hold. I couldn't take in this reversal of roles.

"You OK, Dad?"

"Yeah, I'll be fine."

"Can I get you anything?"

"No. I'm going for a walk soon," I said, as though I were going to climb Mount Everest. It astounded me how fast my muscles had deteriorated. Five—going on six—days in the hospital, and I was so weak I could barely lift myself out of bed. My muscles were like Jell-O. I'd worked so hard, going to the gym and running in the park, building minuscule quads and abs and triceps, and now they were all gone in a matter of days. "All that work for nothing," I thought. "Why bother?"

"Good morning, Mr. Hamlin."

The respiratory therapist showed up to walk me around the nurses' station. That's as far as I could go. I had to be disconnected from the heart monitor; my breathing tubes needed to be hooked up to a portable tank of oxygen; any medicine that was flowing through the IV would be put on a pole that could come with me. I sat on the side of the bed and looked at my thighs. What thighs? I had none. Sitting up made me woozy. What if I threw up in front of my son?

I smiled to show I was strong, the fake bravery of the patient—"How do you feel today?" "Better. Better." Better on a very low scale. The fevers still came, unpredictable in their arrival, making me wheeze like an old man.

"Let's go for a little walk," said the respiratory therapist.

"Sure."

Sometimes if you act like you feel better, you will feel better. Act like you're hopeful and you *will* feel hopeful, pretend you're happy and maybe you'll feel happy. The emotions normally work from the inside out, but sometimes you can make them work from the outside in. Crack a smile, and it'll warm up your soul, laugh and your spirits will rise. I'd pretended to be well before, maybe I could do it now, indulge in the vast conspiracy of wellness that hospitals unconsciously—or maybe consciously—encourage.

I stood up slowly, the respiratory therapist at my side. Physical and respiratory therapists are the most likable people on earth, paragons of equanimity. I suspect none of them ever had to worry about getting picked to be on a team in junior high school or fretted over what to wear on a first date. They had that kind of inborn confidence. They always acted as if things were fine or would be fine with a little work, no problem. This one was no exception.

"Good," she said with every tentative step I took. "That's very good."

"Where are you...from?" I asked. I figured if I asked her about herself I wouldn't have to think about how I felt.

Every step forward took enormous effort and concentration. Every joint ached. Every breath was a struggle. The therapist kept her eye on the oxygen monitor. "Good, good," she said. What was good? Two weeks earlier I had run four miles up and around the park in one of my early morning runs. Now I could barely hobble around the nurses' station. Space had collapsed. My world had shrunk. Goals would be measured in small footsteps, inch by inch.

The therapist was kind and encouraging. "Next time we'll go a little further," she said, walking me back to my room. What I was contending with was the prospect of the long trip I would have to make to get out of the hospital. Distance wasn't just physical, it was emotional. Wellness was so far away. Recovery would be this painful struggle forward every step of the way. There was no magic potion. The doctors were no closer to any reasonable diagnosis. I would have to cling with all my strength to that heaven-sent message: YOU ARE GOING TO GET WELL. God would have to help me because I couldn't do much to help myself. Maybe that needed to be the text of the next e-mail Carol sent: Keep up your prayers, because Rick has just realized how far he has got to go. Perhaps that's what Paul was talking about when he said the Spirit prays for us "in wordless groans." Words were beyond me.

I was escorted back to my bed, exhausted, and discovered that while I was gone, William had made it for me. All those beds we had made for him over the years, the sheets washed, the bedspread tucked in, his stuffed animals piled up in one corner, and now he was making one for me. He sat in the chair, checking messages on his computer, and got up to help. "Thanks," I said. I was grateful. But it also broke my heart.

In the ICU, Carol had taped up opposite my bed a print of two women in 1950s bathing suits doing a circle of flips in an invisible swimming pool, like something from an Esther Williams film. "Rhine maidens," Carol called them. There they were in water portrayed with quick short brushstrokes. "My loop-to-loop girls," was how I thought of them, dancing the light fantastic. They were what I hoped to be, free and fun and floating. They were a prayer and a gift from a friend.

Susan is an artist. I'd seen the original of this print first in her studio in Brooklyn and then in an exhibit framed on a wall. I loved it and told her so. It made me happy. Susan was one of the many who had received Carol's e-mails about my health. She knew I was in dire straits. No visitors yet, but she sent me this copy of her work, e-mailing it to Carol, who had printed it out and put it up. It was my icon, my hope, my wish and belief for myself. My prayer in an image.

You feel so stuck in a hospital room, deprived of all sensory stimulation. The same four walls, the same window, the same tests administered over and over again (blood pressure, temperature, X-ray), the same dull chairs. John Ruskin once said of Constable's paintings when they hung in a gallery that it was as though the wall had been cut open and the sunlight came blazing through. That's how it felt to have Susan's print there, an opening to the world beyond, access to life, beauty, art, love, friends.

Some people ignored the "no visitors" rule or they knew I would have granted them special privileges anyway. Actually, if I'd been the sole gatekeeper, I would have granted hundreds of people special privileges and then felt miserable when I couldn't entertain them. Another failure, another sign of how sick I was. Even when you're a patient and not expected to be at your best, you want to be at your best.

Stacy showed up with her daughter Millie, who I figured was running a race at the Armory next to the hospital.

"How'd it go?"

"Great." Two thumbs-up? Three thumbs-up? I can't remember if Millie won or not, just that she was in her running clothes, and I thought of the times we'd seen her compete at the Armory. But then, the Armory was where they did indoor track in the winter. It wouldn't have made any sense in September. She must have been up in Van Cortlandt Park, one hundred blocks away, and they had stopped by on their way back. It would be like Stacy to act as though they'd just been in the neighborhood. No obligation, nothing special.

They didn't linger. I was grateful for that.

Scott came by. Scott was there a lot. My dearest friend from college, he'd seen me at my best, and plenty of times when I was at my worst. No need to fake it for him. We had more than forty years of friendship through thick and thin, or as another friend likes to say, "May there be more thick than thin." Time for thin.

"What are you doing here?" I asked.

"What are *you* doing here?" he asked.

It's not always easy to visit people in the hospital. You can't just park in front and dart in. Hospitals are also scary for many people, germ-packed petri dishes, harbingers of mortality. Scott came on his way home from work, heading to Westchester from his office on the Upper East Side. Making his way to Washington Heights at rush hour wouldn't be easy. Where did he park? How much did he have to pay?

"That's so nice of you...to come."

"Rick, everybody's been worried about you."

He was there for Carol as much as he was there for me, I told myself. Being a caregiver is not only exhausting, but lonely. Here was a friend to ease the burden, somebody to talk to when I couldn't talk, someone to commiserate with.

"Let me show you...something."

I had been practicing my breathing. I still had the tubes in my nostrils but I had decided that I should always inhale through my nose on a long count and exhale through my mouth. If I did that correctly, breathing would be much easier. If I had to do this the rest of my life with a can of oxygen attached, I would do it. A warm breath of oxygen through the nostrils and deep into my lungs, a smooth exhale of carbon dioxide.

"This is how I'm going to breathe now," I told Carol and Scott. I demonstrated. Scott looked at me like I was nuts, trying to understand, wishing he knew what was on my mind.

"If I can breathe like this, I will be well." I did it again, the tubes of extra oxygen still inserted in my nostrils. Why should breathing right be something so hard? What was I trying to convey?

I saw on Scott's face a look of compassion and bewilderment. I flashed back some forty-odd years to when we were college roommates, and I'd pulled an all-nighter to finish a paper that was due for some class, and I came into our shared dorm room where he was just waking up. He looked at me then, as he did now with love and kindness, and uttered the only thing that made any sense: "You need to get some sleep."

Timothy was leaving for South Africa soon. Friday night his girlfriend Henley had arranged for a surprise good-bye party for him. It would be at our house. I'd somehow fantasized that I would be there too. I'd be in the crowd that burst out "Surprise!" when he came through the door. I'd be able to see some of his old friends, all grown up now. I'd find out what they were doing with themselves.

Carol would go home earlier that night. William would be with her, part of the party. Scott stayed a little while with me, and then I was on my own. "Good-bye, Tim. It must be a sign that I'm getting better, or you wouldn't feel you could leave. I'm not there, but I'm always there. Dads are always there. It's just the way things work out. I hope—I pray—that I'm there for the good, that I'm some sort of inner voice that says, 'You're gifted, you're loved, you're a delight, you're all a dad would ever hope for.' You are. Love, Dad."

Sept. 18, 4:19 p.m.
I am not at the hospital.

Just think about that for a moment, friends. Sunny, warm September afternoon and I am at my desk, looking at the Hudson. For that matter, Rick is not even in his hospital bed, I'm told: word from Will is "they took him down for a sonogram."

This would have been incredibly cumbersome yesterday, tethered as he has been to his blood pressure cuff and his EKG sensors and his utterly essential 02 machine. But this morning they took him off the high-flow machine and gave him one of those little cannula things: the prongs you stick in your nose, attached to a clear hose, attached to heaven knows what and a green-painted tank. And two respiratory therapists walked him around the halls with his two tanks of 02 in a little truncated cart, and he was stepping out briskly.

There is even talk of moving to a "quieter room," which probably means off the step-down ward, and while we will miss the remarkable people there, quiet would be good.

Today's diagnosis hypothesis is a kind of squishy combo thing: underlying immune disorder, which produced alarming symptoms when prodded into action by unidentified viral infection. Whatever. Sounds as if there may be more tests later, once Rick's lungs have healed further.

There is even talk of Rick being able to take a shower. Just imagine what that will feel like after a week in a hospital bed.

Love to you all, C.

CHAPTER EIGHT

Hospital, Day 6

H ave you ever worked in a shipyard?"
"Have you traveled abroad recently?"
"How long ago was it that you were in Africa?"
"Do you have any exotic birds?"
"Do you have any pets?"
"Have you been in the Central Valley?"
"Do you have any allergies?"

One question that no doctor ever asked was, "Have you ever suffered from depression?"

It wouldn't have been there in my chart. You couldn't find it in the digital records that Columbia-Presbyterian was so proud to keep, that information any professional affiliated with the hospital could find at the click of a key. Did anyone ever think to ask it? I never thought to say it. And what if they'd asked, and what if I'd said yes...would it have made any difference in the diagnosis they were trying to put together?

"Yes," I could say, "I've been battling depression for over a year now, maybe a year and a half."

"Really?"

"I've been seeing a therapist."

"Any meds?"

"No. It doesn't feel like that kind of depression. I don't object to antidepressants, although I've never had them. I wouldn't hesitate to take them if they were prescribed. They never have been."

If I'd been on meds, it would have been in my records, right?

"I've been treating this with talk therapy. Funny thing: it was all winding down before this infection hit me. In fact, my last appointment with the shrink was scheduled for the week I got sick."

"Your last appointment?"

"My last for a while. My friend Rick, who is a therapist, has this nice phrase, 'You don't ever stop therapy,' he says. 'You simply take a break from it.' I was at that point and had told the therapist, 'I'm ready to take a break.' Then came this."

"Why do you bring it up?"

"It obviously had some effect on my immune system."

I'm usually more prone to anxiety than depression, forging ahead with nervous anticipation rather than gazing behind in numbing regret. "Feigning frenzy" was how Scott described it in our college days, whether it was feigned or not.

Then, about a year before I landed in the hospital, the veil started to descend. Everything seemed dark, my reactions fearful. On an August weekend in Martha's Vineyard with dear friends, I woke up to sunlight streaming into our bedroom, the curtains billowing in the breeze. Logically I knew the day was something to be enjoyed—beautiful weather, warm ocean water for swimming, the chance to lounge on a porch swing with a good book, the prospect of reminiscing with old friends. Instead I dreaded it. I looked at the clear blue sky with horror. I didn't want to talk to anyone. Didn't want to meet any new people—a rare state for an extrovert like me. First thing in the morning I went for a run to be on my own. Later, when we went swimming, I found myself drifting with the current, glad to be taken away from the group. "How far out could I go without being noticed?" I wondered. At dinner

that night, sitting with people I loved, I found myself counting the minutes, glancing at my watch, wondering how soon
I could politely say, "Gosh, it's so late. I think I need to go
to bed."

I could still make conversation, lobbing questions back and
forth, appearing to be interested in all that was said. I could
smile and laugh, but it was someone else doing it, not me.
Echoing the psalmist, I prayed, "Why are you cast down O
my soul, and why are you disquieted within me?" How could I
be such a stranger to myself?

I came to be obsessed with death that summer. Any life
span I saw, the years attached to historical personages like,
say, George Washington (1732–1799), Thomas Jefferson
(1743–1826), or Theodore Roosevelt (1858–1919), got me thinking how long I had lived and could possibly live, measuring my
life against theirs. *Lord, teach us to number our days so that we
may gain a heart to wisdom.* "George Washington didn't even
make it to seventy," I thought. "Teddy Roosevelt was only a
year older than me when he died." Instead of looking to the
future with wonder and hope, imagining all the things I could
and would do, I saw it with blinders. Life didn't feel like a gift
anymore. I started writing about all the guys I'd known back
in the eighties and nineties, guys my age, who had died from
AIDS. Their loss seemed even sadder now than it had then. All
the things they had missed. "Borrowed Time" I wanted to call
it, although that title was already taken by an AIDS memoir.
Didn't we all live on borrowed time?

On Martha's Vineyard I was determined to find the grave
site of the first Hamlin to come to these shores, back in the
seventeenth century. A kindly *Guideposts* reader with the same

last name, who turned out to be a distant cousin, had sent me a notebook outlining our shared genealogy. He pointed out that our ancestor James Hamlin (1636–1718) was buried in a cemetery in the middle of the island. I hitched a ride to the spot, convinced that his tombstone would be impossible to find, buried under brambles. But no, I found it in minutes and gazed with fascination at the winged skull on the tombstone, taking some sort of comfort in the image of death wearing angel wings. I recalled an octogenarian friend who, in considering death, said she prayed for a "direct flight." Seemed like a good idea.

That August, when most New York psychotherapists decamp to Wellfleet or Woodstock, I found one who was still in town. I met with her every Friday at one o'clock, taking a subway to the Upper East Side from our offices down in the Financial District. There were days I didn't like to stand too close to the edge of the platform, too close to the oncoming train.

"I wouldn't ever commit suicide," I told my shrink, "but I understand now why people do it." I could see what a relief it would be, an escape from the grayness inside, death an odd sort of blessing. Was it possible that depression was a way for us to prepare for death, to learn how to let go? Was I being asked to make better friends with death, to see it as part of the natural cycle of life?

I could look at myself from the outside and seem so normal, nothing apparently wrong. I went running or hauled myself to the gym six days a week (taking an exercise Sabbath on Sundays). I went to the office, edited stories, sat through meetings. Sang in choir, organized a church men's group that met once a month to talk about our concerns and pray for one another. I wasn't shy about sharing my own gloomy state and asking for prayers. I continued my own private prayer practice, stretching the time. Closing my eyes, I would sit on the sofa cross-legged and sink into silent meditation, checking out to check in, trying to let go of all the worries that clouded my head. I rose from the couch, the gloom still there.

I believed that this dark patch, this psychic disconnect, was meant to teach me something—good Puritan soul that I am— and I would ask myself and ask the therapist a million questions to understand why and how I'd gotten here. I'd been in therapy before, had put a few bogeymen to rest. By and large my childhood had been happy. I was loved in a family that is still very close. I could look back and find a few untoward moments of unhappiness, but they felt well explored, talked about in previous therapy sessions. Relinquished. The wounds didn't seem worth picking at anymore. Why this now? What was happening to me? It was affecting my body as well as my soul.

"It feels like some lingering PTSD from open-heart surgery," I proposed to the shrink.

"Let's talk about that," she said.

Dear reader, forgive me for going into this now, another organ recital at this late juncture in this reminiscence that is already overcrowded with medical detail. I've hinted enough at it and talked around it, thinking I wouldn't have to explain too much. It was there in my medical records for all to see. "Bovine valve...aortic root replacement." But when I talk about depression I have to talk about this, the surgery I'd had at the same hospital, Columbia-Presbyterian, eight years earlier.

I was born with a bicuspid aortic valve and developed an aortic aneurysm at age fifty-two. As my cardiac surgeon explained, "If you have a bicuspid valve you've got a fifty-fifty chance of getting an aneurysm." Thanks to my pulmonologist, Dr. DiMango, as I've mentioned, the problem was discovered. She'd asked me to have an MRI for reasons that had nothing to do with my heart and then called me and said, in her memorable words, "Your lungs are fine, but you'd better do something about that aneurysm in your aorta."

I met with Beloved Cardiologist Dr. Ravalli on a Thursday. This was when we had talked about Italy for twenty minutes before he'd delivered the news, "You're going to need open-heart surgery." Carol and I met the cardiac surgeon the following Monday—"Doctor God" she'd dubbed him. I had checked into the hospital that Wednesday and had surgery the next day, December 7, Pearl Harbor Day.

I didn't expect surgery to be a picnic, but nothing had prepared me for how brutal recovery would be. I was healthy, in good shape. I'd had no symptoms (which, upon reflection, was less than comforting). Doctor God spoke euphemistically about the operation and how smooth it would be. "We'll stretch open the sternum," he said. Stretch open? *Saw open* would be more accurate. "It should be a six-hour operation," he said. Six hours? The anesthesiologist put me out at around one o'clock in the afternoon and I didn't wake up in the ICU until after one in the morning, with a nurse named Angel, I kid you not, hovering over me.

"We were planning to go on a trip to Spain after the holidays," we told Doctor God.

"No problem," he said. "I'll fix you up, and then you can go on and live your life."

My body ached, not just my chest but my back and shoulders. They get you up and walking as soon as possible after heart surgery, but I didn't want to go anywhere. I was in the hospital recovering for six days, then came home and recovered for six weeks, never taking naps, walking a bit and then walking a bit more.

I'd heard enough about how depression was often a result of open-heart surgery, but I wouldn't describe what I felt then as depression. I was tired but I couldn't fall asleep at night. It was as though my body were saying, "Don't you check out on me. Remember what happened when they put you out in the OR? Remember what they did to you? Sawed open your chest, hooked you up to the heart-lung machine while you were really dead?" I was eternally wary. The gremlins had attacked once. Maybe they would attack again.

We did not go to Spain.

I described all this to my psychotherapist, reliving it to try to understand it, looking under psychic bedcovers to see if the unacknowledged trauma of open-heart surgery—one of those things that people don't talk about—had led somehow to depression now, eight years later.

I would tell her how wired I was, on edge, for weeks after the surgery. I was like a dog during a thunderstorm, desperate to be around people, wanting to be told that everything was going to be all right. My heart would race at ninety beats a minute on my way to cardiac rehab. "It must be the coffee you have at breakfast," Dr. Ravalli said. "I don't drink coffee," I said. "It's probably your heart anticipating the workout you're going to get at cardiac rehab," he said, ever reassuring.

I remember running into neighbors as I was making my way to the deli or the cleaner's, trying to get some exercise. "What happened to you?" the more honest ones could say. I would explain and tell them about the aortic aneurysm and the surgery that Doctor God had performed. "Well, you look great," one woman said. "Thanks," I said. I saw her a couple of weeks later. "You look so much better now," she said. "You looked terrible last time I saw you. I thought you were at death's door."

Never trust what anyone says to you when you're recovering from illness.

The worst symptom was something I came to call "the black domino," a darkness inside my head. It was especially pronounced when I tried to pray. I would close my eyes to sink into what I hoped would be a healing meditation and instead find myself tumbling down a dark hole. It was as though part of my brain had been blasted out of my head, leaving nothing but pitch black. I could almost locate it, toward the top of my brain.

"Why did you call it the black domino?" my therapist asked.

"I don't know." My brain danced to make connections like you do in a therapist's office. "It just seemed like solid darkness, like a black domino if you broke it up inside. Or maybe it's the way you line them up and push one, and they all fall down."

"Is it still there?"

"It lifted after several months, was gone in a year. But if I think about it long enough, I can still feel where it was." I closed my eyes. I didn't want to find it, didn't like facing it, but maybe that's why I needed to face it. "Right there." My place of comfort had been hijacked, and it made me mad and scared me to death.

A year of talking to the psychotherapist, a year of dragging myself up to her office on East Eighty-Sixth Street and sitting there, digging deep, dumping, dredging up what needed to be dredged. Did I like doing it? Not really. Did I resent the time it took out of my day? Yeah, until I considered how much more time I had wasted by burying things. Did I resent the money it cost? Terribly. Did I think it was necessary? Absolutely. The depression eased, glimpses of light started casting themselves into the gloom, I was mending. I was ready to take a break. And now this.

Why hadn't any doctor asked if I'd been depressed? Surely it had weakened my immune system. Maybe it had made me vulnerable to infection. Wasn't that something the docs would want to know? But then, it wasn't something I wanted to talk about.

Even now.

They were moving me out of the ICU step-down into a shared room at the end of the hall, from Garden South to Garden North. They were lowering my dose of oxygen, they were finishing up the round of antibiotics. I was getting better—all signs pointed that way—but I was only feeling worse. "If this is better," I thought, "I don't like it."

The doctors came around, ordering more tests and then waiting to find out what the tests would say. The specialists arrived with different troops of residents or students, and I would be exhibit A. Don't get me wrong, I was glad of the attention. Whatever I could do to help. If they could only come up with a diagnosis.

I hated saying good-bye to my favorite nurse, Jay, even though he was just down the hall. The shower he had promised would have to wait for someone else to administer it. I dreaded leaving one cocoon of care for another and disliked being so sensitive about it. I hated how a fever could still leave me gasping for breath. How was I ever going to get back to normal?

Trust, trust, trust, trust, I preached to myself. Carol printed out some of the e-mails, and I managed to read them, good wishes from people thinking about me, worried about me, praying for me. *You are loved, Rick,* I told myself. *Feel it. Trust it. Know it.*

Soon William would go back to San Francisco. Soon Timothy would leave for South Africa. Oh, how I'd miss them. "The next time you see your father I won't look like this, I promise. I will be OK." *Receive the love, Rick.*

September 19, 8:27 p.m.

The paradox of recovery: sometimes it's not until you feel better that you actually feel sick.

Are you with me? The docs moved Rick from the step-down unit (as in a "step down" from the ICU) to a general medicine ward, thereby releasing/removing him from lots of systemic support and monitoring. Which is progress. But now that he's not getting as much oxygen and not being checked on hourly etc. etc. he feels, as his mother would say, "pretty punk." Me, I see this as the bumpy road to eventual health. But he did spike a fever this morning and has to work harder to breathe. Plus the poor guy never got his shower.

And let's be realistic: this drama has lasted a full week now. We're all bored and tired, Rick most of all.

We've got personnel changes over the next couple of days. Will returns to SF, Tim heads off to SA (that would be South Africa), and Rick's brother Howard joins the support team here. I will admit that I am exhausted but I am fortified by the generosity and inventive concern of neighbors and friends. I come home: there is strange and wonderful food in my fridge. How cool is that?

We are not out of the woods but I have to believe that all these prayers and loving thoughts are making a difference.

XXX, C.

CHAPTER NINE

Hospital, Days 7 and 8

W e faith people, we tell ourselves stories, retell them, then tell them again. It's gone on that way for millennia. They remind us of who we are and whose we are. Lost in my hospital bed, I looked for signs that what I believed to be true would be true. That this misery and boredom would have some purpose. My body was giving me conflicting messages. My soul wanted to trust in better news.

"Remember how much you worried about Tim? Remember how hard you and Carol prayed? Look how that turned out. Isn't there some lesson you can hold on to now?"

You worry about your grown-up kids as they head into the world. You think you know what's best for them. You want to show them the way. You want to engineer a future for them. And make it happen right away. If you could, you would wave a magic wand that would open all the right doors, even if that would rob them of the necessary learning experiences—terrible notion—that make for a magna cum laude in the School of Hard Knocks. Short of that, you make suggestions, you send links to helpful articles (my dad sent clippings), you make phone calls, you mention that you know someone who would love to talk to them and might have just the right idea for them, knowing as you do that sometimes someone who isn't Dad might be able to get through.

To watch William make the transition from college to career was relatively easy. But then, he was an econ major. The way was paved with campus visits from recruiters who were only too glad to sign up a numbers guy with social skills. He had a job offer before he graduated and took it. Happily.

It's harder, though, for a humanities graduate to determine what the away-from-academia future holds. I should know. I graduated from college determined not to sign on the dotted line of any program designed to turn an English major into an investment banker or stockbroker or even a schoolteacher. I didn't want to have a salaried job for years—and didn't. As I mentioned, I went off to Italy and then did theater and freelance writing. But what do you do when you see your history major son look with bewilderment at the choices after graduation?

"Come home," we told Tim. "You can live with us till you figure something out. You've got loads of talent. There are tons of things you can do. Something great will turn up."

You want to be a blindly encouraging parent while offering occasional doses of practicality, bits of solid advice. Tim seemed so disheartened I didn't even dare do that. The merest hint of a suggestion, and he closed down.

I didn't bring up any mention of faith or prayer or church. Both of our boys had grown up going to church every Sunday, a nonnegotiable. They attended Sunday school—for a couple of years I was their teacher. Timothy sang in church choirs from the time he was four years old to his senior year of high school. I was aware that his faith had lapsed in college, but that didn't seem unusual. I'd had my own flirtation with atheism in college until the urgency of final exams and the lure of the Princeton University Chapel changed all that. You lose your parents' faith so that you can find a faith of your own. To pray that Tim found his way back to God seemed beyond hoping.

It was painful enough to watch him struggle with day-to-day life in the real world.

I felt like I had to tiptoe around him, vacillating between telling him exactly what he should do and keeping my mouth shut for fear I'd destroy any shred of confidence he had. In my prayers I went through a litany of things that God was supposed to do for him. "He'd be a great teacher. He should look into that...He's a fine musician. He should start a rock band...God, have you seen what a superb writer he is? Don't you think he should do something with that? We've got tons of friends in nonprofits—I want him to talk to all of them. Lord, tell him he needs to listen to me and follow my advice."

As fellow blogger Julia Attaway recently reminded me, "Let go and let God" is about *not* dictating but accepting.

Tim found immediate employment as a babysitter, a "manny" in contemporary parlance. He is very good with children, has endless patience, and kids naturally glom on to him. He was hired to pick up a sixth-grader from school a couple of days a week, supervising homework and taking the boy to after-school music lessons and karate. He had another gig for a young family so the mom and dad could have a marriage-saving date night. He was employed by one couple who had adopted a boy from Ethiopia and another couple with two boys who needed an agile referee.

He worked all year taking care of kids. His only immediate goal was to put aside enough money to see more of the world. Wanderlust? I understood that. After all, what did I do when I was his age? Expatriated to Florence. But surely I had more focus back then—didn't I?—more drive, clearer goals. I was going to be a writer or a singer or a citizen of the world.

Something like that. "Tim, perhaps you should…," I'd start to suggest, stopping myself at a kick from Carol under the table to zip it, Dad.

By June Tim had enough saved to see the world with a friend for as long as the money would hold out. We wished him bon voyage. The e-mails came from Spain, France, Morocco, Italy, Croatia, Bosnia, Jordan, Israel, Egypt, India. Curiously enough I worried less about him when he was on the road, even when he was in places noted for political unrest.

He and his buddy spent one week on a beach on the Sinai Peninsula, taking care not to reveal where they were until after they'd left, saving us the worries, unless we wanted to worry about things that had already passed, which is always a possibility. By November they were wrapping up five weeks of third-class rail travel through India, with a few too many nights sleeping in train stations, when I got the e-mail that stopped me in my tracks.

He'd been at shrines that attracted pilgrims from all over the country, Hindus and Moslems practicing their faith. "It's pretty interesting," he wrote, "but it makes me think I should learn more about what I grew up with. I need to understand Christianity better. Is there an Episcopal monastery back in New York where I could spend some time, learning about my faith?"

Wow. Where did that come from? It was certainly never a directive in my prayers. I'm not that clever.

"Sure, Tim," I wrote back, my fingers flying across the keys. "There are some Episcopal brothers who have a monastery up the Hudson somewhere. I'll find the name of it. We know lots of people who've gone there on retreats." There it was online, "Holy Cross Monastery, an Anglican Benedictine Community of Men." I got the snail mail address and the name of the prior.

Timothy came home in late November, wrote a letter to the prior, and on a cold January day he took the train up to Poughkeepsie, got a cab to go across the river, and spent a couple of days with the good brothers at Holy Cross. "Come back and stay longer," they said. He did, spending six weeks with them, reading, praying, saying the monastic offices, sledding on a snow day, doing a little work in the kitchen. It was a transforming experience. He'd never been so happy in his life. They didn't charge him. They welcomed him in the age-old Benedictine tradition of hospitality, taking in the stranger as though he were Christ himself. Tim found his faith. Born again. He came back to New York with a new focus, an inner direction.

He became active in our church, the church where he had grown up. Every Friday he'd work to prepare whatever was being cooked for Saturday's soup kitchen and he'd serve the meal on Saturdays, no matter how late he stayed out on Friday nights with his pals. He volunteered one night a week at a homeless shelter. He read, he worshipped, trying to figure out what he wanted to do next. Seminary maybe, possibly the ministry. He applied for a program called "Young Adult Service Corps" that ended up sending him for ten months to South Africa. There he would be living with the Holy Cross brothers, the same group of men who'd brought him to this new spiritual home.

It was nothing I had dreamed up, nothing I had engineered. I couldn't have come up with something this good.

I would have done better by trusting God than wasting my energy telling Him what to do.

Trust, trust, trust.

I had a roommate in my new room, an older man without much English. I couldn't get much out of him and was relieved that he didn't watch much TV. He was obviously afraid and he wouldn't cooperate with the nurses, wouldn't eat the food. When he was scheduled for a test—a CT scan or echocardiogram—he refused to go. He was terribly alone. Unlike me, he had no visitors. Every day he'd get a phone call from someone and yell into the phone. He was fiercely unhappy, and no one could seem to do anything about it. I admired the way the nurses treated him. They never lost their patience. I tried to talk to him but we had little language in common. I nodded and smiled on my way to the john when I passed his bed.

"I'm sorry that we have made so much noise," I said. Carol had been there, Scott came, someone from church came. He nodded. That was it.

I wanted to see this new room as an exit ramp. I had been given my internal marching orders—I was going to get out of here—but they didn't come with any date stamped on them. How much longer would I be in the hospital? When would I finally get out? When would the fevers leave? When would I get off the oxygen?

I felt well enough to know how rotten I was. I was getting enough good news to know how very bad the news had been, getting enough glimpses of light to feel the contrasting dark. I could finally prop myself up with my laptop and read messages sent to me, warming, loving notes of prayer and concern, but I didn't have enough energy to respond. I didn't have the where-withal to organize the messages in any fashion, forgetting which ones to mark "read" or "unread." I guess this is where the term "executive function" comes in. I had lost mine.

This was the week I was supposed to be in California for that conference. I wanted to let my colleagues know I was thinking of them, but I didn't trust my ability to come up with a decent message. Odd self-consciousness for someone who never hesitates before sending a message to anyone. The blank page had never seemed like an enemy before. Now it was intimidating.

For the first time I logged on to Facebook and posted something:

September 20.

Dear friends, I am now entering my second week at Columbia-Presbyterian Hospital, being treated for a rather baffling lung infection. The staff is superb, and I certainly feel better today than I did a week ago, but fevers persist and my breathing is halting at best. I can't tell you how grateful I am for your prayers, because they seem to tide me over when fatigue makes it hard for me to pray. Keep 'em coming. Forgive me for not responding individually to your kind wishes. I am confident in my doctors and confident in my own faith. I grow weary, I confess, but I do not despair. Godspeed.

I am still amazed at how many people that update reached, more than anything I've ever posted before. The number of comments was astounding, comments I could barely take in.

All those people: friends, family, readers, strangers, friends of friends. Bad news travels fast.

I was reading Tolkien's magisterial *The Lord of the Rings*. I had bought a copy for my Kindle not long before I landed in the hospital, the trilogy in a single volume.

I'd tried to tackle it before when the boys were very young. I had a paperback edition of *The Fellowship of the Ring*, and was reading it on the subway home from work back in the days when New York was not as safe a city as it is today.

It was rush hour. I was on the A train, rumbling under Harlem, the book in my lap. I guess I closed my eyes for a moment, maybe in prayer, maybe in sleep. The next thing I knew some troubled fellow traveler was slugging me in the face for no apparent reason. I ducked my head—didn't ever see him—and darted off the train, carrying my bloodstained book. I wasn't hurt badly but I didn't have any appetite to continue with Tolkien.

Now I'd gone back to it, the stirring drama of good versus evil taking me away from my own shapeless narrative of hospitalization. I once wrote a novel about a dying woman who communicates with her husband from beyond the grave through a series of messages she scrawled in the margins of one of her favorite paperback books, a novel she knew he'd discover at some point after her death. *Reading between the Lines*, I called it.

Reading between the lines of Tolkien, I highlighted passages on my Kindle that spoke to me:

> There is a seed of courage hidden (often deeply, it is true) in the heart of the fattest and most timid hobbit, waiting for some final and desperate danger to make it grow.

Where was my seed of courage?

"Despair or folly?" said Gandalf. "It is not despair, for despair is only for those who see the end beyond all doubt. We do not."

What was the end of this?

Sam said nothing. The look on Frodo's face was enough for him; he knew that words of his were useless. And after all he never had any real hope in the affair from the beginning; but being a cheerful hobbit he had not needed hope, as long as despair could be postponed. Now they were come to the bitter end. But he had stuck to his master all the way; that was what he had chiefly come for, and he would still stick to him. His master would not go to Mordor alone. Sam would go with him—and at any rate they would get rid of Gollum.

Or get rid of mysterious, life-threatening, impossible-to-diagnose lung infections.

Sept. 20, 2:36 p.m.
Dear friends, I'm thinking the narrative drive of this story is starting to sag. There isn't much I can do about the real-time aspect of our drama, so I'm going to Space It Out.
That is to say, communicate less often. So don't freak out—or assume that he's home in his own bed—when you don't hear from me tomorrow. Chances are excellent the status will be quo.

Rick is improving for sure. He did get that shower today and has tottered around the room on his long O2 hose. Less happily he spiked fevers both yesterday and today, so we got a return visit this afternoon from the chief of the rheumatology department, who seemed intent on further diagnostic activity. Not that I can imagine what that would be. I'm getting a faint whiff of "Groundhog Day" here.

Our patient is still not ready for visitors, though I know many of you are very eager. His energy is too limited to make his responding to e-mails a sure bet. So keep us in your thoughts and prayers, and don't get alarmed when there's no bulletin tomorrow.

Lots of love from the entire Hamlin family, C.

CHAPTER TEN

Hospital, Days 9 and 10

T hen the most extraordinary thing happened, a gift that came out of the blue. Maybe this is what people mean when they talk about the blessings to be found in the midst of suffering, how reservoirs of goodness and kindness reveal themselves, how joy tumbles out from the clouds.

Howard wasn't really lurking in the clouds. He was in Annapolis, Maryland, competing in a regatta.

Howard is my older brother and a world-class competitive sailor. For nearly forty years he's been racing 505's and other demanding sailboats.

Sailing is supposed to be mind-numbingly boring as a spectator sport. "Like watching grass grow," they say. Not Howard's kind of sailing. I watched him race off the Denmark coast when we were in our twenties and again off Cape Cod when we were in our forties, and more recently back in California when he was in his early sixties, as he is now. Nobody races his sorts of boats at our age. It takes too much stamina, fortitude, muscle power, endurance. It's just too hard. Not for Howard. He flies down to Australia every winter—their summer—to race skiffs in Sydney Harbour, and then competes in another regatta on Lake Garda in Italy or off the coast of France, practicing in the waters back home in Southern California.

These boats go so fast they are more likely to tip end over end, tripping over a wave bow first, like a kid doing a cartwheel, rather than tip over on their side (guess what a mess that would make of the rigging).

Howard has brought those same speed-racing skiffs to San Francisco Bay for a regatta every year, where spectators can watch the boats plane across the water, racing under the Golden Gate and past Alcatraz. I love the photos of Howard—or Howie, as his fellow sailors call him—hiking so far out in his wet suit that only his toes touch the edge of the boat, his body parallel to the bay. Imagine the sort of strength it takes to do that well or how much pummeling your joints absorb over the years, your knees like rubber bands. It's certainly taken its toll on his body. He doesn't go out of the house without doing forty-five minutes of stretches and exercises every morning. That's what it takes to keep him vertical.

In our family we joke about Howard's high pain threshold and his tireless athleticism. We like to repeat his once-made claim: "If I don't sail or surf or ski I'll develop lower back pain within twenty-four hours" ("Hey, Howard, for most of us it's the other way around"), or we remember the time he told his wife, Julie, after she suggested that maybe they didn't need to drive up to the Sierras to ski for the umpteenth weekend in a row: "Julie, if we don't go this weekend, it'll be lost. You can't make it up." *You can't make it up.* You can't. One time he broke his pelvis skiing in the Sierras and still hobbled on board his flight home, walking into his doctor's office the next day. "You shouldn't even be standing," the doctor declared after studying the X-ray.

Howard has a small real-estate business with an office in Huntington Beach, close enough to the beach so that he can surf for an hour before work. This is his meditation time, as essential to him as my sitting on the couch every morning with my eyes closed. He stares at the incoming waves, sizing them up in the wind or fog, riding the right one, getting connected with God's creation.

Howard was sailing on the East Coast when I landed in the hospital, competing in the North American championship of 505's. He e-mailed Carol and said, "I want to talk."

She called him from the garden courtyard of the hospital, outside when she was taking a break. Howard wanted to know exactly what was going on, and Carol spelled it out, straight-forward. "OK," he said, "I'm coming to help out." He didn't ask, he told her. It was a done deal.

He won the North Americans in Annapolis, as he's won the title seven times before, more than anyone else—something that didn't register with me till many months later—and then he flew up to be with us in New York. I don't know what he did with his boat or what sort of penalty he had to pay to change his flight. He just appeared.

On Monday he walked into my hospital room. "Hey, Howie," I said.

"Hey. How are you?"

"Not great." Pause. "But getting better. I'm getting better."

"Good."

That's the world Howard lives in, akin to the world we were raised in, one of abiding optimism, an inheritance from our parents, especially our sunny-tempered mom. Things are always meant to get better. Hope was in the smoggy, sun-burned Southern California air we breathed.

Howard sat by my bed for three days, relieving Carol of that duty so she could unwind in the gym at least once or twice and not rush to my bedside at the crack of dawn. He could take in what the doctors were saying, ask questions about what tests they wanted to give me, write down notes on what they said and share it with Carol.

But he also just sat there. He was probably doing some work on his computer or phone, in between the doctor visits. It might sound counterintuitive that an adrenaline junkie like Howard could be so good at sitting, but he is. I was reminded of how he sat by our father's bed, holding Dad's hand for hours, when Dad was dying. I needed to get up and move around. Howard could just sit.

It took me back to our childhood, all those years that Howard and I had shared a bedroom.

That room was a converted garage, the sliding glass doors opening up to the driveway, convenient for sneaking out at night. We could go upstairs and tell Mom and Dad, "I'm home," and then go right back out without having to escape through some upstairs window. Howard could also bring in his mini-bikes and go-cart for the night, the faint whiff of gasoline the room's abiding scent. His bed was next to an old rolltop desk, and mine next to an upright piano with tacks on the hammers so it gave a honky-tonk tone when I played "Maple Leaf Rag."

I remember him sitting up in that bed in the early morning of a February day in 1971 when the Sylmar earthquake rattled the Southland, rumbling underground like a roadster, rousing us from sleep.

"Bitchin'," he said. "An earthquake!"

(*Bitchin'* was surfer slang for "cool" or "neat" or "far out.")

A disaster was not to be dreaded but celebrated, a break in the norm, maybe offering up the possibility of canceled classes like snow days, something not regularly afforded Southern Californians.

He was right in his hope that school would be canceled for the day, but for some reason afternoon rehearsals for the high school musical were not. I was in the musical; he was not.

We were as different as two brothers could be. Howard was risk taking and physical; mechanically adept, he never met a gadget he didn't want to take apart. I was bookish and musical, memorizing the lyrics to every original Broadway cast album I could buy.

As a kid he liked building forts in the back forty and digging deep holes for lighting bonfires. I stood by with a cupful of water as though I could halt the blaze if any sparks flew. I put on plays in the backyard, casting the neighbors in productions of "Rumpelstiltskin" and "Snow White," the Seven Dwarves singing "Heigh-ho, heigh-ho" as they marched down through the camellias from their "mines" up by Howard's tree house. He wouldn't have considered taking a role in my amateur productions—nor would I have asked—but he made a curtain that could actually be raised and lowered in the gazebo we used for our stage, a foreshadowing of his talent for rigging sailboats.

We talked at night before going to bed, staring up at the gray ceiling. When he fell madly in love in high school—more than once—he'd sneak out that sliding glass door and then return later, exclaiming to his younger brother, "You don't know what it's like." I would find out.

We would enshrine our loved ones' front yard with streams of toilet paper, fluttering from bushes and trees as a sign of our not-so-secret devotion. Getting "t.p.-ed" was a singular honor. One night I was privileged to join Howard on such an escapade, dodging a cop car, running away from a father's flashlight. How to explain the allure of a roll of t.p. shooting through the branches of an oak tree in the lamplight, leaving a streak of white tail, then landing in the grass with a dull thud? Those thuds were something you listened for as you hurled the toilet paper into the trees. I could still hear them now in a hospital bed, taking comfort in the memory of a less dangerous time.

No, that's not fair. There were all sorts of dangers back then, the risk of having your heart broken (what if the girl didn't want to be t.p.-ed?), the real possibility that you'd humiliate yourself in the high school musical, the potential for the next earthquake to be ten times worse, bringing down the house around you.

"That reminds me," I wanted to say. I wanted to retell my favorite Howard story from childhood. There was no need to, of course. He knew the story; I knew it. And he knows how funny I think it is, how it cracks me up every time I tell it. But we didn't have to talk. We could just be with each other. The best hospital visitor is someone who doesn't need much talking, who doesn't require any entertaining, and yet you can say to him or her a thousand things in silence, and they'll get every word.

Of all the backyard forts Howard built, the most elaborate had an elevator that was meant to take you to the third or fourth floor. The whole thing was a rickety concoction of refrigerator boxes (where did we get those?), old fencing, two-by-fours, and plywood sheets, a recycled lumberyard. It probably wasn't the skyscraper it is in my mind's eye. It couldn't have been more than eight or nine feet tall (it was probably less) because it would have towered over the back fence, calling for an inspection from the fire marshal. In fact, I don't know why Mom and Dad never saw it or came to tear it down. Maybe because they were busy enough with the four of us kids, all two years apart. Maybe because one of the best gifts they gave us in a pre-"helicopter parent" era was to love us by leaving us alone.

Upon completion of this masterpiece Howard wanted to get the elevator to work and he wanted to be the first one to ride it to the top floor. The elevator car was basically a crate with a rope attached, thrown over a beam at the top of the fort.

"Pull," Howard said. He sat in the box, and I pulled the rope. The crate didn't budge.

"Pull harder," Howard said. I pulled with all my strength. Nothing.

He went over to our next door neighbor's house and grabbed a cohort. The two of us pulled. We jiggled the crate a little bit, but we still weren't strong enough to raise it all the way. We needed more manpower. Howard knocked on more doors and got some more willing accomplices. We gathered around the rope. "Pull!" he shouted to all of us. We grabbed hold and pulled and pulled and pulled. Howard rose slowly in the air, the elevator bumping against his skyscraper. He smiled triumphantly at us, the builder enjoying the view.

He finally reached the top and sat there in the crate for a moment, the lord of all he surveyed. Just then the fort wobbled a bit, and then wobbled some more. "Hold on to the rope," Howard said.

We held on to the rope.

But we couldn't stop the shaking. Walls ballooned out, beams started bending, there was a cracking sound, some flimsy boards breaking, and then a terrible shuddering. Sawdust flew in the air, refrigerator cardboard crumbled. The whole

Tower of Babel came crashing down, the rope flying through our fingers, Howard plummeting to the earth, his fort landing around him and on top of him.

We scrambled out of the way and then raced back, lifting up boards and two-by-fours, searching for Howard, fearing the worst, certain to find his corpse. I don't think he was older than fourth or fifth grade, which would have put me in first or second. He'd already broken his arm once by then, and had had his tonsils taken out, and had to be taken in an ambulance from school when he'd fallen on his throat, jumping from bench to bench in the playground, almost strangling himself. What would an ambulance do now when they came to pick him up? What could they do with a dead body?

We finally dug him out and came upon him sitting on the ground with the crate on top of him, the rope at his feet. But he wasn't dead at all. He was laughing, laughing so hard he couldn't stop.

"Howard, you could have killed yourself," one of the older, wiser neighborhood boys said.

"But I didn't," he said, still laughing. That was Howard, the miracle kid, walking away from disaster, laughing.

I could still see that look on his face when the fort was starting to tremble, and all of us were clutching that rope. Sheer terror. And yet he'd survived.

Yes, Rick, you will get out of here. Yes, Rick, you will get well. No, that notion you had of getting better, that wasn't just a phantom. That promise was real. You feel rotten right now, and breathing is still hard when you run a fever, but it won't always be that way. Look how far you've come already. Look at the progress you've made. I couldn't hold on to that promise without help.

"For I was hungry and you gave me food, I was thirsty and you gave me something to drink, I was a stranger and you welcomed me, I was naked and you gave me clothing, I was sick and you cared for me…," Jesus said. That is the gift of the hospital visitor, to give your true self back to you. Howard, Carol, the boys, Scott—they all did that.

"I WAS SICK AND YOU VISITED ME." Those words were on a plaque outside the care facility where my father died, where Howard had sat by that bed for hours.

Both Howard and Carol were there to hear an exchange between two of my doctors.

First there was the arrival of an older specialist I had never met, white-haired and distinguished looking even in his untailored white coat. He had a team of younger fellows with him, and I was, evidently, exhibit X, to be poked and prodded and questioned. They were standing at the head of my bed, beginning their inspection, when at the foot of my bed Dr. Ravalli arrived, my beloved Italian cardiologist. Apparently they knew each other.

"Hello," Dr. Ravalli said.

"Hi, babe," said the distinguished-looking specialist.

Hi, babe? Did he really say that? All three of us heard it, "babe," about as politically incorrect a nomenclature as can be, except, I suppose, when given to another man of the same age.

Many weeks later I asked Dr. Ravalli, "Did he really call you 'babe?'"

"Yes," Dr. Ravalli confessed.

"Is it short for 'Beppe' or something?"

"No, it's just what he calls me."

"Why?" I asked.

Dr. Ravalli shook his head, baffled by the mysteries of American slang and the English language. "I don't know," he said. "I really don't know."

Sept. 22, 4:28 p.m.

Oh my gosh, friends, what you've missed! You might think our days in the hospital are tranquil and lacking in incident but you would be so wrong.

Yesterday was a discouraging day: bad fever in the night and dramatic shortness of breath during the day. I was bummed. But it also provided great entertainment. There was the Fellow Smackdown: when the Pulmonology Fellow left the room to get a portable CT scan cart and returned to find his space at Rick's side occupied by the Infectious Diseases Fellow. They both puffed up their chests and exchanged ranks: "I'm Pulmonology." "I'm ID." ID won, I think because he was leading rounds later that afternoon and was going to use R. for an exhibit. Fortunately I missed that.

Then there was a far more civilized exchange later on when a Very Senior Specialist arrived with a team. This was an elder statesman who spoke directly to Rick and to me, and his school of pilot fish stayed mute, which is the way I like them. Then at the door I spied our Beloved Cardiologist, who entered beaming. He and Senior Specialist knew each other: they exchanged a nod and a handshake, and I had the sense of many words Not Being Spoken. I swear, and witnesses back me up, that Specialist said to Cardio, "Hi, babe," which was very odd between two 60-plus men. But it was like watching two

Mafia dons meeting at a niece's wedding, conveying affectionate respect for each other.

And this morning, Rick actually walked down the hall without supplemental oxygen. (It trailed behind in its green tank, unused.) This, my dears, is immense. The normal amount of oxygen in "room air" is 21%, and from it our healthy lungs extract enough of the important stuff to bring the saturation in our blood to a robust, say, 95% or more. Take a breath. Think about that. Last week Rick was getting forced oxygen at 60% and his saturation rate dipped into the 80s sometimes. So we hit a milestone today.

Yet—lest the mystery aspect of the tale peter out into nothing at all, I present to you: the rash. It appeared this morning. All over his body, except for his face. I think this should be catnip to ID, but it may also bring in another specialist, because surely Dermatology wants in on this party, right? Oh, wait, newsflash from CPMC: Derm says reaction to Nexium. Seems kind of dull to me.

Rick is still too weak for visitors. He had two yesterday and they almost did him in. He just doesn't have the stamina yet to keep a social ball in the air, and you know how important that is to him.

Also, I think we can be sure the prayers are working because the medical community in all its complex glory appears still to be flying blind. So don't stop now.

Lots of love from both of us, Carol

CHAPTER ELEVEN

Hospital, Day 11

I wasn't up to reading Carol's e-mails but I know she had made a point of letting people know that visitors were still discouraged. When she was there two arrived at the same time, strangers to each other: Albert, an eighty-something neighbor of ours, and Edgar, a dapper ninety-five-year-old fellow worshipper. Originally from Barbados, Edgar's been a member of our church since the mid-'60s. When our boys were growing up, he was like a grandfather to them, always ready for high fives at coffee hour.

Edgar knows the whole hymnal by heart, and a couple of months earlier, when a bout of pneumonia landed him in the hospital, I'd gone to visit him on a Sunday afternoon, and we'd sung a few hymns together, savoring the sweetness of the music and the memory of worship, bringing church into the ward. But I couldn't sing now, not a note. I couldn't get enough breath to sustain a phrase.

Edgar sat in a chair opposite me, and then Albert came in and sat in another chair next to him. I could imagine making some sort of introduction: "Edgar, this is Albert. He teaches math at a college. In years that most devote to the leisure of retirement, he teaches a couple classes." "Albert, this is our friend Edgar, a pillar of our church. He used to work for Horn & Hardart, the old automat. Remember that?"

They sat in silence, and I sat in silence. I closed my eyes and opened them. They were still there. "This is a kind thing they are doing," I could tell myself. This was prayer in action.

Accept it, enjoy it, appreciate it. But I was chagrined, embarrassed. I couldn't be the Rick Hamlin I wanted to be, the gregarious person I once was, the extrovert in action.

A friend who does pastoral care on the oncology ward of the same hospital described to me what I was going through. "Rick Hamlin had left the room. Someone else was in bed." I wanted to call that person an impostor, but that person was me as much as I am me.

Is this why tribulation is supposed to be such a good teacher? We have lost one self and haven't gained a new self yet. We are wandering in the desert. We are like Nicodemus, visiting Jesus in the middle of the night, under the cover of darkness, afraid of being seen. And what does Jesus tell us? That we need to be born anew, born of the spirit. We can't do that until we let go of that old self.

I could look out the window and see the building where a good friend had his office, a psychiatrist who runs a program at Columbia University. I could have e-mailed him and told him where I was. "Hey, Robert, guess where I am? Guess what I can see out my window? Guess who is the patient on the sixth floor being visited by every specialist you know and don't know on the Columbia-Presbyterian staff so they can check out his mystery ailment and be the one with the right answer?" Robert's a doctor. Of all people, he would understand my situation.

But I never e-mailed him.

I like to think I'm comfortable with vulnerability, my own vulnerability. I don't have a tough-guy persona. I'm not a stiff-upper-lip type. I thrive on compassion—or so I say—but maybe that's because I don't want to be the patient, don't want to be the recipient of such compassion. I want to be in charge.

I want to set the scene and stage for vulnerability, control it, manage it, present it. I can be honest about all sorts of faults when I'm the writer, but then I'm putting all the bread crumbs out, dropping them in a line that will lead to the conclusion I have chosen. I wasn't in charge in a hospital bed.

My visitors left. I said good-bye to them, and they said good-bye to me. I picked up my Kindle to find a Bible quote, scrolling through verses. It would have been easier to search for it on my laptop. "All who want to save their lives will lose them. But all who lose their lives because of me will save them."

Is it possible that you have to be Nicodemus more than once in your life? You have to sneak out in the dark to listen for wisdom that you thought you already knew. You were the wise man, the rabbi, the Pharisee, but then along comes some greater wisdom, and at least you have the wisdom to recognize it even if you're not ready to welcome it in the full light of day. You can only take this halfway step to sit at the feet of the man who is lit by the glow of his own greater knowledge.

This is the scarier part of being in the hospital, not the body-dying part but the soul-struggling part, letting go of the old you, waiting for some new you that doesn't seem like it could ever find you in this place of drugs, tests, beeping monitors, meals on trays, experts coming and going. You need to be born from above, born anew, born when you thought you were going to die.

Would I ever sing again? Maybe that was one of those things I would have to give up, losing that part of myself. Perhaps I needed to mourn that, all those moments of song. I could find them on my phone, recorded not so long ago. I could log on to Facebook and see them, listen to them, remembering who I once was.

God has given me a lifeline in music, opening me up, straightening me out, making the rough places plain, quieting my soul even as I make noise. Not for nothing does singing the blues put me in the pink. Even sad songs can make sadness bearable, putting thoughts into words and music. A song is a way to remember a text, the brain holding on to what's glued to it by rhythm and tune. Surely the ancient poets chanted the verses of their epic poems because it was easier to remember them that way.

I still find myself humming a high-speed version of the A-B-C song just to be sure that W comes after U and V. Short and long passages of Scripture are only retrievable because someone set them to music. "O clap your hands, all ye people. Shout unto God with the voice of triumph," I sing to myself, with thanks to Ralph Vaughan Williams, who gave me the tune. "The Lord's my shepherd, I'll not want," is set in my head to a melody called "Brother James's Air." Jesus might have said, "I am the bread of life," but the moment I see those words I start humming a hymn that doesn't always scan but always brings us to our feet at church.

In honor of turning sixty I posted a song a day for sixty days on Facebook, videos I took on my phone. I didn't overthink it, for better or for worse. A colleague at the office wanted me to hold off for a week or two, just to do more promotion. I was more afraid that if I didn't jump in—jumping in the deep end—I would never do it. I began on a Friday in May, without any list. "In honor of my sixtieth birthday this year I'm singing sixty songs in sixty days. Here's the first one."

At once I was committed. A promise is a promise. Sixty might prove to be a bigger number than I thought, perhaps a reminder that living for sixty years was longer than I remembered.

The first song, "Precious Lord," I recorded near my office on Fulton Street, with the Freedom Tower in the background—would people notice? I did two takes and that was it. I planned to record each song in a different spot in the city, giving them different settings. It would become a sort of tour of my life. If Gene Kelly and Frank Sinatra could sing "New York, New York, it's a wonderful town" all over the city, couldn't I? It's not like I was shy about singing in public. I'd embarrassed my children enough over the years by breaking out in song in unexpected places.

I remember once being on the A train, heading for work, and hearing an Afro-Caribbean woman singing "Holy, Holy, Holy" as she made her way down the car. She might have been passing out tracts too—I have a soft spot for anyone handing out tracts—but her intention was in the music: "Lord, God, Almighty, early in the morning our song shall rise to Thee." I knew the words well but I didn't recognize the tune. Was it something from the islands?

"How does that go?" I asked her. "Holy, holy, holy" she resumed, and I sang along. To the amusement or irritation of the other commuters? I don't really know. We were having fun with our music. "Do you know this version?" I asked, singing a few bars, and then I had to get off at my stop, not without getting blessed by her, which was as sweet as any song we might have sung.

Subway tunnels are good for singing, but I soon discovered how noisy New York is, the din of traffic and air conditioners and jets overhead competing with my music. It was fun to record "Moon River" outside of Tiffany's in honor of Audrey Hepburn, but the passing buses gave me a lot of competition.

Same problem with "Give My Regards to Broadway" on the corner of Forty-Second and Broadway.

My repertoire is dated. I would be hard-pressed to pull up a tune written in the new millennium. I know vintage Broadway from singing along to stacks of original cast albums; I've absorbed the American Songbook through cocktail pianists and elevator Muzak; I've wallowed in hymns from the time of my birth, but any pop or rock I know was mostly picked up listening to the radio while driving the LA freeways in Mom's old Buick station wagon. My moment of would-be stardom in a rock band lasted for only one rehearsal in seventh grade, when the budding impresario realized that not only did I lack the chops and the keyboard skills, but I was clueless on the style.

That said, coming up with a song a day was easy. There are tons of them in my head. I posted first thing in the morning with something I'd recorded the previous day, never planning too far ahead lest I intimidate myself, or get so overwhelmed I'd want to give up. I was touched by the enthusiasm of friends and followers, their comments making me smile. I changed venues as often as possible but kept coming back to the subway tunnel for the acoustics, often choosing it for favorite old hymns, like "How Great Thou Art" and "Great Is Thy Faithfulness."

I came back again for "What a Friend We Have in Jesus."

I walked down to the end of the Brooklyn-bound J-Z platform. Any moment a train would be coming. You could tell from how many people were waiting. New Yorkers have a sixth sense about crowds on subway platforms. A crowded platform can be good news—"Oh, good, the train should be coming soon"—until it becomes bad news—"Oh drat, there must be some mess-up or delay, because the platform is way too crowded, and my train will probably be cramped, or I might not even get on…"

This was good news. The train rumbled in, and everybody stepped on. There was no other train to take at this platform, nothing else coming down the track. I waited for the noise of the departing subway to disappear down the tunnel, then held up my phone to record "What a friend we have in Jesus/All our sins and griefs to bear/What a privilege to carry/Everything to God in prayer…" (Best comment came from a Birmingham, Alabama, friend who said she couldn't quite recognize the lyrics without their usual Southern twang.) I botched it once and then tried again.

I was halfway through this second take—or maybe it was the third—when I heard someone whistling. The platform was filling up. The next train would be coming. *That guy whistling is really going to ruin this take. I'm going to have to do it all over again*, I told myself. Then I listened a little more closely. He was whistling with me. He was whistling the tune, "Have we trials and temptations/Is there trouble anywhere…?" My partner in crime, my partner in harmony, he was right there with me.

I still messed up a lyric in one place, but this one was too good to redo. I finished up and called out on the platform, "Who was whistling?" I looked both ways. A guy in a yellowish shirt waved his hand at the far front end.

"Thanks," I said. "That was terrific."

When I watched the video I could see him, in his yellowish shirt, walking right behind me to his spot on the platform where he began tuning in.

It made me happy. The whole thing made me happy, all my griefs to bear, a way out of trouble anywhere.

I found a new use for my phone in the hospital. I began taking photos of all my caregivers: the doctors, the nurses, the techs, the janitors, the woman who brought my meals.

"I'm not going to post this picture," I said. "I just want it for me."

There was Infectious Diseases, with his stethoscope looped over the back of his neck, and the night nurse, with two name tags, and my beloved Jay with "RN" in red letters on his white shirt, and the Chinese nurse at the nurses' station who didn't want to have her photo taken at all. She distrusted the whole project. The bearded PT is wearing plastic gloves and green surgicals in my photo. We'd just come back from a walk. "I need to get a picture of your colleague," I told him, "the one who walked with me for the first time." Had she met and found the man of her dreams in the few days since we'd last talked?

Dermatology is wearing a regimental tie, the food lady has a black sweater and a sweet smile. I have two shots of The Attending in her white coat, her hands flying as she talks. Earnest and tireless, she saw me twice a day, even on weekends. You can see the clock on the wall behind the chatty intern who visited me almost every day; it says four thirty. The resident, with his hipster beard, is giving me the thumbs-up. All these shots are taken from the patient's point of view. They remind me of the photos four-year-old Tim took with a throwaway camera when he was lying in traction for twenty-six days, trapped in bed but looking up at one friend or caregiver after another, a healing brigade pasted in a scrapbook. This would be my record, my gallery.

There was the woman in pulmonology who reminded me of a travel agent, and the nurse from San Diego whose father was a cardiologist. She has the clearest of blue eyes and the whitest of blonde hair. She came to New York to study nursing because all she wanted in life was to be a nurse at a big hospital like Presbyterian, and here she is.

When the nurse's assistant came in to take my vitals I asked, "Will you let me take your picture?"

"Why?"

"So I can remember the people who helped me."

"You've got to let me fix my hair and makeup first." *Did she blush?*

She came back a few hours later. Frankly I couldn't detect a shade of difference, but she did a shimmying dance for my camera. The janitor came by, collecting trash, and I took his picture, to his surprise. "These aren't for Facebook or Instagram," I said. "They're just for me."

Like I said, I had always promised myself when Timothy was in the hospital that we would go back and thank the staff. We never did. Once you're out and well you don't want to go back. Ever. I was wiser this time. I wouldn't come back to 6 Garden North and South willingly. But I would carry the people with me the way I carried songs with me. Not just in my head but in my phone.

September 24, 9:24 p.m.

New idea here. I'm thinking that maybe framing Rick's illness as linear narrative was a mistake. Events seem to be too loose and baggy for that. Here's what popped into my head yesterday after a deeply annoying snafu: Rick and I are on the Elderhostel trip nobody wants to take.

Just imagine the listings in that catalog and you can see the qualities in this offering that would drive people away:

1/duration. Way too long. We're heading toward two weeks in the hospital, during which we could have bicycled all over Iceland, I imagine.

2/cost. Nuff said.

3/food. Actually, Rick eats some of it, to keep his strength up. Ew.

4/surroungings. I understand Elderhostels are sometimes rustic, but institutional medical architecture circa 1982...No.

Remember the rash? It got itchy! All over his body, all night long! Dermatology did show up, bringing our roster of medical disciplines to six. He fasted all night Tuesday prior to having a TEE (sonogram, esophagus, better picture of heart; Cardio ordered it) and they screwed up so he didn't have it after 12 hours hungry and thirsty. However he was just taken downstairs for it this morning. Had a CT scan of his abdomen (looking for enlarged lymph nodes) at 1:00 a.m. Possibly looking for TB, for which there is no blood test. Which I didn't know. So that was an educational nugget.

Good news is more walking all over the floor, without oxygen, and I believe no fever yesterday. He's getting better, though still a long way from well. So still no visitors and we're still not answering phones. As ever, feel free to forward this to other concerned friends.

Lots of love to all of you from the whole Hamlin family. If we didn't feel your support and prayers, this episode would be no joking matter.

CHAPTER TWELVE

Hospital, Days 12 and 13

I was right. My inner voice had spoken the truth. I was going to get out of the hospital. It was going to happen. I didn't know when, but soon. I still had a rash, which baffled the doctors—Dermatology was my newest friend. I was incredibly weak, skinnier than I'd ever been, down to 133 pounds. I looked sepulchral in the bathroom mirror, my cheeks sunken, dark circles beneath my eyes. But at least I was able to go to the bathroom by myself, no bedpans, no buzzing for a nurse. I didn't have an IV attached to me twenty-four hours a day. They'd taken me off the regular heart monitor. I didn't need supplementary oxygen anymore. The maddening fevers were diminishing. Still no diagnosis, but did I need a diagnosis if I was getting better? Couldn't I be that mystery patient who was sick and then got better?

Jesus said with faith we can move mountains. "I assure you that whoever says to this mountain, 'Be lifted up and thrown into the sea'—and doesn't waver but believes that what is said will really happen—it will happen. Therefore I say to you, whatever you pray and ask for, believe that you will receive it, and it will be so for you." That's the sort of faith I can never find for myself, but now it occurred to me: It isn't something you do for yourself. It's a gift you're given, God's grace.

Glenn appeared at the hospital one of those last days. Glenn is an old college friend. We'd sung a cappella together on campus. He still lives in New Jersey and drove in to see me. "I can't believe you came all this way," I said.

Glenn is a musician, a poet, and a computer entrepreneur. He's also a prayer person. "Mom's praying for you," he said. "And Aunt Myra." Aunt Myra was a longtime *Guideposts* reader.

The sun was setting, and I wanted to see it. "Let's go for a walk," I said. There was no view of the river from my room.

We walked farther on the sixth floor than I had ever walked before, leaving the safe confines of my ward and entering another. Here, you could see the Hudson River and the George Washington Bridge without any obstructions.

A barge cut through the water, pushed by a tugboat. The rush hour traffic rumbled across the bridge, slower out than in. Life was going on. I needed to reenter it. It was like taking a big breath before you dive into a cold lake on a hot day. You know you need to do it; you know you'll be glad of it. But you linger on dry land, waiting, taking more than one big breath, wondering if you're ready.

"They have a much better view here," Glenn said, "than you do on your side of the building."

"They do," I said.

He brought me a book, *Good Poems for Hard Times*, edited by Garrison Keillor. I wished Glenn had brought me one of his own poems. We sat in the lounge that faced the river, the September sunlight bathing the room. How many such beautiful days had I missed from here? How could I recover them all? I thought of Howard's infamous words, "You can't make it up."

This time wouldn't be lost forever. I was determined to make it count for something. Even doing nothing can be a blessing. "Wasting time with God," Tim calls it. Sitting with an old friend in a hospital lounge, ignoring the rash itching beneath the hospital gown, clinging to the promise of returning health, believing in healing, wanting to trust it.

There weren't many other patients there or family members.

"What is this ward for?" I asked a nurse.

"Oncology," she said.

Glenn and I looked at each other. Oncology got the better view. They needed it. But then, didn't we?

Jim showed up, another college friend and former roommate. He lives down in DC. I couldn't figure out how he managed to be at the hospital. "I had a business trip up here," he said. "And my interview this afternoon got canceled. I figured that was a sign that I was meant to come visit you."

When he worked in New York we used to have lunch once a month. In addition to talking about our jobs and families, we talked about our faith. For a buttoned-up lawyer, he has a surprising, winsome, childlike love of God and an enthusiasm for Scripture. Wherever he is, he always finds some Bible study to join. That would be like him, to see this chance to visit me as a sign.

"Your timing is a little off," I said. I was lying on a gurney, being wheeled off to another floor for another test, a transesophageal echocardiogram or a TEE, to get a better view of my heart. I didn't like the idea of them putting a tube down my esophagus, but if it helped in coming up with a diagnosis, I would do it. I would do anything. "I've got to do a test. I haven't eaten for hours. Have to do it on an empty stomach."

The aide started pushing me down the hall.

"I'll come with you," Jim said, walking fast.

It reminded me of the one time I'd visited him in his hometown of Kalamazoo, Michigan. He and his dad met me at the bus station on a cold November day. We had only a half hour before we had to head back to Princeton. "Let me show you the town," his dad said, looking at his watch. "We'll run."

And we did, jogging through the empty streets of downtown Kalamazoo on a Sunday morning to see the sights.

Jim was almost jogging now, making the most of the time we had. Life was precious, not a moment to waste. Who knew when we'd see each other again and under what circumstances? You jogged with your friend down bright halls, answering his questions about the kids, work, and Bible study.

Jim stayed with me till the last minute, until I was rolled into a cold, dimly lit room that made me think of the OR when I'd had heart surgery.

"Would you like a blanket?" they asked.

"Please." This was like the blanket they gave me in the OR right before heart surgery because I was freezing, my teeth chattering. I knew back then that they'd take it off as soon as the anesthesia took hold, as soon as they could "stretch" the sternum and saw through it, as soon as they put me on the heart-lung machine. But until then we could act as though I were an old man in winter, sitting on a park bench, needing a blanket to stay warm.

Pam came the last night I was in the hospital. Carol had left, and I'd finished dinner. It was getting dark outside and surely time for her to go home and have dinner with Jeff, her husband, but she stayed.

I wanted to know how her sons were doing.

She asked me about our boys.

I wanted to know about how her work was—she's a documentary filmmaker and her latest project sounded interesting.

She asked me if I was writing anything particular before I landed in the hospital.

I wanted to know what Jeff was doing.

She asked about Carol.

We've known each other almost forty years. Carol says she is the only one of our friends who manages to get us to talk more about ourselves than anyone else. That must be some achievement, but it says more to me about her powers of listening. We met senior year in college when she sang with the women's a cappella group at Harvard, the Radcliffe Pitches, and I sang with the Princeton Footnotes, and we had a concert together. Then she was a neighbor in Washington Heights when our boys were first born. She showed up in the middle of the night to be with William while we rushed to the hospital to await the birth of Tim.

We'd celebrated Thanksgivings together year after year.

"What if I can't do some of the things I used to be able to do?" I asked.

"Like what?"

"Running."

"In time."

"Singing."

"Can you sing now?"

I shook my head. My voice was hoarse from the TEE, that tube down my throat.

How much was I willing to bargain with God? Was I ready for some horse-trading? I had my life. I'd come closer to death than anybody would like, but I was still alive, still kicking, breathing. I would get to go home. "You've given me my life back, God, but what kind of life is it going to be?"

Recovery from heart surgery had been different from this. As soon as possible they'd had me up and walking around the ward. The physical therapist took me up and down steps even in the hospital. When I was released to go home after heart surgery the instructions were: Walk, walk, walk and walk some more. No naps. Get some exercise. It was push, push, push.

Now I had to marshal my forces, had to be careful not to go too far. It was rest, rest, rest. My stamina was gone.

"Do they know what you had?" Pam asked.

"No. They're still trying to figure that out. But I got better." My new mantra, the only way I could explain it: the doctors kept me alive, the prayers healed me.

There was a lot more spiritual healing and emotional healing that needed to happen, my psyche and soul catching up to what Western medicine had done for my body. The old me was gone. I couldn't trust my body anymore the way I once had. Would I always be second-guessing it? Would every slight cough or cold, would the smallest fever scare me into thinking that I was going to land in the hospital again, unable to breathe?

I didn't want to live in fear. I would have to keep working on my faith, dig deeper, love more, trust more, let go more. All of it would have to come by the grace of God because the doing wasn't going to do it.

Pam left. I was alone in the night, the breathing of my hospital roommate coming through the curtain. I had to wait for the night nurse to check me out one last time and then I could sleep—attempt to sleep, really, because I never slept well in the hospital.

The old Rick Hamlin was gone. The new Rick had to be rejiggered and remade. Re-hatched. "Born from above," as the Bible puts it.

With Carol's help I crafted a letter to the staff, and she printed it up so the head nurse would have a copy in her files. "To the staff at 6 Garden North...

"In the nearly two weeks that I was a patient I was continually touched by your passion for your work. Whether you were cleaning the floors (bravo, Peter) or taking someone's vitals or listening for a heartbeat, a job was never sloppily or casually done."

This would be a way to move forward, living with gratitude, gratitude every minute.

"You were great at listening to questions, answering them whenever possible, getting more information if necessary. You rely on machines because they are necessary, but never did I feel that someone was looking over my head at my 'numbers' rather than at me, the person in the bed."

I didn't want it to sound fawning, but authentic, from the heart. Someone once told me that the most important thing to put in any thank-you note were details, so that you didn't sound vague. Easy enough in this case.

"You also seem to like each other and respect each other. I liked hearing you greet each other and laugh with each other. When people like each other, you like being with them. That creates a healing environment."

Maybe that's why I felt so lonely at night. I didn't get to hear other voices, didn't get that sense that life was still moving forward. It was just me in my hospital bed.

"You work for a huge organization, but to my amazement, I didn't feel like a cog in a wheel, a paper that needs to be moved around from desk to desk. This must take enormous work on your behalf, because there is surely much paperwork that must be done. But you made me feel that I was a person, not a number.

"You have many patients to care for. I am grateful that I was one of them. I hope I don't ever have to come back as a patient again, but if I do, I would be grateful to be among you again."

OK, that last line wasn't completely accurate. I wouldn't EVER want to be a patient. Never again.

Sept. 25, 6:56 p.m.

And then, poof! We're home. Just like that. Well, there was a glitch, of course, not just the usual paperwork but at the last minute we were held up a couple of hours because Rick needed to be given a last-ditch set of pills for scabies, of all things, which someone on the floor has. Scabies, which in animals is called "mange." Lest he come from the hospital mangy.

We spent some time this morning with the extraordinary attending doctor who was in overall charge, trying to formulate what this was. Here's what she came up with:

"Respiratory failure and severe systemic inflammation caused by idiopathic infection." I.e., Rick got really really sick and nobody knows why. We did add one more specialty to our roster of the medical disciplines when an allergist came in this morning to discuss The Rash and its possible antecedents, but she was such a late entrant and the symptom was so comparatively minor that she didn't have a chance of ownership. Rick will follow up with pulmonology and his internist.

He went around the floor this last couple of days taking pictures of the people who have taken care of him. They were thrilled—this was clearly a novelty. And we have now a little album of smiling faces. We grew very, very fond of these people: docs, cleaners, aides, nurses, therapists, med students. If you need to be gravely ill, try to get onto 6 Garden North at Columbia-Presbyterian.

Your own smiling faces, your thoughts, your prayers, your food and your cards and your chocolate and well-wishes and flowers have all kept us afloat. And you praying people can now slip in one more prayer—of thanksgiving. We don't expect much in the way of long-term issues, though the worriers among us will be sure to keep that eventuality covered.

Rick can now communicate directly, so go to it, folks, I'm bowing out. But not without one additional story.

A nursing student friend of ours came to see us when Rick was still in the step-down unit on heavy-duty oxygen. She figured out very quickly, she said, that he was the favorite on the floor. So much so that when she left the room, one of the younger nurses asked, "Is he famous?" And she said firmly, "Yes."

We've spent a lot of time in the last two weeks with people who were not as supported as we were. So at the end of this two weeks, here's how we feel:

Lucky.

Much love,

Carol

CHAPTER THIRTEEN

Home

W rite about Italy." That was my prescription. "Remember your experience in Italy. Recall the time. Recover it, immerse yourself in it, dream about it, see it again. Remember the people and the place. Put the words down."

I was home, but with very little energy. Stamina had gone out the window. I didn't know if I'd ever get it back. There was no possibility of putting myself on the subway train and dragging myself into the office, as much as I would have liked that, as much as I yearned to see my colleagues, to sit at my desk, to attack a manuscript that needed fixing, to interview a story subject, to gab in the kitchen with another editor. That would have to wait.

I felt guilty about being home, but bless my dear colleagues, they preempted me and reminded me that I was on sick leave and that I was absolutely not to consider coming in. In e-mails they insisted that I was not to *think* about work until I was really well. I knew I was being read the riot act: "You are Absolutely Forbidden to come to the office until you are so well that there will be no risk of any relapses, Hamlin. Don't push it. Stay put."

What was I to do instead?

First thing in the morning, after sitting in silence for half an hour, after brushing the cat, after cooking myself a bowl of oatmeal and eating it over the opened pages of the *New York Times*, I opened my laptop, sat on Carol's big yellow exercise ball at the dining room table, and wrote about Italy. I was on assignment. I might say that my muse had put me up to it, but really, it was a God thing, a divine command.

I felt rotten. My body still ached. My breathing wasn't up to par. And I was so tired, too tired to concentrate for long on a book. Even Tolkien would have put me to sleep. But I could write and, oddly enough, the writing took me out of myself. It released me from second-guessing about where the aches were coming from and wondering what they meant and fearing that I was plunging down mortality's rabbit hole again.

Italy was the perfect subject. I was once again the twenty-two-year-old kid who landed in London—it was cheap—and took the ferry across the English Channel, heading toward the Continent, imagining I was a modern J. M. W. Turner, tying himself to a mast in the midst of turbulent seas to experience a storm up close—though there was no storm that October day. From France I took a train down to the Italian peninsula, changing trains in Milan and getting into a car that was marked FIRENZE, Florence my final destination. I savored the views: the golden hills of Tuscany framed by gray cypress, dotted with dark green olive trees, crisscrossed with vines, the fruit getting heavy, ready for the harvest.

The landscape hadn't changed in hundreds of years; it looked like the background of some cinquecento portrait of a saint or Jesus sitting on his mother's lap. My guidebook described "the diaphanous light," and even if I didn't know what the word meant, I understood it. God was shading the hills with his own celestial paintbrush.

I didn't know a soul in Florence, had no practical prospects at all, had no idea what I was going to do, but in a matter of days I found friends and a place to live, a church where I could worship and a choir to sing in, and a job as a teacher of English as a foreign language. I ended up staying for two years, singing, teaching, supporting myself, becoming someone new, starting out from scratch on my own.

I began to see the wisdom of this "only-for-me" writing assignment. I was being taken back to a time when I was born anew, forging a new identity as I would have to forge one now. Back then I didn't know enough to be scared, to know how harebrained my "I want to live in Italy" notion was. I just did it, drawing on hidden resources and the grace of God.

Fear was the enemy now, worse than any bodily fatigue. I was glad to be back in my own bed, glad to have Carol next to me, glad to gaze out the bedroom window to the Hudson River and the Palisades beyond, but this spot, this sanctuary, was the very place I had become mortally ill, my temperature rising, the "idiopathic infection" taking hold of me and shattering my self-assured view that death was a long way off. I had been in this bed when my breathing got worse and worse, and my temperature soared until I went off to the ER. I would wake up now in the middle of the night and look at myself just to see if I was still alive, my soul checking on my loud beating heart. I knew without asking that Carol was doing the same thing: looking at me in the middle of the night to see if I was breathing. Was I still here?

I have a friend from church whose husband, after a losing battle with depression, took his own life in their apartment. As she was waiting for the police to finish their inquiry and waiting for the ambulance to take the body, she invited friends to sit with her in the living room. She is a musician, a wonderful

singer, and as stunned and numb as she was from her dev-
astating loss, she started singing hymns and they joined her,
claiming faith in the midst of sorrow. In the weeks and months
that followed she had to teach herself to see her home as the
sanctuary it had always been and not the scene of tragedy. She
even invited a priest to bless the home, like Jesus driving a
demon out of a possessed soul.

Fear was my demon, and I would do all I could to drive it
out, reclaiming the places of my life. Morning after morning I
would sit at my laptop at the dining room table and remember
what it was to be reborn, to start from scratch. It had happened
more than once in my life. It would happen again.

All those friends who had prayed for us, now they showed
their love in an even more tangible fashion. They brought us
food. For weeks we did not have to cook a meal or even go to
the store to buy lunch and dinner. Food simply appeared at
our door.

Word had gone out through our congregation, our apartment complex, our network of friends. FreshDirect or Blue
Apron boxes arrived just when we wondered if we should heat
up the Tupperware leftovers from someone else's generosity
that was still in the fridge. Someone would call and say they
were coming with mac and cheese or a roast or a pizza, and
then also bring soup and sandwiches and some homemade
brownies and a bottle of wine. Whenever possible I was glad
to sit and talk, but nobody stayed for dinner. We were on our
own, and that was good.

My younger sister, Diane, flew out just as I was coming
home, and her presence was a blessing, another adult, another
pair of hands, someone else who could wash the dishes or do

the laundry, jobs I normally never minded doing. But now just to take the trash down two floors to the basement left me winded. No way could I come back up without pausing on the landing halfway there. Would I ever climb those stairs again without running out of breath?

We were flooded with cards and gifts, flowers, books, boxes of chocolate, more wine. I lingered over each card, reading the words to myself, the good wishes the prayers. "One more person who prayed for me," I would think. It was humbling and touching and also embarrassing.

I couldn't take it in, all that kindness, all that warmth and affection and generosity. It was too much.

Invariably I wrote back, sending e-mails or mailing a postcard or note, and then—this sounds so callous and ungracious—I would throw the card away. I'm not sure what the issue was. Was I trying to get myself out of Sick Land? Was I tired of being the patient? Was I ashamed of being vulnerable? Mostly I felt too indebted. I was being given more than I could ever return. I was being told in a million ways how loved and cherished I was, and I couldn't take it.

One day, after going through a stack of cards, sending off e-mails to the givers, I took them to the kitchen wastebasket and paused. *Don't,* I simply told myself. *Rick, keep these. Keep all of them. Not forever. But for now. Receive the love, Rick. It is as rich and unearned and satisfying as God's own love.*

This was who the new Rick was supposed to be. This was how I would be born anew. By knowing that I was loved, incredibly, impossibly, unimaginably, from above and beyond, and from close by in dozens of ways. The stack of cards and notes was to build and build until I could somehow hold the message, the hardest one for me to take in, probably because it would mean letting go of my ego and accepting that who I am is not the result of all my tireless good work and charm. I said it at the beginning of this memoir: "It's not what you do, it's what God does. It's not how hard you try, it's how willing you are not to try."

Believe it, Hamlin. PRAY IT. Take it in.

I began a long series of return visits to my various doctors down at the hospital so they could check on my progress.

The first visit was with my pulmonologist, Dr. DiMango. It was only the first week after I'd been released from the hospital, and Carol and I took the bus down to her office. She was incredibly thorough, as always. We sat with her for a good hour as she logged on to the computer and looked through all of my tests. She turned back to us and gave us the only theory we've gotten of what might have caused this disastrous infection.

"I think you had an allergic reaction to the sulfa drugs you were given."

"The sulfa drugs."

"Yes, what they gave you for the boil on the back of your leg."

"Could I get that sick from an allergic reaction?" I asked.

"Yes," she said, "if it goes unaddressed. It's just a very good thing that you went to the Emergency Room as soon as you did."

One thing we did right.

We thanked her. A couple of weeks later I came back for some tests on my lungs and my breathing. This time I came by myself. "You can always tell they're doing better," she said, "when they come without their spouse."

I laughed.

I saw the Beloved Cardiologist and the Wise Internist, Seth, greeting his office staff with joy. I took their pictures to add to the gallery of caregivers on my phone, although I did not bring back the Columbia-Presbyterian sweatshirt Seth had given me that day I was in his office, shivering from fever.

On all these trips I had a foreboding sense whenever I looked up to the sixth floor of Garden North, my home for those two agonizing weeks. For years this corner of Washington Heights had seemed like sacred ground because it was where our children had been born. I would never forget the joy I'd felt walking that fifteen-block stretch from our hospital to our apartment, filled with the wonder of their births. No more. Newer memories crowded out those happy days. I glanced up at the skyway over Fort Washington Avenue that leads to Garden North, and could remember being pushed down its corridor at 2:00 a.m. on my way to the ICU step-down unit, that night when my health seemed at its most perilous. Instead of thinking with gratitude, "Gosh, this is the place where I got better," I recalled those terrifying moments of hopelessness. My body remembered what my mind wanted to forget, my bones knowing their own mortality like Jesus foreseeing what was ahead. If only I could remake this domain. That was a challenge of being truly healed.

One sunny fall day I was coming back from a test at the sprawling medical campus—another look at my clearing lungs—and that day I had enough strength to walk those fifteen blocks instead of taking a cab or a bus, so I paused in a park along the way, sitting on a bench in an urban sliver of green. Basking in the sun, I gazed at a surfboard of native schist rising out of the grass. I remembered how these benches used to be full of the old German-Jewish residents, refugees from World War II who lived here when we'd first moved to the neighborhood. Most of them had long since died or moved to Florida, but they were the ones who'd welcomed us when we first came here. Our lovely next-door neighbor Hildegard, who had escaped from Frankfurt, wryly claimed, "You're refugees from the Upper West Side." I suppose we were.

Now I was the gray-haired man sitting on a park bench, watching kids running up and down the dark whale's back of schist, jumping from it, laughing like our kids used to. This was our Promised Land back when they were young, our Canaan, the place we had claimed as our own, the place that sustained us and made us happy. I felt I needed to claim it all over again. I would not let new fears rob me of the joys of the past or the joys to be found on a glorious fall day.

"These fifteen blocks are still sacred to me, Lord. You are still here as you were here in the middle of winter, when the snow was melting and Will was born and Tim was born. You are here now."

This was the spiritual work of recovery.

After I finished my morning sessions of writing about Italy, I would venture out and walk—ever so slowly at first—to the park up to the north of us, Fort Tryon Park, where I normally ran when I was well. No running now. No running yet. *But enjoy the day, Rick. Be grateful. Be glad. You are loved. You are unconditionally loved by the Greatest Lover in the universe.* Love so amazing, so divine, as the hymnist put it, demands my soul, my life, my all.

I wanted to recover my singing voice too. I gave myself a musical project. Just as I had sung a song a day for sixty days to celebrate turning sixty, I would sing a song a day for Advent and post them online. Alisa, a pianist and composer, recommended a couple of songs that we could record together. I downloaded the music and put myself at the keyboard, learning the notes, doing it when Carol was out of the house because I didn't want her to hear my scratchy-sounding tones.

It was hard at first to find the right register to sing in, the places where my voice felt comfortable. The old mix of head voice and chest voice was gone, a new one had to be found. I suspected that the tube they sent down my esophagus for that last big test in the hospital, the TEE, had done something to the vocal cords. But I was determined to get my voice back.

Learning a new piece of music, memorizing lyrics, getting the intervals, was another source of healing. "Emmanuel," I sang, "our God is with us. And if God is with us, who can stand against us..." Sustaining the notes started to come easier, finding the breath, making music again. My stamina still had a long way to go, but singing was coming back. I could make music again. At least for myself.

I returned to work. On my first day there I took a picture of myself at my desk, my cheeks still a bit drawn, and posted it on Facebook, letting everybody know the good news. I was back in the office. The picture got plenty of comments and kind wishes, but what amused me most—this will show you how small-minded I can be—was that though it was well received, it got a lot less traffic than that first post I did in the hospital, alerting people to my dangerous illness. Note to self: bad news gets more hits than good news. No journalistic surprise there.

I was so glad to see my colleagues, grateful for their prayers, grateful for all the work they had done covering for me in my absence. We're a small editorial team putting together the magazine, and with a zillion deadlines every month the work can't just take a pause and come to a rest. On it goes. Once again I had that sense of indebtedness. No way could I pay everybody back. *Accept it, Rick*, I told myself. *Receive it. Be grateful.* Gratitude was the only way I could pay it back.

"Welcome back," my colleague Kelly said that first happy but tiring day when a half day was more than enough. "If I find you still here at five after three, you're fired!" she said.

I took some secret pleasure in knowing that I had anticipated a couple of deadlines, and that in my absence my colleagues had logged on to my computer and found two short articles that were due when I was in the hospital. I would have done more work on them, but heck, I was glad they could be used.

I returned to church, but it was a while before I had the energy to return to choir. I wanted, though, as soon as possible, to visit Wesley, the homebound ninety-four-year-old Tuskegee Airman and consummate musician who had been a member of our church. I wanted to be sure I was well enough that I wouldn't pass along any germs to him.

On a Sunday afternoon I took the subway up to his place in the Bronx. He looked weaker and thinner, his voice softer. He winced in pain when I touched his shoulders in the hospital bed. His best friend from World War II, his best buddy, had died since I'd seen him last, and he felt the loss, but we sang again together, Wesley making harmony with whatever

I picked out of the hymnal. He would not be long in this world.

"I'm sorry that I was away for so long," I told him. "I was sick and in the hospital."

"I know," he said. "I prayed for you."

I saw him a couple more times; each time he was weaker. He went into the hospital, came home, and was on hospice care. One day in the middle of the week I got a call from a fellow parishioner, "Can you come visit Wesley? I don't think he'll be around much longer."

"I can't come up right now," I said, "but I'll be there this weekend."

I hung up the phone, and then had second thoughts. What if he didn't make it to Saturday?

I called right back. "Let me sing to Wesley now," I said to his caregiver who answered the phone. "I'll sing one of the hymns he liked. If you can hold the phone up to his ear, I'm sure he'll hear it." They say that hearing is one of the last of our senses to go.

I darted into a conference room at the office and closed the door and sang "Amazing Grace" into the phone. It was around 1:00 in the afternoon. "God bless you, Wesley," I said, promising to call back later with another song, another hymn.

That afternoon at around 5:00 I was in Times Square on my way to an appointment and I picked up my phone. This time I wanted to sing "Be Thou My Vision," another one of his favorites. I dialed, got his caregiver, identified myself, and asked if I could sing for Wesley. Could she hold up the phone for him to hear?

"He passed," she said, tears in her voice.

"He died?"

"Just this afternoon, shortly after you called."

"I'm so sorry," I said. "Thank you for caring for him. Thank you," I said, not sure I could say anything else.

I stood in the street and sang the words to myself, to anyone who was passing me in Times Square. It was that last verse I wanted to sing for him. "High King of Heaven, my victory won/May I reach Heaven's joys, O bright Heav'n's Sun!/Heart of my own heart, whate'er befall,/Still be my Vision, O Ruler of all."

His victory was won.

EPILOGUE

Healing

You want something different, you want change. You don't want to live in fear. You can't just banish the dark thoughts with a snap of your fingers. You want to be bathed in light inside and out, basking in its glow. You give yourself the daily discipline—the delight—of sitting on the sofa with your eyes closed, connecting to God above as much as the God within. You listen to your heart beating, keeping count as you keep count of your days. The busyness of your life catches up to you at the very moment when you want to forget all the busyness. You become anxious at this very time when you're doing battle with all anxieties.

You are sitting here to let it all go and yet you're holding on to the nattering self-talk. Letting go alone won't work. You have to give it up. "You take it," you say to the divine. "Take all this garbage and do something with it. Transform it the way you turn our compost into mulch." You, the praying person, put yourself in a one-way tug-of-war with God, wishing he would win and leave you lying in the grass without a rope to hold, not even the hard knot of your thoughts.

You could say to your more secular friends that this is meditation, which is a notion that seems to be acceptable in multiple circles, from Hollywood screenwriters who haul themselves off to Indian ashrams to the ranks of engineers in Silicon Valley who have been taught that meditation is a boost to their creativity, a way to increase their company's net worth. But this meditation—this prayer time—is pure

Resurrection thinking. You're claiming new life. You've made yourself a Jesus follower, for better or for worse, and like the disciples, you know that your faith doesn't mean squat without the Resurrection. You are praying to a God who became a man and knows what you're going through because he went through it all and ten times worse; then he died and rose from the dead, changing everything.

Like the disciples, you have trouble at times believing. You don't always recognize him—this Resurrected One—in your midst. You could be on the road to Emmaus, listening to him, walking with him, entranced by his words, but you don't know him until he breaks bread with you, and then he simply vanishes before your sight, a phantom of your thoughts. You didn't even have a chance to embrace him. Even if you were like Mary Magdalene in the garden, taking in the empty tomb, you didn't recognize your savior, the one you loved, until he said your name.

You had it all wrong. He is your teacher and friend and source of transformation. That's who you're addressing as you sit here in the silence, the garbage truck outside cranking up its mechanical arm, dumping the trash into its middle, swallowing it up, as you dump your trash into God's pit.

It's not as though you expect a clean slate. Even when your sixth-grade teacher wiped the chalkboard clear there were hints of the equations and vocabulary words left there, the pentimento of previous lessons and teachers. "Rabbi," Mary called him. "Teacher." She knew him when he called her by name.

We flew to South Africa for Easter week, flew there to be with Tim. We don't normally get travel insurance on flights. It's too expensive; it's like betting against yourself; it seems a bad omen. But we got travel insurance for this trip. It all seemed so risky. I was well, but was I well enough to take a fifteen-hour overnight flight to Johannesburg and then another shorter flight, once we got there, to Cape Town? Talk about stamina. Talk about endurance.

I went to the doctor for a checkup beforehand, just to make sure it was all right. What did he request? The usual shots for a foreign land, and that was it. Wasn't there more to be afraid of? There it was, the fear still there, the fear after all these months of recovery, rebuilding strength, running again, singing in the choir, serving on committees, having dinner with friends, writing, going to the museum, seeing movies, being New Yorkers, but wondering still if I was pushing it, doing too much too soon, doing more than I should ever do.

"We're going to South Africa to be with our son," I explained.

"You'll need to get a hepatitis shot," Seth said.

We would only make this trip for Tim.

The flight was grueling, but we got there in one piece, and soon the adrenaline of being in a new place took over.

Cape Town was gorgeous, the views from atop Table Mountain stupendous, the history of the place riveting, the visit to the cells at Robben Island where Nelson Mandela was imprisoned for eighteen years poignant. We had high tea in the colonial outpost of the Mount Nelson Hotel—the Nellie—with an Anglican priest who had done time in our parish in New York. The church is so often on the wrong side of history, but in this place, for a time, the Anglican Church was on the right side, arguing for justice, making a stand for equality. But our priest friend was still angry. He'd grown up "colored" in the crazy ghettoizing patchwork of apartheid, and even though he had good work and a good education, he spoke with bitterness about the joblessness of his twenty-seven nieces and nephews, only a third of them with work.

How long it takes for a ship to turn around even after it has turned.

We went from there to a game park to see the wild animals, going on a photo safari to take pictures of giraffes and zebras and a magnificent lion, lying improbably next to a barbed-wire fence. There was something ersatz about this game park in the Eastern Cape, and only when we got to the monastery where Tim had been living did we get a fuller story.

"It's not that old," one of the guests pointed out. "Eighteen years ago, several of the farmers in that area got together and decided to let their land go wild. They decided they'd make more money out of it as a game park than letting their wild stock graze. Also, if it were a game park, they wouldn't be obliged to house and offer jobs to the people on their farms."

The Holy Cross brothers were invited to South Africa by Archbishop Desmond Tutu shortly after the fall of apartheid, with the hope that they could be a new model for community in a country that needed to reinvent itself. They established themselves on a hilltop outside of the university city of Grahamstown, planting gardens, creating a refectory among low-lying, suburban-looking houses, building a simple sanctuary with a plate-glass window that faced due east to catch the rising sun.

We got there on Maundy Thursday, joining a half dozen other guests who were making their Holy Week retreat. We ate our meals in silence with the brothers, joining them for the offices.

Tim showed us where he lived, the rambling guesthouse where he had a room, where he Skyped his girlfriend back in America, the library with its shelves of spiritual references. We went for long walks in the sunburned hills, the terrain reminding me of central California, give or take a few baboons. We visited the school where Tim worked five days a week, opening it at six thirty in the morning, playing with the kids, working in the office, shepherding the kids when needed. This school, founded by the brothers, was for children from kindergarten through third grade, the classes taught in Xhosa, preparing them for entry into the regular state schools after that, giving them the tools they would need to succeed.

We were the lucky ones, the blessed, parents who could see the place our son had made his home and be with the people who had been his team of support these last few months. The brothers gave him the opportunity to preach on Sundays, the teachers and staff called on his skills as a writer for grant applications, the kids called him "*Bhuti* Tim," "Brother Tim," because he was their light-skinned brother for a season.

Was I like Mary Magdalene at the empty tomb, not recognizing the good news when it was already in front of me? Did I not see that this was what Resurrection could look like? A new life for Tim, a new one for me, a new one for the kids and families to whom the brothers and the school staff reached out.

Good Friday we celebrated with the brothers in the sanctuary, reliving the horrible moments of the Crucifixion, rereading the Gospel account. Parts of the service were in Afrikaans and Xhosa, the Lord's Prayer prayed in three languages at once. The congregation included neighbors who supported the brothers and their good work. And then there were some of the kids, reverencing the cross, kissing the feet of Jesus without a shred of self-consciousness. *Let the children come.*

The Easter vigil started well before dawn on Easter Day. The brothers had broken their silence the day before to give us our parts in the liturgy, different Bible lessons to read aloud, our only light coming from the stars and the Paschal candle. There was a breeze that autumn morning, and the flame struggled to stay lit as we gathered around it in the garden. "The light of Christ," we chanted. "Thanks be to God." Three times, each time a little higher: the light of Christ, thanks be to God. We'd done this service dozens of times before back in New York, but always on the Saturday night leading into Easter. How much better it was here, on Easter Sunday, in a garden like the garden where the women came early on Easter morning, bringing spices to anoint the dead body.

The sky lightened. We moved in a procession closer to the sanctuary, neighbors joined us, the crowd clamoring for Easter, ready to claim it for themselves. Whether the brothers knew how to time it, or whether this was simply the accident of the season, the sun rose at exactly the right moment, shining into the window of the sanctuary just as we proclaimed, "Alleluia. The Lord is risen. The Lord is risen indeed."

The rest of the day, we made ourselves a feast, cooking in the refectory, the brothers pouring glasses of good South African wine, all of us chatting happily together after three days of dining in silence.

The Lord had risen indeed.

That next day, when I went for a jog across the hills, keeping my eye on the road for any poisonous snakes, lest I accidentally step on one, I thought to myself, "The Lord is risen. The Resurrection is here. Claim it. Own it."

I had been sick, I got well. I had almost died, I was alive. I had tumbled into a fit of despair, I had found hope again. I had lost my ability to pray, I was prayed for. I was afraid, I was reassured. I had been lost, I was found. I had everything to be thankful for and to celebrate. Alleluia. I had stumbled through Calvary and landed in a verdant garden of warmth and love and happiness. Other illnesses would surely come, other dark days descend, but this I would not lose. Hold on to it. Keep it fast. The Resurrection is not something seasonal that comes around every spring. The Resurrection was once and for all. I would live it like that.

People still ask, "How are you?" "Fine, fine," I answer breezily. "You still look pretty skinny to me," they'll say. "I've always been skinny," I answer. Sometimes I wonder if it was wise to go so public about a medical disaster. Shouldn't we have kept silent about the whole thing, limiting our news to just a few close friends? I could have eased back into life as though I'd been away on sabbatical. Could have said I was on the other coast looking after family matters.

But you can't get away with such deception in this digital age of tell-all social media and viral e-mails. Besides, we needed every ounce of the support that came through them, all those prayers. I didn't read Carol's e-mails till months after I got out of the hospital, and they still startled me with their immediacy. I wanted to pray for that guy and his wife in their agonizing situation, what I'd come to term, with the levity afforded by distance, "my medical misadventure."

What I hope this remembrance does is fill in the gaps left by not-so-tell-all social media. Getting better is a lot of work; prayer is too. Recovering from a medical crisis means addressing the spin of trauma, not just sweeping it under the carpet or burying it with quick responses of "I'm fine, I'm fine." I'm grateful for the work of talk therapy, am glad I have friends with whom I can be brutally honest, despite my first instincts of sunny temper. I hope my men's group at church will tell you how boring I can be with my complaints. "There goes Rick again, talking about his slow recovery, impatient to be well."

Not long ago I was asked to preach on the passage from Romans, Paul's exhortation, "And not only that, but we also boast in our sufferings, knowing that suffering produces endurance, and endurance produces character, and character produces hope, and hope does not disappoint us, because God's love has been poured into our hearts through the Holy Spirit that has been given to us."

I had to get over my usual reaction to this passage, that it's another tiresome example of muscular Christianity, that we're supposed to stiff-upper-lip our way through life, that all our suffering produces character if we let it. Don't I know—don't you know—people for whom suffering has produced nothing but misery and more misery? This sort of transforming process Paul writes about seemed like the worst sort of wishful thinking.

The challenge of preaching about the passage was to see that it's not a matter of toughing misery out, it's not about waiting and wading through suffering in the hope that somehow, magically, it will produce this much-vaunted quality of character. As Paul goes on to point out, it's not something we do; it's something done in us and for us. It all happens because "God's love has been poured into our hearts." It's the work of the Spirit.

Which is what healing is.

I recently signed up for a seminar at our church to learn how to do healing prayer. I'd been immersing myself enough in the Gospels to see that if I wanted to really be a follower of Jesus I should be willing to do what Jesus asked, and the disciples did, to offer to heal with prayer.

I had to stifle feelings of being an impostor. Me a healer? Fat chance. But Leigh, our leader, said one thing that truly made sense to me. "It's not you who heals, it's God. When you pray for someone else to be healed, you are opening yourself up to be used by God. What it takes is surrender."

Surrender. That's pretty much where I am in prayer. Surrendering, waving a white flag in the trenches of my life, shutting down to open up, certain that the only true victories to be claimed are found in loss. I do feel healed. Sometimes fear will intrude, and a memory will startle me. Then it's time for some talk therapy and more prayer, to loosen the bonds of trauma, to shrink it down to a manageable size. Because I don't want to face fear—especially fear of death—with trembling. I yearn to be open to the truth, the whole truth, the biggest truths.

Shock comes to me when I discover a person inside me who is glad to let go, who loves life desperately and yet is equally eager to lose it, who savors this world with his whole heart and yet holds on to it with a loose grip, who knows the God within so well that the anxieties and noise outside hardly matter.

I like to think that the next time I'm hit with some medical situation that plunges me down mortality's rabbit hole I will be better prepared. I will know where I am and where I need to turn for help. But I'm not at all certain that's true. I just have to trust.

In the meanwhile, I will ask for lots of prayers. Tons of them. From anyone I've ever met and lots of people I've never known. Put me on every prayer list out there, read my name aloud in churches and synagogues, copy and paste that e-mail about me and pass it along, re-post that notice that appeared on Facebook. Thanks to all that I'm alive.

"Brothers and sisters," Paul wrote in his Second Letter to the Corinthians, "we don't want you to be unaware of the troubles that we went through in Asia. We were weighed down with a load of suffering that was so far beyond our strength that we were afraid we might not survive. It certainly seemed to us as if we had gotten the death penalty. This was so that we would have confidence in God, who raises the dead, instead of ourselves.

"God rescued us from a terrible death, and he will rescue us. We have set our hope on him that he will rescue us again since you are helping with your prayer for us."

Pray for me. I'll pray for you. It's just what we do.

ABOUT THE AUTHOR

Rick Hamlin is the executive editor of *Guideposts* magazine, where he has worked for over thirty years. He is the author of three novels, the spiritual memoir *Finding God on the A Train*, *Ten Prayers You Can't Live Without*, and *Pray for Me*. Rick and his wife, the writer Carol Wallace, live in New York City, where they have raised their two boys. He has been a long-time contributor to the best-selling devotional *Daily Guideposts* and regularly blogs on prayer at Guideposts.org.

A NOTE FROM THE EDITORS

We hope you enjoyed *Prayer Works: A Lifetime Spiritual Journey* by Rick Hamlin, published by the Books and Inspirational Media Division of Guideposts, a nonprofit organization that touches millions of lives every day through products and services that inspire, encourage, help you grow in your faith, and celebrate God's love.

Thank you for making a difference with your purchase of this book. Your purchase helps support our many outreach programs to military personnel, prisons, hospitals, nursing homes, and educational institutions.

We also create many useful and uplifting online resources. Visit Guideposts.org to read true stories of hope and inspiration, access OurPrayer network, sign up for free newsletters, download free e-books, join our Facebook community, and follow our stimulating blogs.

To learn about other Guideposts publications, including the best-selling devotional *Daily Guideposts*, go to Guideposts.org/Shop, call (800) 932-2145, or write to Guideposts, PO Box 5815, Harlan, Iowa 51593.